Euskadi Ta Askatasuna

CAUSES AND CONSEQUENCES OF TERRORISM SERIES

Series Editors:
Laura Dugan
Gary A. Ackerman
Anthony Lemieux

BOOKS IN THE SERIES:

From Freedom Fighters to Jihadists: Human Resources of Non-State Armed Groups
Vera Mironova

ISIS Propaganda: A Full-Spectrum Extremist Message
Edited by Stephane J. Baele, Katharine A. Boyd, and Travis G. Coan

Insurgent Terrorism: Intergroup Relationships and the Killing of Civilians
Victor Asal, Brian J. Phillips, and R. Karl Rethemeyer

Extremist Islam: Recognition and Response in Southeast Asia
Kumar Ramakrishna

Proto-State Media Systems: The Digital Rise of Al-Qaeda and ISIS
Carol Winkler and Kareem El Damanhoury

Becoming Jihadis: Radicalization and Commitment in Southeast Asia
Julie Chernov Hwang

Roots of Counterterrorism: Contemporary Wisdom from Dutch Intelligence
Constant Willem Hijzen

Published in partnership with The National Consortium for the Study of Terrorism and Responses to Terrorism and the University of Maryland

Euskadi Ta Askatasuna

A Case Study on Terrorist Dynamics and the Fight to Survive

NELL BENNETT

OXFORD
UNIVERSITY PRESS

OXFORD
UNIVERSITY PRESS

Oxford University Press is a department of the University of Oxford.
It furthers the University's objective of excellence in research, scholarship,
and education by publishing worldwide. Oxford is a registered trade mark of
Oxford University Press in the UK and in certain other countries.

Published in the United States of America by Oxford University Press
198 Madison Avenue, New York, NY 10016, United States of America.

Library of Congress Cataloging-in-Publication Data

Names: Bennett, Nell, author.
Title: Euskadi Ta Askatasuna / Nell Bennett.
Description: College Park : University of Maryland National Consortium for the
Study of Terrorism and Responses to Terrorism (START), 2025 |
Series: Causes and consequences of terrorism | Includes bibliographical references and index.
Identifiers: LCCN 2024037512 (print) | LCCN 2024037513 (ebook) |
ISBN 9780197764237 (paperback) | ISBN 9780197764220 (hardback) |
ISBN 9780197764251 (epub) | ISBN 9780197764268
Subjects: LCSH: ETA (Organization)—History. | Terrorism—Spain—History.
Classification: LCC HV6433.S72 E85307 2025 (print) | LCC HV6433.S72 (ebook) |
DDC 363.325092/39992—dc23/eng/20241031
LC record available at https://lccn.loc.gov/2024037512
LC ebook record available at https://lccn.loc.gov/2024037513

DOI: 10.1093/9780197764268.001.0001

For Kiero

Contents

Acknowledgments

First and foremost, I would like to thank Associate Professor Adam Lockyer. This book simply would not have been possible without your support, guidance, inspiration, and patience. I would also like to thank Dr. Yves-Heng Lim, whose encouragement, feedback, and advice were invaluable. I thank Associate Professor Julian Droogan for encouraging me to pursue this research. I would also like to thank Macquarie University, in particular the Library, the Faculty of Arts, and the Department of Security Studies and Criminology.

I am very grateful to Oxford University Press, and to the editors of the Causes and Consequences of Terrorism series, for including this book in the series. I thank Professor Laura Dugan, Associate Professor Gary Ackerman, and Professor Anthony Lemieux for giving me the opportunity to share this research. I am very grateful to my editors at Oxford University Press, Nadina Persaud and Kayley Gilbert, for their generosity and guidance. I would also like to thank the anonymous reviewers for making this a better book.

This book would not exist if it were not for the *Lazkaoko Beneditarren Fundazioa*. Thanks to Aita Juan José Agirre, Miren Barandiaran, and the archive staff for granting me access to the collection and for assisting me in my research. I must also give my most sincere *eskerrak* to my Euskera teacher, Neka, for teaching me the difference between *nahi* and *behar* and how to make *gazta tarta. Eskerrik asko bihotza!* I also thank Sr. Encarna and Sr. Sole at the Hospederia Santa Ana de Lazkao for providing me with a home away from home.

I would also like to thank my family and my husband, David, for putting up with me while I worked on this book. And of course, my Tenterfield terrier, Kiero, who sat with me, day after day, month after month, as I squinted over documents and typed away. *Nire mundu osoa zara.*

I could not have done this without you all.

List of Abbreviations

CCOO	Euskadiko Langile Komisioak / Euskadi Workers' Commissions
EE	Euskadiko Ezkerra / Basque Country Left
EIA	Euskal Iraultzarako Alderdia / Party for the Basque Revolution
EPK	Euskadiko Partidu Komunista / Basque Communist Party
ETA	Euskadi Ta Askatasuna / Basque Homeland and Freedom
ETA-m	Euskadi Ta Askatasuna militar / Basque Homeland and Freedom military
ETA-pm	Euskadi Ta Askatasuna político-militar / Basque Homeland and Freedom political-military
IAM	Ikasle Abertzaleen Mugimendua / Patriotic Students' Movement
LAB	Langile Abertzaleen Batzordeak / Nationalist Workers' Committee
LAIA	Langile Abertzale Iraultzaileen Alderdia / Party of the Revolutionary Patriotic Workers
LOAPA	Ley Orgánica de Armonización del Proceso Autonómico / Law on Harmonisation of the Autonomous Process
LOFCA	Ley Orgánica de Financiación de las Comunidades Autónomas / Law on the Financing of Autonomous Communities
PNV	Partido Nacionalista Vasco / Basque Nationalist Party
PSOE	Partido Socialista Obrero Español / Spanish Socialist Party
UCD	Unión de Centro Democrático / Union of the Democratic Centre
UGT	Unión General de Trabajadores / General Union of Workers

1
Introduction

Long-standing terrorist groups and insurgencies account for a substantial proportion of global conflict. These campaigns, often labeled "intractable conflicts," continue because the opponents claim that military struggle is the only viable course of action for achieving their objectives. However, in many cases, there is evidence that the nonstate groups are fighting even though they know they cannot win. One example of this is the Irish Republican Army. In 1971, more than thirty years before their eventual demobilization, IRA Chief of Staff Ruairí Ó Brádaigh acknowledged that the terrorists were incapable of "pushing the British into the sea."[1] The British strategy of containment and attrition was gradually isolating the militants from their constituency.[2] In 1991, IRA member Danny Morrison wrote, "I think we can fight on forever and can't be defeated. But of course, that isn't the same as winning or showing something for all the sacrifice."[3] Two years later, the IRA were engaged in secret talks with the British government because they knew that military victory was impossible.[4] Despite signing the Good Friday Agreement in 1998, the IRA did not relinquish their weapons until 2005.[5]

Another example is that of the Peruvian terrorist group Sendero Luminoso, or Shining Path. Formed in 1960, the group reached its height in the 1980s. The capture of their leader, Abimael Guzman, in 1992 and the introduction of a government amnesty law greatly weakened the organization. However, Sendero Luminoso was not defeated. Rather, the hardliners returned to the Peruvian highlands to continue the armed struggle.[6] It was clear that the organization, in its reduced state, was not capable of overthrowing the central government. And indeed, in 2011 Sendero

[1] Alonso, *IRA and Armed Struggle.*
[2] Bosi and Della Porta, "Processes of Disengagement," 90–91.
[3] Ibid; Danny Morrison in Patterson, *Ireland since 1939*, 320. See also Hart, *I.R.A. at War*, 175.
[4] White, "Peace Process"; Pruitt, "Readiness Theory."
[5] Bosi and Della Porta, "Processes of Disengagement, 90–91.
[6] Burch, "Natural Resources," 2–3.

Euskadi Ta Askatasuna. Nell Bennett, Oxford University Press. © University of Maryland National Consortium for the Study of Terrorism and Responses to Terrorism (START) (2025). DOI: 10.1093/9780197764268.003.0001

Luminoso leader Comrade Artemio gave an interview in which he called the Peruvian government "the winners of the war."[7] In spite of this knowledge, the terrorist group persists.

The Kurdistan Workers' Party (PKK) launched its assault on the Turkish government in 1984. Though their numbers rose to around 10,000 in the 1900s, in 1998, Turkish scholar Henri J. Barkey and extremism expert and CIA analyst Graham E. Fuller said the group "cannot win the armed struggle in any military sense." By the 2000s, their numbers had halved, rendering victory a remote possibility, and yet they persisted.[8] In 2013, Güneş Murat Tezcür opined, "the militants are in no position to dislodge the Turkish state from the territory they contest with the exception of some mountainous border zones."[9] Despite four decades of conflict and minimal prospects of achieving a military victory, the PKK continue.

These are just some examples of terrorist groups choosing to continue to fight despite having no real prospect of achieving a territorial victory. There are many others.

When Colonel Karuna left the Liberation Tigers of Tamil Eelam (LTTE) in 2004, he told the rebel leader that the terrorists could never win.[10] Yet, the organization persisted for five more years. Lashkar-e-Taiba continue to fight for Kashmiri freedom, despite negligible prospects of territorial victory. After more than three decades, the militants refuse to "be worn down and surrender to reality."[11]

These examples prompt the question: Why is it that so many terrorist groups continue to use violence well after all hope of success has vanished?[12] Why do so many conflicts continue beyond the point at which the militants can expect to obtain a net benefit from violence?[13] The puzzle of terrorist persistence remains an underexamined area of conflict studies.[14] I argue that

[7] *The Guardian*, "Comrade Artemio Interview"; BBC News, "Peru's Shining Path Defeated"; Aquino, "Peru's Shining Path Rebels."

[8] Bulut, *A Checkmate, Not a Stalemate*, 54.

[9] Tezcür, "Prospects for Resolution."

[10] Ramesh, "Tamil Tigers Finished"; NewsX, "Interview with Col. Karuna."

[11] Braithwaite and D'Costa, *Cascades of Violence*, 256.

[12] For additional examples see Ovalle, "Was FARC Militarily Defeated?"; Anderson, "Why Victories in Battle."

[13] Mullins, *Twenty-Five Years of Terrorism*; Reshi, "Kashmir Insurgency"; Murua, *The End of ETA*.

[14] Some studies that have examined resilience in insurgencies include Weinstein, *Inside Rebellion*; and Metelits, "'Bourdieu's Capital.

organizational theory advances the best explanation for this seemingly irrational behavior. Over time, terrorist groups that may have begun as a group of committed idealists led by charismatic leaders will frequently become increasingly bureaucratic organizations.[15] The survival of the organization itself can supplant the original political objectives as the terrorists' primary goal.[16] I argue that this organizational dynamic provides a compelling explanation for conflict persistence.

In order to understand terrorist persistence, it is important to distinguish cases in which it is rational for militants to continue fighting. In cases like that of the Taliban in Afghanistan or the Vietcong in Vietnam, the militants knew that the foreign power would eventually have to withdraw. In such instances, the militants win if they do not lose. They know that the government will be vulnerable after the foreign power inevitably withdraws.[17] For example, when journalist Christina Lamb asked Afghan villagers why they accept benefits from the US troops but attack their bases at night, one explained, "In the end, they'll be gone, and the bad guys will still be here."[18] Similarly, in wars of annihilation or genocide, the rational rebel may choose to fight on despite low prospects of victory because pursuing a peaceful strategy would mean certain death.[19]

However, in other struggles, such as that of the IRA, Sendero Luminoso, FARC, or the Red Brigades, there comes a point at which the terrorists are able to see that victory over the regime is unattainable and government amnesties and pardons should make disbanding an attractive option.[20] In such cases, the rational alternative would presumably be to participate in a peace accord, if satisfactory terms are offered. And yet, so often militants refuse to lay down their arms.[21] I argue that organizational theory helps provide the missing link that explains terrorists' decisions to carry on in the face of diminishing prospects of success under any reasonable circumstances.

[15] Weber, *Economy and Society*, 224.
[16] Beetham, *Max Weber*, 66; Osterman, "Overcoming Oligarchy,"626.
[17] Mack, "Why Big Nations Lose Small Wars," 177–178; Arreguín-Toft, "How the Weak Win Wars," 123.
[18] Lamb, "Chronicle of a Defeat Foretold."
[19] Davis and Ward, "They Dance Alone," 473.
[20] Horchem, "Decline of the Red Army Faction," 71; Crenshaw, "How Terrorism Declines," 83; Peña, "Las FARC."
[21] Huff, *Why Rebels Reject Peace*.

Rational Choice and Organizational Theories of Terrorism

Rational choice theory is a dominant theoretical framework in terrorism studies.[22] Researchers who view terrorism from a rational choice perspective typically see terrorists as utility maximizers who use violence when the expected political gains, minus projected costs, outweigh alternative forms of political activism.[23] In determining whether to engage in violence, terrorists are assumed to calculate the costs of the various alternatives, including nonviolent protest and political participation.[24] Their objective is to impose sufficient costs on the targeted constituency so that its government will concede to their demands because concessions are perceived to be less costly than withstanding ongoing attacks.[25]

In this book, I employ the definition of terrorism used in the Global Terrorism Database. That is, "the threatened or actual use of illegal force and violence by a non-state actor to attain a political, economic, religious, or social goal through fear, coercion, or intimidation."[26] I use this definition of terrorism because it is widely used and recognized. However, I am aware that the very concept of terrorism is contested. I am using an objective definition of terrorism to examine a specific subcategory of political violence. However, in making the decision to adopt this definition, I considered competing definitions and subjectivist arguments that the very concept of "terrorism" is nothing more than a political construct.[27] Indeed, Will H. Moore argues that the application of the term "terrorist" to a group implies that its organizing system of beliefs is "terror," which thereby dismisses any legitimate political objectives that the dissident group may seek to advance.[28]

I appreciate that the application of the term "terrorist" to Euskadi ta Askatasuna (ETA) could be misconstrued as an attempt to minimize the role

[22] Heath et al., "Calculus of Fear"; Dugan and Chenoweth, "Moving Beyond Deterrence"; Wood, "Opportunities to Kill?"; Hultman, "Battle Losses and Rebel Violence"; Lichbach, "Will Rational People Rebel?; Lichbach, "Deterrence or Escalation?"; Anderton and Carter, "On Rational Choice Theory," 276; Bader, "Harsh State Repression."

[23] Abrahms, "What Terrorists Really Want," 78; Shapiro, "Terrorist Decision-Making," 6; Crenshaw, "The Causes of Terrorism," 380; Stohl, "Counterterrorism and Repression," 62.

[24] Muller and Weede, "Cross-National Variation," 625.

[25] Arce and Sandler, "Terrorist Signalling," 573. For an alternative perspective on rebel motivation see Wood, *Insurgent Collective Action*; Petersen, *Resistance and Rebellion*; Jacques and Taylor, "Male and Female Suicide Bombers," 307; Gallimore, "Unresolved Trauma"; Pape, *Dying to Win*; Kruglanski and Orehek, "Role of the Quest."

[26] START (National Consortium for the Study of Terrorism and Responses to Terrorism), "Data Collection Methodology."

[27] Shanahan, "Definition of Terrorism," 104.

[28] Moore, "Tilting at a Windmill?," 4.

that the organization played in the Basque Country, particularly during the 1960s to the 1980s, when ETA had substantial popular support. Indeed, a 1978 opinion survey conducted by Euskobarómetro showed that 48 percent of Basques viewed ETA as patriots or idealists.[29] However, in this book I use the term as a means of categorization to distinguish the form of violence perpetrated by ETA from different kinds of political violence and because it is the term that most accurately describes their violent actions during the years under analysis. I also use the term because the findings of this book are relevant to conflict resolution, and "terrorism" is a term that is commonly employed by policy makers and scholars in that field.[30]

For the purposes of this book, I distinguish terrorism that occurs as a result of wars of occupation. This is because there are different motivating factors at play in wars of occupation. A people under the rule of a temporary occupying power may find it rational to continue fighting regardless of the prospects of achieving a military victory over the invader.[31] Under these circumstances, it might always be rational for the terrorists to continue until the occupier withdraws.[32] I also distinguish conflicts in which the incumbent regime's objective is the annihilation of a targeted population. In such instances, fighting with little or no prospect of success could be a rational course of action.[33] As an example, for Polish partisans, surrendering to the Nazi regime would mean certain death.[34] In such cases, resistance against the odds is a rational decision.

My focus is on conflicts in which the terrorist organization challenges the sovereign power of the state which they inhabit and in which the terrorists and their constituencies are not forced to choose between fighting or annihilation.[35] Put simply, these are conflicts between terrorists and governments that cannot "leave" and in which the terrorists are not in a position of having to choose between fighting and death. This is what James D. Fearon and David D. Laitin refer to as "separatist" conflicts, or conflicts that are "between a group that controls a recognized state apparatus

[29] Muro, "ETA during Democracy," 39.

[30] A similar approach is taken by Renanah Miles Joyce and Virginia Page Fortna. See Joyce and Fortna, "Extremism and Terrorism," 2.

[31] Petersen, *Resistance and Rebellion*, 32–45.

[32] Lockyer, *Foreign Intervention*.

[33] Kalyvas, *Logic of Violence in Civil War*, 151–152.

[34] Krakowski, *War of the Doomed*.

[35] This is similar to Richard Shultz's category "Revolutionary Terrorism" in Shultz, "Conceptualizing Political Terrorism," 9–10.

and another that does not, where the latter seeks greater political autonomy or secession from the state."[36] This category of terrorism is neither rare nor peripheral to the study of civil conflict. Indeed, Fearon and Laitin found that separatist/autonomy-related violence was the predominant form of large-scale ethnic violence between 1945 and 1994.[37]

Under classical rational choice theory, militants are understood to interact with environmental conditions and adapt their strategies in accordance with opportunities and constraints.[38] They are anticipated to lay down their arms when the cost of engaging in violence outweighs the benefits.[39] According to T. David Mason and Patrick J. Fett: "If G [incumbent government] (or R [rebel organisation]) chooses to continue to fight, it must be the case that G (or R) expects to win eventually."[40] According to this logic, parties to a conflict will be amenable to a negotiated settlement when their subjective estimated utility of a negotiated settlement is greater than their subjective expected utility from continuing the conflict.[41] As Fearon has observed, "war is costly and risky, so rational states should have incentives to locate negotiated settlements that all would prefer to the gamble of war. . . ."[42] However, this approach does not explain why so many conflicts persist beyond the point at which the militants can reasonably anticipate victory and in which the incumbent government is offering amnesties and pardons. Neither does this approach explain why so often terrorists choose to continue fighting over generous demobilization agreements and potential lucrative positions in the legitimate political system.[43]

Protracted conflicts often confront the leaders and the rank-and-file members with diminishing rewards for increasing risks. Indeed, in 1989 Jeffrey Ian Ross and Ted Robert Gurr observed that rebel groups rarely achieve their stated political objectives, but that this "chronic failure" did not explain "either the sporadic recurrence of revolutionary terrorism . . .

[36] Fearon and Laitin, "Weak States, Rough Terrain," 9.

[37] Ibid., 10.

[38] Bosi and Della Porta, "Processes of Disengagement", 83; Kalyvas and Kocher, "Dynamics of Violence."

[39] Becker, "Crime and Punishment."

[40] Mason and Fett, "How Civil Wars End," 548.

[41] Ibid., 547; Crocker, *Taming Intractable Conflicts*, 7; Mason, "Insurgency, counterinsurgency"; Brym and Andersen, "Rational Choice," 483; Fitzsimmons, "Hard Hearts and Open Minds?"

[42] Fearon, "Rationalist Explanations for War," 380.

[43] Ibid; Gawthorpe, "All Counterinsurgency Is Local," 848; Cramer, "Homo Economicus," 1845; Schultz, "Breaking the Will"; Connable and Libicki, *How Insurgencies End*, 19–20; Sinno, *Organizations at War*, 2.

or the fact that some such movements have been much more resilient and persistent than others."[44] Similarly, Ben Connable and Martin C. Libicki observed that "[i]nsurgents lose slowly; as their effectiveness declines, it does so at a decreasing rate."[45] Impending defeat is often signaled by increasing defections and reductions in resources, external support, and safe havens.[46] Thus, terrorists generally have years to observe their declining effectiveness and popularity and watch their prospects of victory slowly slip away.

I argue that a blind spot in contemporary counterterrorism theory and practice is that it tends to overlook the fundamental characteristic of terrorist groups. That is, that they are organizations.[47] For, as Abdulkader H. Sinno observed: "Ethnic groups, social classes, civilizations, religions and nations do not engage in conflict or strategic interaction—organizations do."[48] Organizational theory has shown that once individuals form a collective, they become subject to unique organizing principles and drivers. The overarching objective of all organizations is to ensure their own survival. As James Q. Wilson says, "Whatever else organizations seek, they seek to survive".[49]

The will to survive is a unique characteristic of organizations and is the result of incentive structures that develop once a group of like-minded individuals arrange themselves into a bureaucracy.[50] Once an organization is formed, group members, and leaders in particular, become the recipients of incentives.[51] These benefits can only be maintained if the organization remains intact. Therefore, group members are motivated to protect the organization, even if this comes at the expense of advancing the goals that the

[44] Ross and Gurr, "Why Terrorism Subsides," 408.
[45] Connable and Libicki, *How Insurgencies End*, 213.
[46] Ibid; Staniland, "Whither ISIS?," 34–35.
[47] Shapiro, *Terrorist's Dilemma*, 2; Shapiro and Siegel, "Moral Hazard, Discipline," 40–43; Gates, "Recruitment and Allegiance," 111. Studies that have examined the organizational characteristics of militant groups include Staniland, *Networks of Rebellion*; Staniland, "Organizing Insurgency"; Humphreys and Weinstein, "Handling and Manhandling Civilians in Civil War"; Bueno de Mesquita, "Terrorist Factions," 399–400; Pearlman, "Spoiling Inside and Out"; Zech, "Counter-Terrorizing," 256–257.
[48] Sinno, *Organizations at War*, 3.
[49] James Q. Wilson, *Political Organizations*, 10.
[50] Merton, *Social Theory and Social Structure*, 255; Zald and Ash, "Social Movement Organizations."
[51] Tullock, "Paradox of Revolution," 92; Eastin and Zech, "Joining the Counterinsurgency; Bahney et al, *An Economic Analysis*, 4–6; Bahney et al., "Insurgent Compensation"; Olson, *Logic of Collective Action.*

organization was formed to pursue. Why should terrorist organizations be any different from political parties,[52] NGOs,[53] businesses,[54] or government agencies?[55] I argue that terrorist organizations are no different. That is, despite terrorist groups frequently employing rhetoric that emphasizes self-sacrifice and the greater political good, over time the overarching aim of the organization becomes ensuring its own survival.[56] This fundamental objective explains the apparent irrational behavior of parties to persistent conflicts.

The Benefit of Better Understanding Civil Conflict Termination

Intrastate conflict is the most common form of conflict in the world today.[57] The majority of violent struggles take place within the bounds of a single state and involve a challenge to the incumbent's rule by one or more rebel organizations.[58] Valuable research has been conducted on civil war onset and duration.[59] This has found that civil conflicts have increased in duration since the end of World War II.[60] In 1947 the average civil war lasted just two years. By 1999 that had increased steadily to approximately fifteen years.[61] Indeed, many have gone on much longer. Conflicts in West Papua and Jammu and Kashmir have continued for more than three decades, and there has been conflict in the Philippines for more than fifty years.[62]

[52] Moskovich, "Goal Displacement."

[53] Khieng and Dahles, "Resource Dependence"; Henderson, "Negotiating for Survival."

[54] March, *Explorations in Organizations*, 27–29.

[55] Ansar, "Fate of Ideals"; Tremblay-Boire, "Change Can Be Good," 3–4. See also Warner and Havens, "Goal Displacement," for a discussion of the way that organizational maintenance goals can displace professed goals, especially at 547–548.

[56] This concept has been discussed in Vinci, *Armed Groups and the Balance of Power*, 37–38; Crenshaw, "Theories of Terrorism," 19; Cordes et al., "Trends in International Terrorism," 50.

[57] Council on Foreign Relations, "Understanding Intrastate Conflict"; Howard and Stark, "How Civil Wars End," 132.

[58] Collier, Hoeffler, and Sambanis, "Collier-Hoeffler Model," 2–3; Paul et al., "Paths to Victory," xvii; JLyall and Wilson, "Rage Against the Machines," 67; Stevenson, "Northern Ireland."

[59] Walter, "Bargaining Failures," 259.

[60] Wood, "Civil Wars," 251–252.

[61] Fearon and Laitin, "Ethnicity, Insurgency and Civil War," 75. However, Laia Balcells and Stathis N. Kalyvas observed that civil wars are becoming shorter, though not less lethal, and that conflicts like Vietnam and Afghanistan may be outliers: Balcells and Kalyvas, "Does Warfare Matter?," 32–33. See also Wood, "Civil Wars," 251–252.

[62] Zech and Eastin, "Household Economics of Counterinsurgency"; Mullins, *Twenty-Five Years of Terrorism*, 111–128; Reshi, "Kashmir Insurgency," 9–12.

The prevalence and longevity of civil conflict may be explained in part by international power structures.[63] Ann Hironaka argues that the proliferation of weak states after World War II, combined with an increase in interstate intervention, has exacerbated internal conflicts. While the causes of conflict are rooted in local issues, Hironaka argues that international conditions "play a critical role in perpetuating the conflict."[64] In spite of their proliferation, there is still much about civil war termination that eludes researchers. As Elisabeth Jean Wood observes, "a key aspect of conflict resolution is as yet inadequately understood: how does the underlying shift in the conditions of the conflict (toward 'ripeness' for settlement, such that a 'mutually hurting stalemate' is in place) occur?"[65]

Part of the reason for the increase in conflict duration is that civil conflicts are becoming increasingly difficult to settle.[66] Of conflicts since 1944 that were formally resolved, conflict resumed between the parties in approximately 42 percent of cases without peacekeepers and in around 39 percent of conflicts in which peacekeepers had been deployed.[67] Not only is it difficult to bring the parties to the negotiating table, in the majority of conflicts, the parties are unable to reach a mutually binding agreement. Barbara F. Walter found that between 1940 and 1992 only one third of negotiations to end civil wars resulted in settlements. This was not because the parties could not resolve their differences. Walter found that of those conflicts, 62 percent resulted in a settlement agreement, yet more than half of those agreements were never implemented.[68] Despite having reached a compromise position, the parties nonetheless chose war over peace.[69]

There are competing explanations for this low rate of conflict resolution. Some, like Walter, argue that credible commitments play an important role.[70] Others argue that internal and external spoilers can derail peace processes.[71] Others suggest that incomplete information, bargaining problems, or fixed cleavages could be to blame.[72] However, as Walter observes: "A host

[63] Howard and Stark, "How Civil Wars End."
[64] Hironaka, *Neverending Wars*, 2. See also Shafer, *Deadly Paradigms*, 4–5.
[65] Wood, "Civil Wars," 253.
[66] Hartzell, Hoddie, and Rothchild, "'Stabilizing the Peace"; Jones, *Waging Insurgent Warfare*, 5.
[67] Fortna, "'Does Peacekeeping Keep Peace?," 271.
[68] Walter, *Committing to Peace*, 3–5.
[69] David E. Cunningham argues that the intervention of international actors and peacekeepers can induce parties to implement peace accords: Cunningham, *Barriers to Peace*, 222–225. See also Fortna, *Does Peacekeeping Work?*
[70] Walter, "Designing Transitions," 133; Hoddie and Hartzell, "Civil War Settlements."
[71] Stedman, "Spoiler Problems in Peace Processes"; Walter, "Bargaining Failures," 259.
[72] Morrow, "Signalling Difficulties"; Boukhars, "Logic of Violence," 123.

of additional factors determine how strong and resolute players are likely to be, such as how much pain each side is willing to bear."[73] Thus, there is a gap in the literature that has real-world policy implications. Back in 2016, then president of Colombia, Juan Manuel Santos, beseeched FARC members: "Anyone with doubts, best leave them aside and join the peace accord, because it's the last opportunity they will have to change their lives, because otherwise they will end up, I assure you, in a grave or jail."[74] And yet, almost five years later it was estimated that between 2,500 and 3,000 FARC members were still active in Colombia.[75]

Kelly M. Greenhill and Paul Staniland argue that intrastate conflicts will only become more difficult to combat in the future. Conflicts including those in Afghanistan, Iraq, Chechnya, and Somalia are connected to broader international conflicts. Militants in these states have the benefit of technology that allows for international recruitment and effective dissemination of propaganda. The recruitment pools for terrorist organizations are not limited to their geographically defined population base.[76] Thus, it essential that scholars and policy makers understand the key characteristics of terrorist organizations and what motivates their members to keep fighting. Addressing the gap in the scholarly literature on conflict resolution will better equip leaders and policy makers to negotiate and implement successful peace accords.

The findings of this book have relevance for scholars and policy makers outside of the fields of conflict resolution, counterterrorism, and counterinsurgency. In essence, this book demonstrates the applicability of organizational theory to the study of illicit organizations. This has significance for criminologists, as the theoretical approach could be equally applied to organized crime groups and gangs. I also prompt researchers in the field of organizational studies to expand the scope of their research and consider unlawful organizations, as there is little substantive difference between legal and illegal organizations. Additionally, this book presents a detailed discussion of a pivotal period in Spanish political history, one which has received little attention in English-language publications. The empirical discussion, and the references to primary documents, are therefore relevant to scholars of twentieth-century Spanish and Basque history.

[73] Walter, "Bargaining Failures," 259.
[74] Reuters, "Colombian FARC Rebel Unit."
[75] Aljazeera, "Colombia Accuses FARC Dissidents."
[76] Greenhill and Staniland, "Ten Ways to Lose," 416. See also Salehyan, *Rebels without Borders*; Fair, "Diaspora Involvement in Insurgencies"; and Byman et al., *Trends in Outside Support*.

Methodology and Research Design

In this book I elaborate a causal explanation of terrorist persistence by analyzing an instrumental case study.[77] An instrumental case study is the analysis of a particular unit to "provide insight into a particular issue, redraw generalizations, or build theory."[78] All case studies involve the detailed analysis of a single unit in order to understand a larger class of similar units.[79] However, an instrumental case study is distinguished by the fact that it is employed to provide an answer to a predetermined research question. Thus, instrumental case studies are distinct from intrinsic case studies, which may be analyzed because of a pre-existing interest in the case.[80] Additionally, I will be adopting a longitudinal approach to observe changes in the decision-making of one organization over a period of six years.[81] I will use this case study to address the puzzle of terrorist persistence. Specifically, I will ask why certain groups continue fighting when they have no rational prospects of success and when there are benefits to demobilizing. To do this, I will analyze the decision processes of one organization. This will enable me to assess the competing considerations that the terrorists weighed and the cost-benefit analyses they made when determining whether to continue with armed action.

Although a defining feature of a terrorist organization is that they are an *organization*, remarkably little work has been conducted on whether or the extent to which organizational dynamics contribute to conflict persistence. For this reason, the case study that I present in this book is what Alexander L. George and Andrew Bennett refer to as a "plausibility probe." It is a study on a "relatively untested" theory "to determine whether more intensive and laborious testing is warranted."[82] I have selected the case study methodology because it is best suited to directly analyzing the decision behavior of a terrorist organization. Decision-making is a complex social process that involves multiple actors (individuals and groups), interests, and constraints.[83] An advantage of the case study approach is that it allows the researcher to "introduce nuance and complexity into the understanding of a given topic."[84]

[77] I adopt the definition of a causal explanation as a "theoretical concept independent of the data used to learn about it" from King et al. *Designing Social Inquiry*, 76.
[78] Grandy, "Instrumental Case Study," 473.
[79] Gerring, "What Is a Case Study," 342.
[80] Stake, *Art of Case Study Research*, 3–4.
[81] Yin, *Case Study Research*, 32.
[82] George and Bennett, *Case Studies and Theory Development*, 75.
[83] Almond and Genco, "Clouds, Clocks," 518.
[84] Collier and Mahoney, "Insights and Pitfalls," 71.

Patrick J. Haney argues that there are many problems and processes that required the kind of detailed analysis that only a case study permits. These problems are not amenable to the use of large-*N* or statistical analyses.[85] The influence of internal organizational dynamics on conflict duration is one such problem. Nicholas Sambanis observes there is a "significant gap" between micro-level and macro-level understandings of civil war.[86] This gap is increased when cross-national statistical analyses are used to ascertain the relationship between micro and macro phenomena.[87] Sambanis argues that case studies can assist in better understanding the processes that lead to conflict.[88] By focusing on one organization and tracking its decision processes over a significant number of years, I am able to more accurately capture the complex social and organizational processes that constitute terrorist decision-making.

There are limitations to using data from just one conflict.[89] As John Stuart Mill stated: "Observation, in short, without experimentation . . . can ascertain sequences and co-existences, but cannot prove causation."[90] Another limitation is what David Collier and James Mahoney refer to as the risk of "*overestimating* the importance of explanations discovered in case studies of extreme observations."[91] However, in order to test the theoretical model, it is necessary to make a detailed study of terrorist decision-making processes as they occurred. There are significant risks involved in grouping historical cases to create a larger data set. As Ian S. Lustick noted, interpretations of historical data vary, and once this is considered the "actual number of 'cases' expands from the number of episodes to the number of accounts of those episodes." Thus, differences in historical opinion can distort findings in aggregate studies.[92] The instrumental case study method allows me to scrutinize the evidence, examine the questions that were posed to the militants, arguments that were raised, and the proposals that were accepted. For this research project, the benefits of a granular approach outweigh its potential limitations.

[85] Haney, *Organizing for Foreign Policy Crises*, 28. See also Cunningham, Gleditsch, and Salehyan, "It Takes Two," 571; Mahoney, "More Data, New Problems."
[86] Sambanis, "Using Case Studies," 259.
[87] See also Wood, "Civil Wars," 252–253.
[88] Sambanis, "Using Case Studies,"259.
[89] Arjona and Kalyvas, "Rebelling Against Rebellion," 4; Kalyvas, "Promises and Pitfalls," 398.
[90] John Stuart Mill in Holland, "Statistics and Causal Inference," 950.
[91] Collier and Mahoney, "Insights and Pitfalls," 72.
[92] Lustick, "History, Historiography, and Political Science," 605.

Case Selection

Constructing a case study analysis involves selecting a case from a population of theoretically appropriate cases.[93] As Stanley Lieberson states, the choice of case in a small-*N* study is extremely important because studies that examine only one or a small number of cases necessarily make deterministic rather than probabilistic claims.[94] Thus, it is important that the selected case be representative of the broader class, to the extent that this is possible. There are many cases that could be used for this book. Organizations such as the IRA, the Red Brigades, FARC, and the Naxalites, to name but a few, would all make appropriate case studies to test the organizational model.

The case of ETA was selected for this study because it shares many key characteristics with other post–World War II terrorist groups. It operated between 1959 and 2011, and it was heavily influenced by the anti-imperial movements of the postwar era.[95] Like many other terrorist organizations, ETA was part of a nationalist and a separatist movement. The organization emerged out of the Basque nationalist movement, which was based on the ethnic and cultural uniqueness of the Basque people and a rejection of the nation-building policies of the Spanish central government.[96] ETA also makes a useful case study because the use of violence remained a contentious issue within the organization until the dissolution of the more moderate branch in 1982.[97] Thus, the issue of whether and to what extent the organization should use violence was a recurring topic of debate. ETA's internal disagreements regarding the use of violence reached a crisis point in 1973. The militant faction of ETA placed a bomb at a busy Madrid café, which killed thirteen people. This caused ETA to split into two factions, ETA militar (ETA-m) and ETA político-militar (ETA-pm).[98] ETA-m was the more hard-line, militant faction. ETA-pm was more moderate and believed in a combined political-military solution in which armed action would be subordinate to and in support of political objectives.[99]

[93] Haney, *Organizing for Foreign Policy Crises*, 29.
[94] Lieberson, "Small N's and Big Conclusions," 316.
[95] Zabalo and Saratxo, "ETA Ceasefire," 367; Whitfield, "Basque Conflict and ETA," 4.
[96] Lingelbach, "Defiant Basques," 111.
[97] Llera, Mata, and Irvin, "ETA: From Secret Army," 115.
[98] Soldevilla, "Agur a las Armas," 74.
[99] Romero, "El Proceso de Liquidación," 4.

I focus on the trajectory of ETA-pm. This choice is significant, because ETA-pm was the strongest branch of ETA during the Spanish transition from the Francoist dictatorship to representative democracy.[100] This was a time of great political upheaval, and ETA was required to decide how, and even whether, it would continue its operations in the new political regime. Between 1976 and 1982, ETA-pm faced four key decision points. I will therefore analyze the internal debates that took place in 1976, 1977, 1981, and 1982. I acknowledge the argument that labeling ETA-pm a terrorist group is an oversimplification. ETA-pm engaged in a range of activities including labor organizing, youth work, and cultural promotion. However, while ETA-pm's activities were not limited to terrorism, the violent actions of the organization align with the definition employed in this book.

While ETA-pm is the formal unit of analysis, there are also informal units of analysis. According to John Gerring, informal units are "all other units that are brought into the analysis in a peripheral way. . . ." It is not possible to study ETA-pm without also discussing their political party, Euskadiko Ezkerra (EE), the militant branch ETA-m, and the ETA-pm's own internal militant faction, the Komando Bereziak.[101] These informal units provide useful points of comparison. However, the focus of this book is ETA-pm. I made the choice to present a detailed analysis of the decision-making processes of one organization, and therefore I have not employed a cross-unit case study research design. The reason for this is that I want to be able to accurately portray the complexity and "messiness" of actual organizational decision-making.[102]

As this is a structured case study analysis, I will be focusing on certain aspects of the case.[103] I do not present a descriptive historical analysis of the period 1976–1982 in Basque politics, or even Basque radical politics. Neither is it a history of ETA-pm. Rather, it is a targeted analysis of ETA-pm's decision-making regarding their use of violence. There are various historical events that took place during this period that are relevant to this discussion. Developments such as the first general elections, the peace movement, the attempted military coup of 1982, and certain legislative developments

[100] Soler, *La Transición Sangrienta.*

[101] Gerring, "What Is a Case Study?," 344.

[102] Merton, *Social Theory and Social Structure*, 251–253; Lindblom, "Science of 'Muddling Through,'" 82; Simon, *Administrative Behavior*, 101–104; Etzioni, "Mixed-Scanning"; Lipsky, *Street-Level Bureaucracy*, 29–32.

[103] George and Bennett, *Case Studies and Theory Development*, 67.

influenced ETA-pm's decision-making.[104] These need to be understood in order to make sense of the internal debates. However, historical context is only provided as an aid to interpreting the arguments. To that end, secondary sources have been used to provide historical background to the transcripts and documents that are analyzed. Where available, contemporaneous newspaper reports have been used. These have been supplemented with scholarly works, with an emphasis on works from Basque and Spanish academics and historians.

Data Collection

My research into ETA-pm led me to a small private archive named the Lazkaoko Beneditarren Fundazioa, which is attached to a Benedictine monastery in a village called Lazkao in Gipuzkoa. Lazkao is situated in the mountains of the Basque Country and is home to approximately 5,600 inhabitants. The archive was established by a Benedictine monk, Aita Juan José Agirre Begiristain. It contains an extensive collection of documents relating to ETA. Aita Juan José Agirre has been celebrated for his preservation of Basque political history and is considered one of the leading authorities on ETA.[105] The Fundazioa houses an extensive collection of ETA's internal documents. Among these documents, I found original records from three internal debates that took place within ETA-pm in the late 1970s and early 1980s. At these debates, members of the organization gathered to discuss a variety of issues, including the future of the organization, the utility of violence and ceasefires, the Basque people's attitudes to ETA's activities, target selection, recruitment, resources, rival organizations, and political matters.

Aita Juan José Agirre has a long history of engagement with Basque politics. This has brought him unwelcome attention over the years. In fact, he was arrested by the Civil Guard in 2005 on the suspicion of being an ETA collaborator.[106] However, his trusted position within Basque society has meant that his archive has been the recipient of many anonymous donations of internal ETA documents. The records of the ETA debates in the early 1980s were one such donation. These documents include the minutes that were

[104] Llera, "ETA, Ejercito Secreto."
[105] Azkarraga, "Juan Jose Agirre"; Soldevilla, Barandiaran, and Casanellas, "La documentación de (y sobre) ETA."
[106] *El Pais*, "Puestos en Libertad."

taken at these internal debates. They provide an actual contemporaneous record of the discussions that the members held before deciding whether to continue to engage in political violence. The minutes and transcripts allow the reader to be a "fly on the wall" during these historic debates.

The records are highly significant because a large proportion of the discussions were taken down verbatim. Disputes, arguments, and dissenting views were all recorded. There is evidence of musings, ranting, rambling, jokes, jibes, and personal attacks. The candid nature of this material means that researchers do not need to contend with the issue of post hoc justification, which can affect the reliability of sources such as terrorist memoirs and interviews.[107] The transcripts from the debates of the early 1980s were all the more remarkable because they had not been published in any form. The only way that these documents could be accessed was by physically viewing them in the Lazkao archive. Some of these documents have been referred to in historical works on ETA.[108] Indeed, some of the documents were used in a dissertation by Gaizka Fernández Soldevilla on ETA's affiliated political party, Euskal Iraultzarako Alderdia (EIA).[109] Many of the documents dating up until the year 1978 have been published in the collection of ETA primary sources titled *Documentos Y.* However, the documents from 1980–1982, during which time ETA-pm debated the utility of political violence and whether they should disband, remained unpublished. The remote location of the archive, and the fact that the documents were written in Spanish, may account for the fact that they had not been previously examined by terrorism scholars outside of Spain. The documents had not been translated into English. Thus, in order to analyze them, I was required to make my own translations. The minutes of the debates from the 1980s must be viewed in the context of the internal documents of ETA-pm from its inception in 1976 until its dissolution in 1982. The Lazkao archive holds internal documents, official communications, pamphlets, and propaganda materials from this period. They are written in a combination of Spanish and the Basque language, Euskera. These documents enable the reader to chart the organization's decision-making process from its inception to its dissolution, over a period of approximately six years.

[107] Jerolmack and Khan, "Talk Is Cheap"; Kalyvas, "Urban Bias," 168; Atran, *Talking to the Enemy.*

[108] For example, Hamilton, *Women and ETA*; Moro, "Gerra iraultzailetik nazionalismo"; Ortuñez, "Revitalización del Partido Comunista"; Giacopucci, *ETA pm: El otro camino.*

[109] Soldevilla, *Historia de una Heterodoxia Abertzale*; Soldevilla, Barandiaran. and Casanellas, "La documentación de (y sobre) ETA."

The ETA documents are highly significant for the study of terrorism and political violence because accurate and reliable data on the internal processes of terrorist organizations are notoriously hard to come by.[110] A common difficulty faced by researchers who seek to uncover the motivations of terrorist groups is how to access reliable information about their decision-making processes.[111] It goes without saying that terrorists operate clandestinely to avoid detection and infiltration.[112] Thus, it is difficult for scholars to obtain accurate information about their internal processes.[113] Stathis N. Kalyvas has observed that written sources from civil conflicts are rare and are typically limited to government records.[114] However, with these documents, I am able to present a candid depiction of the internal deliberations of a terrorist organization as it grappled with the issue of whether to continue to engage in political violence.

Structure of the Book

This book commences with an overview of the literature on terrorist decision-making processes and organizational approaches to understanding terrorism. This is followed by a chapter that presents the theoretical framework employed in this study: the organizational survival approach to terrorism. This model holds that terrorist groups are organizations first and foremost and that the overriding objective of organizations is to ensure their own survival. The chapter explains how this approach helps to elucidate why certain conflicts persist when rational explanations would predict their conclusion.

The literature review and theory chapters are followed by the book's empirical component, which comprises seven chapters. Each chapter examines a particular decision point in the trajectory of ETA-pm. In Chapter 4 I provide background to Assembly VII, a debate that took place in 1976 within ETA-pm at which the organization decided to establish a legitimate political party. In Chapter 5, I examine the arguments presented at Assembly VII

110 Kalyvas, *Logic of Violence in Civil War*, 48–51; Chenoweth and Ulfelder, "Can Structural Conditions Explain?," 21.

111 Sageman, "Stagnation in Terrorism Research," 571; Silke, "The Devil You Know," 2; Oots, "Bargaining with Terrorists," 147; Bueno de Mesquita, "Political Economy of Terrorism," 14; Piazza and Walsh, "Physical Integrity Rights and Terrorism," 413–414.

112 Zech and Gabbay, "Social Network Analysis," 214–216; Shapiro, *Terrorist's Dilemma*," 3–6.

113 Silke and Petersen, "The Golden Age?," 692–693.

114 Kalyvas, "Urban Bias," 168.

and the internal debate that resulted in ETA-pm adopting a more moderate political position. In Chapter 6 I consider the debates that ETA-pm conducted concerning whether to support the first general election under the new democracy. Chapter 6 looks at the internal discussions on how to adapt the organization's military strategy to the new political circumstances. In Chapter 7 I discuss ETA-pm's admissions of failure and the decision to call a ceasefire. Chapters 8, 9, and 10 examine the three debates that took place between 1981 and 1982, which led to a further division of ETA-pm into two distinct organizations, one of which dissolved in late 1982. All these chapters use the original internal documents of ETA-pm to show the competing considerations that informed the decision-making processes at each juncture. Chapter 11 provides a brief overview of the outcome of the final debate that took place within ETA-pm and tracks the organization's trajectory to its ultimate dissolution.

The book concludes with a summary of the results of the empirical analysis and information on the primary sources to facilitate further research. In the summary of results, I argue that the original records of the debates demonstrate that most of the ETA-pm membership were motivated by a desire to maintain their organization and to continue operations. This was their paramount concern and was considered more important than the nationalist cause and the desires of the Basque people. I then provide a discussion of the implications of these results for academics and policy makers. I argue that the organizational survival approach can help to explain why some conflicts continue beyond the point at which it is in the terrorists' interests to continue operating. I then provide a discussion of the theoretical and empirical limitations of this study and provide recommendations for future research. The book concludes with an appendix that includes a discussion of the documents that are used in this book, along with their location and options for access. I believe that these documents can provide important insights into the way that terrorist and other illicit organizations operate. I therefore encourage researchers to access the original documents and use them as the basis for further analysis.

2

Current Understanding of Terrorist Mobilization and Persistence

Finding evidence of terrorist decision-making, such as the ETA-pm internal documents, has long been the holy grail of terrorism and political violence researchers.[1] As directly observing terrorist groups' private deliberations has been impossible, researchers have had to use the data they could find or interviews with former militants.[2] Researchers have then made inferences on the terrorists' decision-making.[3] Having direct access to the terrorists' decision-making processes and being able to "listen in," so to speak, with transcripts and minutes gives researchers a more accurate picture of the incentives, constraints, and considerations that caused the terrorists to make the decisions they made.

Despite data constraints, terrorism and political violence scholars have developed a variety of compelling explanations for conflict persistence. The dominant framework within the literature is rational choice theory.[4] This approach has yielded valuable research on terrorist mobilization and operations.[5] However, its fundamental premise, that conflict should end when the costs outweigh the benefits, is called into question by the historical record. Even once militants have agreed on suitable terms for demobilizing, in most conflicts, hostilities resume.[6] Joakim Kreutz examined data from civil wars

[1] Kalyvas, "Urban Bias in Research," 168; Sageman, "Stagnation in Terrorism Research," 571; Schuurman and Eijkman, "Moving Terrorism Research Forward"; Schuurman, "Conducting Qualitative Research."

[2] Lidow, *Violent Order*; Orsini, "Interview with a Terrorist."

[3] Chenoweth and Ulfelder, "Can Structural Conditions Explain?," 21; Oots, "Bargaining with Terrorists," 147; Bueno de Mesquita, "Political Economy of Terrorism," 14; Piazza and Walsh, "Physical Integrity Rights and Terrorism," 413–414.

[4] Keeney and von Winterfeldt, "Identifying and Structuring the Objectives of Terrorists." Rational choice theory is also the dominant approach in organizational studies: Georgiou, "The Goal Paradigm," 292; Regan and Norton, "Greed, Grievance, and Mobilization," 323.

[5] See, for example, Mason and Quinn, "Sustaining the Peace"; Doyle and Sambanis, "International Peacebuilding"; Chang, *Study of Political Coercion* ; Humphreys and Weinstein, "Who Fights?"; Hirsch, "Sacrifice for the Cause"; Thomas, "Rewarding Bad Behavior"; Peter Krause, "Political Effectiveness."

[6] Walter, *Committing to Peace*, 3–5.

Euskadi Ta Askatasuna. Nell Bennett, Oxford University Press. © University of Maryland National Consortium for the Study of Terrorism and Responses to Terrorism (START) (2025). DOI: 10.1093/9780197764268.003.0002

between 1946 and 2012 in ninety-nine countries and found that of conflicts that had been terminated, postresolution stability was only maintained in 43 percent of cases. In the 52 percent of cases that were resolved by signed peace agreements on agreed terms, conflict resumed within ten years.[7] This begs the question: why do militants choose war over an acceptable (and agreed upon) peace? This is the gap in the research that I address in this book. Specifically, I argue that organizational dynamics play a key role in conflict persistence. The focus on micro and macro factors in the terrorism literature has yielded valuable insights. However, more attention is due to the meso or group-level factors. This book advances one framework for examining the organizational drivers of persistent conflicts.

There has been significant research on the internal dynamics that contribute to conflict persistence.[8] These approaches problematize the unique characteristics of organizations. Organizational studies of conflict encompass research on internal dynamics of terrorist organizations, including intragroup competition, splitting, merging, and factionalism.[9] These studies complement rational choice research by examining structural factors and internal dynamics that influence organizational decision-making and goal setting.[10] Organizational studies suggest that the internal dynamics of terrorist organizations may have as much if not more influence on the groups' trajectories as external factors, including government responses.[11]

Rational Choice Explanations

According to classical rational choice theory, individuals make decisions in order that they may optimize their own well-being while, at the same time, minimize costs.[12] Researchers who view conflict from a rational choice perspective typically see terrorists as rational utility maximizers who use violence when the expected political gains, minus projected costs, outweigh

[7] Kreutz, "Civil War Outcomes," 2. See also Högbladh, "Peace Agreements 1975–2011," 43; Kreutz, "When Armed Conflicts End."

[8] On organizational approaches see Zald and Lounsbury, "The Wizards of Oz"; Spicer and Böhm, "Moving Management"; Polletta, *Freedom Is an Endless Meeting*; Bolleyer, "The Irish Green Party"; Boucek, "Rethinking Factionalism."

[9] Pearlman and Cunningham, "Nonstate Actors, Fragmentation, and Conflict Processes"; Asal et al., "Why Split?"; Ishiyama and Batta, "Swords into Plowshares."

[10] Cunningham, "Actor Fragmentation."

[11] Brenner, "Recognition and Rebel Authority"; Rudloff and Findley, "Downstream Effects."

[12] Dugan and Chenoweth, "Moving Beyond Deterrence," 597.

alternative forms of political activism.[13] According to this approach, terrorist organizations are assumed to have relatively stable and consistent goals. They are expected to weigh the relative costs and benefits of the tactical options reasonably available to them, and they are projected to select the option that they anticipate will yield the maximum utility.[14]

Under classical rational choice theory, terrorists are assumed to be rational (or at least boundedly rational)[15] actors who use violence to achieve a political end. In determining whether to engage in violence they calculate the costs of the various alternatives, including nonviolent protest and political participation. The costs include the structure of the political system, in particular the degree of "openness" in the system, and the ways that the government responds to dissent.[16] Their objective is to impose sufficient costs on the targeted constituency so that its government will concede to their demands because concessions are perceived to be less costly than withstanding ongoing conflict.[17]

By the same logic, terrorists are predicted to demobilize when the cost of engaging in violence outweighs the benefits.[18] Hence, counterterrorists typically seek to develop capabilities that can inflict unacceptable costs on the opponent. Yet research on the efficacy of repression and deterrence is mixed.[19] Some have even argued that it does not work. Laura Dugan and Erica Chenoweth have observed that "empirically, unwanted behaviors continue—and indeed often increase—despite the threat of punishment." Indeed, they went so far as to argue that repressive policies have never resulted in a decrease in terrorism and have sometimes caused an escalation of violence.[20] This could be because, as Ted R. Gurr argued, "[r]epressive policies increase anger and resistance; denial of the right to use conventional politics and protest pushes activists underground and spawns terrorist and revolutionary resistance."[21] This is particularly applicable to indiscriminate deterrence or repression, which typically targets the broader community

[13] Abrahms, "What Terrorists Really Want," 78; Shapiro, "Terrorist Decision-Making," 6; Crenshaw, "Causes of Terrorism," 380.

[14] Eisenhardt and Zbaracki, "Strategic Decision Making," 18.

[15] On bounded rationality see Simon, *Models of Bounded Rationality*, 291–294.

[16] Muller and Weede, "Cross-National Variation," 625.

[17] Arce and Sandler, "Terrorist Signalling," 573.

[18] Becker, "Crime and Punishment"; Felson and Clarke, "Opportunity Makes the Thief"; Dugan and Chenoweth, "Moving Beyond Deterrence," 597.

[19] Opp and Roehl, "Repression, Micromobilization," 523.

[20] Dugan and Chenoweth, "Moving Beyond Deterrence," 597–598.

[21] Gurr, "Some Observations on Resistance," 283–284.

to which the offenders pertain and may compromise the legitimacy of the repressor.[22]

Organizational theory posits that these rational choice models tend to overestimate the information gathering and processing abilities of individual decision makers, as well as to underestimate social influences on decisions in organizational contexts.[23] Herbert A. Simon argued that adaptive behavior causes individuals and organizations to "satisfice" rather than "optimize." Thus, it is essential to consider their environment as well as their preferences, incentives, and constraints.[24] In Paul A. Anderson's critique of the traditional rational choice approach, he argued that the model needs to be imbued with the behavioral dimensions of individual information processing as well as the social and symbolic interactions that occur within organizations.[25]

Similarly, Charles E. Lindblom argued that rational choice theory assumes decision makers to be capable of assembling all relevant values or objectives, assessing the effects of all potential outcomes on those values and undertaking a systemic comparison of the relative merits of all alternatives. This, he argued, could only be possible for the simplest problems and even then, in a modified form.[26] When faced with complex social problems it is rare that decision makers will agree on the values and objectives that are to be pursued. This contradicts the traditional conception of decisions as means-ends processes whereby means are selected to advance predetermined ends.[27]

Another criticism that is frequently made of rational choice approaches is that they assume terrorist groups are collectively rational. The group is viewed as a unitary actor with stable preferences that is able to evaluate competing options without internal dissent.[28] Accordingly, it should be relatively easy to interpret the behavior of a terrorist group because their actions should reflect the sum of their goals and constraints. Organizational approaches, in contrast, assume that although groups may act rationally, the decisions they reach may still be suboptimal. This can be the result of information deficits, evaluation constraints, time limitations, and internal

[22] Dugan and Chenoweth, "Moving Beyond Deterrence," 600; Daxecker and Hess, "Repression Hurts," 560; Snow et al., "Frame Alignment Processes."
[23] Anderson, "Decision Making by Objection," 201–202.
[24] Simon, "Rational Choice.".
[25] Anderson, "Decision Making by Objection."
[26] Lindblom, "Science of 'Muddling Through,'" 79–80.
[27] Ibid., 81–83.
[28] McCormick, "Terrorist Decision Making," 482; Sobek and Payne, "A Tale of Two Types."

dissent, all of which can cause members to choose a course of behavior that may only satisfy the minimum requirements for achieving the groups' objectives.[29]

Rational choice theory can provide compelling explanations for conflict persistence. Dan Reiter argued that bargaining provides a helpful metaphor for understanding the relationship between two warring actors.[30] Reiter applied a realist perspective to conflict resolution, which holds that the lack of international enforcement mechanisms means that compliance with peace agreements is likely to be rare. Accordingly, parties may choose not to agree to negotiated settlements and instead pursue absolute victory, which in the case of conflict can result in long-standing wars of attrition.[31]

Barbara F. Walter breaks the conflict resolution process down into three stages: the initial negotiation stage during which the parties determine whether they will engage in peace talks; the bargaining stage during which they decide whether they will reach an agreement; and the implementation stage in which they choose whether and how to execute the agreement.[32] Walter argues that the implementation stage is both the most important and most underexamined part of the conflict resolution process. Walter observes that as part of the implementation phase the militants would be required to relinquish their arms and any conquered territory. This puts them at high risk of exploitation and surprise attack. Therefore, unless the militants are certain that the agreement will be upheld, they are unlikely to lay down their arms. It is possible to subvert even the most carefully designed enforcement measures, and this could explain the fact that so few conflicts resolve into stable peace.[33]

Katherine Glassmyer and Nicholas Sambanis examined conflicts in which militants were integrated into the national army after disarming. The logic behind these programs is that by joining the national armed forces the militants are granted a means of controlling the coercive power of the state. However, in their analysis Glassmyer and Sambanis found no evidence that this approach resulted in longer-lasting peace settlements.[34] Monica Duffy Toft presented the theory of "mutual benefit and mutual harm." According to this argument, conflict resolution is more likely to result in enduring

[29] Cohen et al., "A Garbage Can Model,", 1–4; Langley et al., "Opening Up Decision Making."
[30] Reiter, *How Wars End*, 8.
[31] Ibid., 23–25.
[32] Walter, *Committing to Peace*, 19.
[33] Ibid., 20–21.
[34] Glassmyer and Sambanis, "Rebel: Military Integration."

peace when it involves a settlement that contains credible mechanisms for punishing those who defect from the terms of the agreement, as well as a credible system for distributing benefits to the signatories. Under this system, survivors are granted the right to inflict direct harm on any defectors.[35] Bargaining theory presents a logical framework for understanding how militants behave when they want to reach a peace agreement but lack the necessary assurances to demobilize. However, it does not explain cases in which militants prefer conflict over peace despite credible commitments.

Rational choice can also provide persuasive arguments when the content of the terrorists' utility is expanded to incorporate more intangible elements. While "thick" rational choice theory emphasizes narrow self-interest, "thin" approaches examine the preferences of the individual and allow for psychological considerations.[36] Thus, notions of identity, emotions, and the desire for revenge can be utility that the terrorists seek to maximize by maintaining armed conflict. Bryan Caplan developed a model of "rational irrationality" to fit apparently irrational behavior into the rational choice framework. He argued that some actors have an additional utility function, which he called "fidelity to cherished beliefs." This means that they prefer to believe certain things, even if the evidence does not support them. This can provide the necessary justification and incentive for continuing to engage in conflict even when it no longer appears logical to do so.[37]

Another common hypothesis that fits within the "thin" rational choice approach is that of relative deprivation.[38] Gurr famously applied relative deprivation and the frustration-aggression model in *Why Men Rebel* and argued that political repression is a form of relative deprivation, which leads to discontent and, in turn, rebellion.[39] While commonly applied to conflict onset,[40] relative deprivation has also been used to explain persistent and intractable conflicts. One example of this is Lingyu Lu and Cameron G. Thies's analysis of economic inequality and conflict duration. Lu and Thies used the Armed Conflict Dataset (1960–1992) to demonstrate that inequality resulted in deadlier and more protracted conflicts.[41] Another example

[35] Toft, *Securing the Peace*, 17, 154.
[36] Hechter and Kanazawa, "Sociological Rational Choice Theory,". 194; Hug, "Further Twenty Years of Pathologies?"; Lehtinen and Kuorikoski, "Unrealistic Assumptions," 119–120.
[37] Caplan, "Terrorism," 98.
[38] On the difference between perceived and actual deprivation see Crosby, "Model of Egoistical Relative Deprivation."
[39] Opp and Roehl, "Repression, Micromobilization," 522; Lichbach, *The Rebel's Dilemma*, 4.
[40] Cederman, Weidmann, and Gleditsch, "Horizontal Inequalities."
[41] Lu and Thies, "Economic Grievance."

is a study by Daniel Druckman and Cecilia Albin that examined different kinds of peace accords. They found that those that use distributive justice to address existing inequality led to more durable peace.[42] Of course, this study only examined cases in which parties had managed to implement a peace agreement. It did not address the majority of conflicts in which no peace agreement was ever enacted.

The relative deprivation framework does not discount the importance of rational choice calculations. Rather, it changes the content of the utility that militants seek to maximize.[43] Many different theories have been advanced to explain the specific psychological processes by which perceived deprivation perpetuates violent conflict. These include the frustration-aggression hypothesis, lack of just deserts or distributive justice, alienation, class consciousness, or identification with a dissident group.[44] Heavy-handed government policies can create the desire to strike back or take revenge. The need for vengeance can arise from incidents the individual has experienced personally or suffering that has been inflicted on the broader community or identity group.[45] Conflicts of long duration can create deep divisions between the militants and the state, thereby further perpetuating the conflict.[46] Thus, pre-existing ethnic and social cleavages have been identified as predictors of conflict persistence and the resumption of hostilities after conflict resolution.[47]

However, the utility of the frustration-aggression hypothesis has been challenged by a body of scholarly work that casts doubt on the strength of the link between frustration and aggression.[48] Joan Neff Gurney and Kathleen J. Tierney have observed that there has been little attention paid to the fact that there may be other responses to deprivation-induced frustration than collective aggression.[49] Thomas F. Pettigrew also criticized Gurr's application of relative deprivation to collective protest. According to Pettigrew, Gurr overlooked the social psychological genesis of relative deprivation and the fact that it is a phenomenon applicable to individual responses and

[42] Druckman and Albin, "Distributive Justice."
[43] Gurr, "Some Observations on Resistance,". 282–283.
[44] Lichbach, *The Rebel's Dilemma*, 4.
[45] Jacques and Taylor, "Male and Female Suicide Bombers," 307.
[46] Gallimore, "Unresolved Trauma."
[47] Westendorf, *Why Peace Processes Fail*"; Boukhars, "Logic of Violence," 123.
[48] Miller, "Frustration-Aggression Hypothesis"; Berkowitz, "Whatever Happened?"
[49] Gurney and Tierney, "Relative Deprivation," 36.

not to group activity. Pettigrew opined that Gurr's use of macro-level economic and political indices obscured actual human reactions. As he put it, "macro-units are too broad to determine individual data, and individuals have unique properties that cannot be inferred from macro data."[50] This is an additional reminder of the importance of examining granular data from inside actual terrorist organizations to understand their decision-making processes.

According to rational choice theory, conflict should end when one party suffers costs that outweigh any benefits (real or perceived) from persistence. In the words of I. William Zartman, "when the parties find themselves locked in a conflict from which they cannot escalate to victory and this deadlock is painful to both of them (although not necessarily in equal degrees or for the same reasons), they seek a way out."[51] In a 1989 discussion of the decline of domestic terrorist groups in the United States and Canada, Jeffrey Ross and Gurr applied Andrew Mack's general analysis of the strategy of conflict.[52] Mack's thesis was that the outcome of conflict was determined by the relative strength of the contending parties. Strength was understood to mean both military and political capabilities, with "political capabilities" including affiliations with political parties and popular support.[53] Ross and Gurr adopted Mack's argument that this loss of political strength was a more frequent contributor to the decline in militant organizations than military defeat.[54] This ties in with the classic tenet of counterinsurgency canon that a sure-fire way of undermining a rebellion is to win the hearts and minds of the populace. However, under rational choice theory the populace itself is made up of rational actors who also make cost-benefit analyses. As Stathis N. Kalyvas has argued, violence is an effective means of garnering popular support. Civilians may have political preferences, but their ultimate priority is to stay alive. Thus, in a competitive political environment they will cooperate with the group that makes the most credible threats.[55]

Martha Crenshaw discussed Ross and Gurr's use of Mack's framework. She noted its utility but argued that it gave rise to numerous questions about the interrelationship of internal and external variables. For her explanation of the decline of terrorist groups she adopted three variables:

[50] Pettigrew, "Samuel Stouffer and Relative Deprivation," 13.
[51] Zartman, "Ripeness," 228.
[52] Ross and Gurr, "Why Terrorism Subsides," 408.
[53] Mack, "Utility of Terrorism."
[54] Ross and Gurr, "Why Terrorism Subsides," 408–409.
[55] Kalyvas, "Paradox of Terrorism," 138.

government responses (including pre-emption, deterrence, and conciliation), the organization's strategic choices, and the group's organizational resources. Crenshaw argued that a nuanced understanding of terrorist persistence must encompass the group's external, internal, and organizational characteristics.[56]

Organizational Approaches

While studies that focus on the strategic interaction between states and challengers typically take a "black box" approach, researchers are increasingly examining the influence of intragroup dynamics on violence.[57] Such studies attempt to move away from the assumption that nonstate groups are substantive entities with fixed goals and identities. But they rather treat the objectives, interests, and divisions between groups as outcome of contentious processes and not just a reflection of their ideological cause or strategic objective.[58]

Recently, organizational behavioral theories have become increasingly popular in political violence research. This approach is premised on the assumption that violent groups function much like nonviolent groups of similar size and scope.[59] An example of this is Abdulkader H. Sinno's book *Organizations at War*, in which he applied contingency theory from management studies to the Afghan conflict. Sinno contended that there are considerable similarities between corporations and warring organizations. Both compete with other organizations to get a larger share of the market, or in the case of civil conflict, popular support.[60]

Another similarity between legal and illegal organizations is the way they treat their members. Mancur Olson argues that political organizations work to further the common interests of their members and that "the assumption that organizations typically exist to further the common interests of groups of people is implicit in most of the literature about organizations."[61] Terrorist organizations operate much like political organizations. They also seek to

[56] Crenshaw, "How Terrorism Declines," 80.
[57] McCormick, "Terrorist Decision Making"; Eisenhardt and Bourgeois, "Politics of Strategic Decision Making," 737.
[58] For example, see Sindre, "From Secessionism to Regionalism"; Daly, "Dark Side of Power-Sharing"; Bakke et al., "A Plague of Initials," 266; Vogt et al., "From Claims to Violence."
[59] Crenshaw, "Terrorism Research," 563.
[60] Sinno, *Organizations at War*, 10.
[61] Olson, *Logic of Collective Action*, 7. See also Bentley, *Process of Government*, 211.

achieve their members' political goals. What sets them apart from legitimate political organizations is their use of violence to advance their objectives.[62]

A classical (and indeed, rational choice) definition of an organization is "the arrangement of personnel for facilitating the accomplishment of some agreed purpose through the allocation of functions and responsibilities,"[63] or even, "the structural expression of rational action."[64] However, there is a long history of scholarship that has sought to add nuance to this conceptualization.[65] Back in 1948, Philip Selznick argued that this understanding of organizations overlooks their human element. Selznick observed that organizations are at once "an economy" meaning a system of relationships that define the availability of scarce resources that can be manipulated to maximize effectiveness. But they are also social systems made up of individual people who will inevitably respond to situations as human beings, thereby undermining the pure rationality of their structure.[66]

Selznick conceptualized organizations as aggregates of subgroups, bound together by incentives.[67] Selznick argued that the ends and means of the subgroups may conflict with those of the leadership and that there could be conflict within the organization over the distribution of power.[68] The organization itself is constantly required to adapt to the changing environment and adjust its internal organization. Organizational goals are understood to change in accordance with internal and external pressures.[69] This understanding of organizations gained substantial traction in organizational theory. Andrew M. Pettigrew considers organizations to be open political systems made up of specialized subgroups.[70] And indeed, John W. Meyer, W. Richard Scott, David Strang, and Andrew L. Creighton used the subunit structure to decouple the concept of bureaucracy from centralization to argue that bureaucracies can and frequently do develop in decentralized organizations.[71]

[62] Oots, "Bargaining with Terrorists," 148.
[63] Gaus, "Theory of Organization, 66.
[64] Selznick, "Foundations of the Theory of Organization," 25.
[65] For an alternative perspective see Meyer and Rowan, "Institutionalized Organizations."
[66] Selznick, "Foundations of the Theory of Organization," 26.
[67] On the development of the subunit structure, see Boeker, "Development and Institutionalization."
[68] Cameron, "Critical Questions," 70.
[69] Selznick, "Foundations of the Theory of Organization"; Gaertner and Ramnarayan, "Organizational Effectiveness," 102. For examples of studies that treat organizational goals as the product of internal and external factors see Rootes, "Transformation of Environmental Activism"; Rucht and Roose, "Neither Decline nor Sclerosis"; Drago, "Predicting Organisational Objectives."
[70] Pettigrew, *Politics of Organisational Decision-Making*, ch. 2.
[71] Meyer et al., "Bureaucratization without Centralization."

The social aspect of organizations is also vital for understanding terrorist behavior. Shared identity and camaraderie have been identified as motivations for mobilization and persistence.[72] The same can be said for organizations. In his 1937 book, *The Folklore of Capitalism,* Thurman W. Arnold argued that organizations need four things to survive: a creed or set of rituals that makes each member feel an integral part of the group, a set of attitudes that make the creed effective, institutional habits by means of which the members automatically work together, and mythology or tradition that gives the creed a force beyond that of human creation. These four essential elements hold the group together with a sense of shared identity and purpose.[73]

Social and political psychology research can help to explain why people join terrorist organizations. Michael Hogg and Dominic Abrams observe that the simple act of joining a group is rewarding, noting that there is "a very powerful human motive for social contact that causes people to affiliate."[74] This draws on social identity theory that posits that people understand their own identity by reference to their group memberships. Groups, therefore, serve as a means of constructing and protecting the identities of their members.[75] Henri Tajfel and John Turner described groups, or "social categorizations," as "cognitive tools that segment, classify, and order the social environment," thereby allowing the individual to define their place in society.[76] Social identity theory does not examine extremism, but it does set out the conditions under which groups can become competitive and assertive. It can therefore be applied to the interactions between the incumbent organization (the state) and the challenger nonstate group.[77] Hogg and Janice Adelman argue that a group can become radical when the things that the group stands for come under threat, or when the group perceives itself as deprived in relation to other groups. The result can be that members strengthen their identification with the radical group at the expense of their ties to other more moderate groups.[78]

[72] Kruglanski and Orehek, "Quest for Personal Significance"; Giezendanner and Ingelaere, "Understand Ex-Combatants' Political Participation?," 9.

[73] Arnold, *Folklore of Capitalism*. See also Shils and Janowitz, "Cohesion and Disintegration."

[74] Hogg and Abrams, "Towards a Single-Process," 179.

[75] Islam, "Social Identity Theory."

[76] Tajfel and Turner, "'Integrative Theory of Intergroup Conflict," 59.

[77] Hogg and Adelman, "Uncertainty-Identity Theory," 437–438.

[78] Ibid., 441.

In *Inside Rebellion,* Jeremy M. Weinstein discussed the relevance of organizational culture to conflict persistence. Weinstein suggested that when faced with mounting losses, militant groups "draw on the shared beliefs and behaviors of the identities or networks that brought them together to reinforce their long-term orientation and prevent defection to the opposing side."[79] The psychology of the organization can also explain how state repression leads to the continuation of terrorist activities. The atmosphere of chaos and crisis that can be the result of state violence and oppression can in fact foster group cohesion.[80] In such circumstances group members may feel further alienated from the state and more reliant on the group for physical and emotional support. Recruits may continue to support the organization and participate in rebellious activities to share the cost of rebellion, despite the increasing risk and personal cost of doing so.[81]

In *Organizations at War,* Sinno argues that the internal power distribution in warring organizations creates incentive structures within the organization.[82] These incentives motivate the behavior of the individual members, which in turn affects the organization's overall performance and its ability to survive. Sinno found that certain structures make organizational success more likely and thereby increase the odds of the organization outlasting its rivals.[83] This book used organizational theory to develop a valuable method of predicting the relative success of warring groups. However, it did not explain why some groups choose to fight on when the odds are against their succeeding.

Henning Tamm also examined the internal structures of terrorist groups. Tamm found that external sponsors can help foster group cohesion when they allocate resources to the group leader but can create divisions when those resources are instead diverted to internal rivals. This can lead to coups and splitting.[84] Internal divisions can contribute to terrorist persistence, because as Crenshaw has observed, splitting is a form of terrorist propagation.[85] Ethan Bueno de Mesquita notes that terrorists and terrorist groups often have shifting and unstable structures and are generally

[79] Weinstein, *Inside Rebellion*, 263. See also Gates, "Recruitment and Allegiance," 115.

[80] For example, Paul D. Kenny found that periods of more intense fighting between British forces and the Provisional Irish Republican Army correlated with higher levels of cohesion. Kenny, "Structural Integrity and Cohesion," 552.

[81] Hirsch, "Sacrifice for the Cause," 245.

[82] Sinno, *Organizations at War*, 11.

[83] Ibid.

[84] Tamm, "Rebel Leaders."

[85] Crenshaw, "How Terrorism Declines," 80.

constituted by heterogeneous factions that splinter as the political landscape in which they operate changes.[86] These divisions have important influences on organizational decision-making.[87] Factions often disagree over the utility of violence as opposed to negotiated settlements. If one faction accepts government concessions, other factions may become more extreme to signal their continuing resolve and to undermine the peace process.[88] This gives rise to the "spoiling" phenomenon that can prevent conflict resolution.[89]

There are compelling arguments that spoiling is a significant cause of conflict persistence. Wendy Pearlman contends that it can be the result of internal power struggles within rebel organizations. Pearlman states that nonstate entities typically comprise numerous factions vying for power.[90] According to her "internal contestation model," spoiling is more likely to occur in groups that do not have an institutionalized system of legitimate representation. This is because a system of representation settles the issue of who has the right to speak on behalf of the group. When such a system is lacking, rivals and contenders within the group may seek to influence the group's policy by forming alliances and factions within the group and by engaging directly with the incumbent regime.[91]

Adding to the research on intra-organizational dynamics, Kathleen Gallagher Cunningham, Kristin M. Bakke, and Lee J. M. Seymour found that such factors, including factionalism, rivalries, and contestation, are as important a driver of conflict as government action. Thus, conflict resolution and peace building are "as much about dynamics within groups as between these groups and the states they challenge."[92] Literature on the decline of organizations has been of assistance to this field of inquiry. Albert O. Hirschman argues that members who are dissatisfied with the group's leadership have two options: voice or exit. Voice is the articulation of complaints to change the group's direction. Exit, which typically occurs after attempts to exercise voice have been unsuccessful, refers to either joining a rival organization or splintering off to create a new group.[93] Crenshaw finds

86 Bueno de Mesquita, "Terrorist Factions," 399–400.
87 Nilsson, "Partial Peace," 21–22.
88 Kydd and Walter, "Sabotaging the Peace," 264–265.
89 Newman and Richmond, *Challenges to Peacebuilding.*
90 Pearlman, "Spoiling Inside and Out," 84.
91 Ibid. See also McLauchlin and Pearlman, "Out-Group Conflict, In-Group Unity?," 2.
92 Cunningham et al., "Shirts Today, Skins Tomorrow," 87.
93 Crenshaw, "Theories of Terrorism," 22.

that both exit and voice can hasten the decline of an organization; thus leaders must safeguard the loyalty of their members, typically with incentives or coercion.[94]

It is also important to note that the spoiling literature is grounded in rational choice theory. The underlying assumption is that militants will scuttle a deal if it is in their interest to do so. Kelly M. Greenhill and Solomon Major used rational choice theory to posit that spoiling is a function of incentives and constraints. If militants perceive that they can get a better deal by continuing to fight, or if leaders can no longer convince their followers to accept a negotiated settlement, then spoiling will occur.[95] This thesis is applicable in cases in which militants can receive tangible benefits from continuing the conflict. However, it does not provide a satisfactory explanation for instances in which militants reject generous peace accords to their own detriment.

Pearlman and Theodore McLauchlin examined the effects of government action on intra-organizational dynamics and found that repression can disrupt the equilibrium within the organization. This can either lead to greater cooperation among its members or greater conflict, depending on the members' satisfaction with the pre-existing internal power distribution. If the group members were relatively satisfied with the institutional arrangements, the repression will be perceived as a challenge to be surmounted and will cause the members to redouble their efforts to unify the movement.[96] However, where members were dissatisfied, repression will provide an opportunity for those members to express their opposition to the status quo.[97] The dissidents may try to take advantage of the disruption caused by the repression to set up new leadership, finance, or organizational structures, which could in turn generate conflict within the movement's ranks. As Pearlman and McLauchlin observe, this has important implications for conflict resolution. Civil wars have been found to last longer when they involve multiple factions.[98] This creates the phenomenon that David E. Cunningham labeled "veto players" who have the ability to derail settlement negotiations. Cunningham found a strong correlation between the number of veto players

[94] Hirschman, *Exit, Voice and Loyalty*; Crenshaw, "Theories of Terrorism," 22–23; Bekker, "Protest as an Act of Love," 8.

[95] Greenhill and Major, "Perils of Profiling," 12–14.

[96] McLauchlin and Pearlman, "Out-Group Conflict, In-Group Unity?," 2.

[97] Ibid.

[98] Ibid., 48.

and the duration of civil war, thus giving further weight to the argument that spoiling is a predictor of persistent conflict.[99]

One possible explanation for why terrorist groups tend to continue beyond the point at which the benefits outweigh the costs is simple inertia. Michael T. Hannan and John Freeman hypothesized that most aspects of organizations suffer from the strong pressure of inertia. They defined organizational inertia as responding relatively slowly to threats and opportunities in the environment. This is due to internal factors including sunk costs in equipment and personnel, the dynamics of political coalitions, and ingrained standard operating procedures. Inertia is also caused by external factors, such as legal and other barriers to entry and exit, as well as fear that radical change could threaten the organization's legitimacy.[100]

Hannan and Freeman argue that part of the reason for organizational inertia is that successful organizations are generally reliable and accountable. These are characteristics that require that the organizational structure be reproducible. Reproducibility increases over time in step with internal learning, socialization, and the establishment of standard operating procedures. This reproducibility can cause increased inertia. Thus, established and successful organizations are more likely to be resistant to change.[101] Howard Aldrich and Ellen R. Auster built on the work of Hannan and Freeman and found that the internal conditions of organizations can increase inertia. These include the specialization of personnel, which is a defining feature of bureaucratization and decreases internal diversity, and the institutionalization of standard operating procedures. Organizations may also develop resources to provide a buffer from external conditions, thus making them less reliant on their environment.[102] This supports Weinstein's thesis that resource-rich terrorists are less beholden to their constituents and thus less concerned with maintaining popular support.[103]

Terrorist organizations may also be reluctant to change their strategic direction because they have already invested in organizational capabilities that are "difficult to create and costly to adjust."[104] As Rebecca M. Henderson and Kim B. Clark note, organizational change forces members to "ask a new set of questions, to draw on new technical and commercial

[99] Cunningham, "Veto Players and Civil War Duration."
[100] Hannan and Freeman, "Structural Inertia," 150–151.
[101] Ibid., 153–155; Singh and Lumsden, "Theory and Research in Organizational Ecology," 168.
[102] Aldrich and Auster, "Even Dwarfs Started Small," 170.
[103] Weinstein, *Inside Rebellion*.
[104] Henderson and Clark, "Architectural Innovation," 9.

skills, and to employ new problem-solving approaches."[105] Hannan and Freeman also explain why leaders could be disinclined to disband their organization. Creating an organization requires the accumulation of capital, support, entrepreneurial skills, and legitimacy. Once these resources have been invested, they are difficult to recover. Indeed, most of these scarce resources are lost when an organization dissolves.[106] In addition, institutionalized power distributions result in vested interests that "harden" as organizations age.[107] This in turn lowers the organization's sensitivity to changes in the environment and its willingness to change course.[108]

Conclusion

This chapter has presented a discussion of the literature on terrorist persistence. Rational choice approaches have made valuable inroads in understanding conflict termination. While the framework has given rise to a wealth of important research, the focus on using "means" to obtain "ends" often overlooks the fact that the chosen "means" may actually affect the "ends" that are ultimately pursued. In addition, cost-benefit analyses provide satisfying models, but their predictions are not always supported by history. "Thin" rational choice theorists have attempted to circumvent this obstacle by expanding the concept of utility. Such approaches have provided more nuanced understandings of individual decision-making processes. However, they also have the tendency to overlook the fact that an organization is more than just the sum of its parts.

Additionally, the rational choice assumption that militants will lay down their weapons when it is in their best interest to do so fails to account for cases in which terrorists choose to continue fighting in the face of mounting costs. This gap in the literature has prompted researchers to examine the internal dynamics of terrorist groups. Organizational approaches have allowed scholars to consider diverse factors including internal power struggles, factionalism, splitting, and merging. Compelling arguments have been made that these intra-organizational dynamics have as much, if not more, influence on conflict duration as government responses. I adopt this approach to argue that the unique characteristics of terrorist organizations

[105] Ibid.
[106] Hannan and Freeman, "Structural Inertia," 159.
[107] Aldrich and Auster, "Even Dwarfs Started Small," 170.
[108] Singh and Lumsden, "Theory and Research in Organizational Ecology," 180.

contribute to the phenomenon of persistent conflict. Indeed, I argue that the very fact that terrorist organizations are *organizations* is a significant factor that is too often overlooked. In the next chapter, I will present the theoretical approach that is employed in this book. The "'organizational survival approach" employs key organizational dynamics to provide novel explanations for persistent and intractable conflicts.

3

The Organizational Survival Approach to Terrorism

In this chapter, I introduce the theoretical framework for this book, which is called the organizational survival approach. It is a hybrid theoretical construct that draws heavily from organizational theory. According to the organizational survival approach, terrorist organizations have both public goals, meaning the professed goals that they claim to be pursuing, and internal goals, which are the goals that concern organizational maintenance.[1] I argue that the internal goals of terrorist organizations are primarily concerned with the survival and expansion of their organization. When the survival of the organization is threatened, organizational maintenance becomes the priority, even when this conflicts with the terrorists' public goals. The organizational survival approach provides an alternative to typical rational choice models that assess the success or failure of a terrorist organization by its ability to achieve its publicly professed goals.[2] Instead, it posits that there are structural features of terrorist organizations that incentivize members to perpetuate conflicts to preserve their organizational integrity. This, therefore, provides an explanation for why conflicts often persist beyond the point at which the benefits of violence outweigh the costs.

This chapter explains the organizational survival approach and discusses the role of goal displacement in terrorists' determination to continue fighting. Goal displacement is well established in organizational theory and can

[1] Arnold, *Folklore of Capitalism*, 356–357.

[2] Fortna, "Do Terrorists Win?," 523; Kydd and Walter, "Strategies of Terrorism," 52; Merari, "Terrorism as a Strategy"; Dudouet, "Dynamics and Factors of Transition"; Do and Iyer, "Geography, Poverty and Conflict"; Kilcullen, "Countering Global Conflict," 601–604; Phelan, "Engaging Conflict";. Emerson, "Desert Conflict," 678. For an alternative view of terrorist objectives that incorporates organizational maintenance, see Acosta, "Live to Win Another Day." This approach is also the dominant method by which the efficacy of legitimate organizations are assessed: Yuchtman and Seashore, "A System Resource Approach," 892; Cameron, "Critical Questions." 67.

Euskadi Ta Askatasuna. Nell Bennett, Oxford University Press. © University of Maryland National Consortium for the Study of Terrorism and Responses to Terrorism (START) (2025). DOI: 10.1093/9780197764268.003.0003

provide important insights for civil war studies. The research on goal displacement has shown that once individuals form a collective, they acquire special interests that may conflict with the objectives they came together to pursue. The predominant interest is the survival of the organization. The reason for this is that once a person acquires a position within an organization, they become the recipient of benefits.[3] Individuals have been shown to weigh losses more heavily than gains, so once positioned within an organization they resist any change that could result in a loss of these benefits, even if they were to be rewarded with commensurate gains.[4] The theory presented in this chapter explains why terrorist organizations often attempt to survive against competitors by becoming more conservative. This is contrary to studies that argue that terrorists may decide to engage in more violent attacks when faced with competition to maintain media attention, notoriety, and popular support. Instead, I will argue that terrorists seek to expand their base by courting more moderate sections of society. However, when the survival of the organization is in jeopardy, it may well become more radical and engage in more brutal or indiscriminate attacks.[5]

This chapter is divided into two parts. The first explains the organizational survival approach and the concept of goal displacement. The second part applies this theory to terrorist groups. It shows how organizational theory can be used to explain mobilization to violent extremism and conflict persistence. The chapter will close with a brief discussion of some of the benefits to the organizational survival approach. I argue that an important aspect of resolving a conflict is knowing what the adversary *really* wants. This requires an in-depth understanding of the internal dynamics of the terrorist organization, as these dynamics create unique incentive structures for their members. These incentive structures can cause members to be hesitant to accept negotiated settlements or amnesty agreements. Thus, counterterrorism practitioners who are seeking to encourage terrorists to demobilize should address these organizational incentive structures and create alternatives for militants that compensate them for any perceived loss of utility and that overcome the status quo bias.

[3] Aldrich and Auster, "Even Dwarfs Started Small," 170.

[4] Kahneman and Tversky, "Prospect Theory"; Weyland, "Risk Taking in Latin American Economic Restructuring"; Kahneman et al., "Endowment Effect."

[5] Crenshaw, "Theories of Terrorism," 22–23; Chenoweth, "Democratic Competition," 16–30; Nemeth, "Effect of Competition," 3–5; Biberman and Zahid, "Why Terrorists Target Children."

Incentive Structures of Conflict

The organizational survival approach fuses organizational theory with rational choice understandings of conflict to provide researchers with a more complete picture of terrorist incentive structures. It argues that the paramount objective of terrorist groups is to maintain the integrity of the organization. All stated aims are subordinate to this objective. The significance of this model is that it provides an alternative explanation for some of the apparently "irrational" behavior of terrorist organizations. To resolve conflicts, scholars and policy makers need to be able to understand terrorists' reasons for fighting. I argue that a thorough appreciation of terrorist incentive structures is not complete without an understanding of the organizational drivers of conflict. I emphasize the organizational aspect of conflicts because, ultimately, organizations are what fight wars. Not individual militants, not amorphous ethnic groups, not structureless collections of bandits and militants, not incumbent officials.[6] As Sinno has observed, engaging in conflict requires the performance of a range of complex processes, including recruitment and mobilization, logistical coordination, and the manipulation of information. These are tasks that can only be performed by organizations.[7]

Peace agreements with the incumbent regime frequently mean the dissolution of the military organization of the militant movement or the integration of the militant's military organization into the national army.[8]According to the organizational survival approach, in such a scenario the organization, or at least the militant organization within the wider movement, would scuttle the deal to preserve the organization and maintain the status quo. This may provide part of the explanation for why, as Pearlman has observed, thirty-one of the thirty-eight peace agreements signed between 1988 and 1998 did not last more than three years.[9] For such an agreement to succeed, the members would need to be offered benefits that would be sufficient to overcome their reluctance to relinquish the benefits that they received from the organization and to overcome any status quo bias.[10]

[6] Sinno, *Organizations at War in Afghanistan and Beyond*, 4.
[7] Ibid.
[8] Banholzer, "When Do Disarmament," 10–13; Schulhofer-Wohl and Sambanis, *Disarmament, Demobilization, and Reintegration Programs*; Muggah, "Innovations in Disarmament," 8; Berdal and Ucko, "Introduction to the DDR Forum."
[9] Pearlman, "Spoiling Inside and Out," 79.
[10] Fleming et al., "Overcoming Status Quo Bias," 6007; Korobkin, "Status Quo Bias," 618.

One difficulty for governments seeking to reach a peace agreement with terrorists is credibility.[11] Conflicts, and protracted conflicts in particular, tend to erode trust between the warring parties. If the militants relinquish their arms, they may have legitimate concerns that they are leaving themselves and their constituents open to state reprisals. They may also have little faith that the government will follow through with the promised benefits.[12] Thus, a risk averse terrorist may make the rational decision to reject even an apparently generous peace offering. This approach can also help to explain why conflicts persist after they have lost the support of their base.[13] While conflicts may begin with the intention of advancing their constituents' cause, as the organization develops, the original goals of the movement may come into conflict with the desire to maintain the integrity of the organization.[14] This can alienate the constituency and create the apparently paradoxical situation in which an armed group is purportedly fighting for a people who oppose their activities.[15]

At the heart of the model is an understanding of goal formation that is derived from organizational theory. This approach conceptualizes goals as the results of organizational processes. Goals are produced through the social dynamics within the organization and in consequence of external pressures, opportunities, and constraints.[16] This is in contrast with the dominant approach in conflict studies that typically assumes terrorist goals to be relatively static and independent of the internal dynamics of the terrorist organization.[17]

Goal Displacement

The pursuit of clearly articulated goals has been touted as a prerequisite to a successful conflict. As Mao Zedong wrote in *On Guerrilla Warfare*, "Without a political goal, guerrilla warfare must fail, as it must if its political objectives

[11] Brigadier Vere Hayes, "Establishing the Credibility," 2–12; Addison and Murshed, "Credibility and Reputation," 13.

[12] Walter, "Critical Barrier"; Hartzell et al., "Stabilizing the Peace"; Toft, "Ending Civil Wars," 34.

[13] Or indeed, even if they never had it to begin with. For example, see Stroll, *Rigoberta Menchu*, 44.

[14] Sanín, "Criminal Militants?," 20.

[15] For an example of militants using violence against the opposition of their base, see Alonso, "Modernization in Irish Republican Thinking," 138. For a discussion of the complexities of popular support during civil wars, see Kalyvas, "'New' and 'Old' Civil Wars," 109–113.

[16] Yuchtman and Seashore, "A System Resource Approach," 894.

[17] Lutz and Lutz, "How Successful Is Terrorism?," 4–5; Abrahms, "What Terrorists Really Want."

do not coincide with the aspirations of the people. . . ."[18] The reason that rational choice models tend to accept terrorists' public goals as their primary objectives is that under orthodox rational choice theory, objectives are equated to utility that is presumed to be stable and consistent.[19] Organizations, according to this view, are constructs created for the efficient advancement of established objectives.[20] However, this is not the only way of understanding terrorist goal setting. An alternative is to view organizations as complex organisms. Although they may have been created to accomplish certain goals, these organisms generate needs of their own.[21] This view has been termed "the natural systems model." This is because it understands organizational objectives to be the result of complex systems within the organization.[22] According to this perspective, once organizations have been created, they take on a distinctive identity.[23] This identity includes shared values, norms, accepted systems of operation, and modes of behavior.[24]

Members of the organization become invested in the perpetuation of this organizational identity. Thus, the survival objective is not just about mere persistence.[25] The survival of the organization is about maintaining the unique characteristics of the group in the face of changing external circumstances.[26] Terrorist groups do not typically begin with the objective of becoming perpetual organizations.[27] In the beginning, the organization's objectives will reflect their public goals. However, once a group of like-minded people form an organization with a leadership structure and a bureaucracy, they become subject to the unique drivers of organizations. The driver relevant to this discussion is referred to in organizational theory as "goal displacement."

Goal displacement refers to a phenomenon that occurs in organizations in which the main goals of that organization are disregarded in favor of goals that are associated with maintaining or advancing the organization itself.[28]

18 Zedong, *On Guerrilla Warfare*, 43. See also Guevara, *Guerrilla Warfare*, 54–55.
19 Green and Shapiro, *Pathologies of Rational Choice Theory*, 20.
20 Gaus, "A Theory of Organization," 66.
21 Selznick, *Leadership in Administration*."
22 Panebianco, *Political Parties*, 7.
23 Glynn, "When Cymbals Become Symbols," 286.
24 Selznick, *Leadership in Administration.*
25 Dutton and Dukerich, "Keeping an Eye on the Mirror," 520.
26 Selznick, *Leadership in Administration.*
27 For a discussion of mobilization into militant movements, see Bosi and Della Porta, "Micromobilization into Armed Groups"; White, "Peaceful Protest to Guerrilla War"; Opp and Roehl, "Repression, Micromobilization, and Political Protest".
28 Warner and Havens, "Goal Displacement," 539.

Goal displacement is a long-established component of organizational theory, yet in spite of this, limited attention has been paid to it in conflict studies. In a 1966 paper, Mayer N. Zald and Roberta Ash identified the "institutionalization and goal displacement model of organizational transformation" as the dominant approach to the sociological study of the transformation of social movement organizations.[29] Despite its prevalence in organizational theory, it has had limited influence on the study of conflict. One of the few scholars to apply the theory is Donatella Della Porta, who used it to describe individual motivation in violent political activism.[30]

Zald and Ash referred to this model as the Weber-Michels model. This is because it was based on Max Weber's *Essays in Sociology* and Robert Michels's *Political Parties*.[31] The model is as follows: as a social movement group attains an economic and social base the original charismatic leadership is replaced by a bureaucratic structure that has a stake in maintaining the organization regardless of its ability to maintain its stated goals.[32] The goal transformation process under the Weber-Michels model is a shift toward conservatism. Ambitious and targeted goals may be substituted for more attainable and diffuse goals to give the organization a broader sphere of operation. Organizational maintenance involves shifting attention to resources and personnel. The original goals of the organization are also subordinated to societal norms to avoid conflict with the wider society.[33]

The reason why organizations are thought to become more conservative in their operations is because it is anticipated that the bureaucracy will perceive this as the best way of expanding and maintaining its membership base. Weber warned that it "is a fundamental error to imagine that bureaucracy has the characteristic of being independent of any social basis. It finds its social basis in those power groups that control the organization of society."[34] If a bureaucracy is beholden to the power groups in its environment, it can be anticipated that it will seek to adapt its operating procedure to be able to exist in peace with those groups.

[29] Zald and Berger, "Social Movements in Organizations"; Nyden, "Democratizing Organizations."
[30] Della Porta, *Social Movements*, 165.
[31] Gerth and Mills, *From Max Weber*, 297–301; Michels, *Political Parties*; Zald and Ash, "Social Movement Organizations."
[32] Zald and Ash, "Social Movement Organizations," 327–328. See also Jordan, "Attacking the Leader."
[33] Zald and Ash, "Social Movement Organizations," 327–328.
[34] Weber, *Economy and Society*, 224.

Robert Michels discussed the "conservatization" of organizations in his 1949 book *Political Parties.* Michels is thought to have developed this idea after considering the German socialist movement of the pre–World War I era and its failure to pursue the revolutionary social policy for which its base was agitating.[35] Michels took the view that this was due to conservatism on the part of the organization's leadership and bureaucracy, which did not want to jeopardize the organization's survival by adopting a controversial policy.[36] In elaborating the theory of goal displacement, Michels argued:

> The interests of the body of employees are always conservative, and in a given political situation these interests may dictate a defensive and even a reactionary policy when the interests of the working class may dictate a bold and aggressive policy: in other cases, although these are very rare, the roles may be reversed. By a universally applicable social law, every organ of the collectivity, brought into existence through the need for the division of labor, creates for itself, as soon as it becomes consolidated, interests peculiar to itself. The existence of these special interests involve a necessary conflict with the interests of the collectivity. Nay, more, social strata fulfilling peculiar functions tend to become isolated, to produce organs fitted for the defence of their own peculiar interests.[37]

Thus, Michels argued that once individuals form an organization their position within the organizational structure will influence their interests. These interests may well conflict with the objectives of the constituency. If the members' overriding interest is to maintain their position within the organization, this would cause them to prioritize the interests of the organization over the interests of the base that the organization was created to advance. A similar tendency toward conservativism was observed by James DeNardo in this analysis of the Boston Tea Party movement. DeNardo found that to appeal to a broader social base, the Boston Committee of Correspondence abandoned the more aggressive tactics that had been favored by more radical Bostonians.[38]

In contrast, Kim Voss and Rachel Sherman found that innovation was possible, even within the highly bureaucratized labor unions of the United

[35] Hands, "Roberto Michels," 167.

[36] Ibid. This thesis is not without its critics. See, for example, Koelble, "Party Structures and Democracy," and Leach, "'The Iron Law of What Again?," 319.

[37] Michels, *Political Parties*, 353.

[38] DeNardo, *Power in Numbers*, 224–225.

States. They found that several factors explained the revitalization of the labor movement, including organizational crises and new leadership. This, they argued, indicated that the "iron law of oligarchy" was more malleable than some scholars, including Michels himself, had originally thought.[39] However, as Darcy K. Leach observes, "Those with power are always conservative in the sense that they have an interest in conserving their power, but where conservation of power depends on maintaining a mass membership, the avowed goals of the organization will take on whatever political content is most likely to attract more members."[40]

Another explanation for organizational shift, whether toward conservatism or radicalism, is Selzick's notion of coöptation. This is a process by which organizations absorb new elements into the leadership or the policy-determining structure to avert threats to the organization's survival. If an organization sees that its survival is threatened because of a change in market conditions, it can adapt its structure by incorporating new components that will bring the organization in line with market demands.[41] This can either be a formal or an informal process. Formal, when it is required to safeguard the legitimacy of the organization and some public demonstration is required. Informal when it is simply in response to pressures in the environment.[42]

At the heart of Michels's argument is that there is a fundamental tension in the relationship between the organization and its base. This is because the very nature of the organization will cause it to prioritize its own position, resources, and integrity over the concerns of the people it purports to serve. At times these two objectives may not be mutually exclusive. Indeed, the health and growth of the organization may be bolstered by helping the constituency. However, at key inflection points, such as toward the end of a civil war, the interests of the organization and its constituents can conflict. In the words of Gerald R. Salancik and Jeffrey Pfeffer: "Power is used by subunits . . . to enhance their own survival . . . Because of the processes by which power develops and is used, organizations become both more aligned and more misaligned with their environments."[43] It can therefore be argued that

[39] Voss and Sherman, "Breaking the Iron Law."

[40] Leach, "The Iron Law of What Again?," 319.

[41] Kristin Elisabeth Fabbe applied this concept in her analysis of secularization in nineteenth-century Greece, Turkey, and Egypt: Fabbe, *Disciples of the State*, 41–42.

[42] Selznick, *TVA and the Grass Roots*, 259.

[43] Salancik and Pfeffer, "Who gets Power," 4.

although organizations may be constituted to advance certain objectives, they are not structures best suited to goal fulfillment.[44]

The "Front" and "Back" of Terrorist Organizations

To understand why organizations' public goals may differ from their internal goals, one must look closely at the characteristics of organizations. Amitai Etzioni said that organizations are social systems. Goals, by contrast, are cultural entities. Etzioni argued that cultural entities tend to be more stable than social systems.[45] Therefore, the organization's stated objectives can maintain a position of prominence in the organization's communications. Yet, their actual goals may have shifted because of internal dynamics. As Etzioni stated, organizations do not fail to realize their public goals because of internal mismanagement or external conditions. Rather, it is because *"[t]hey are not meant to be realised."*[46]

Etzioni said that one of the reasons why organizations do not seek to accomplish their public goals is that it is impracticable for them to do so. Organizations have finite resources, and they are only able to dedicate part of those resources to goal advancement. The rest must go toward maintaining the organization through recruitment, fundraising, and other administrative tasks.[47] Etzioni argued that if an organization were to invest sufficient resources into their stated goals so as to effectively pursue them, the administrative function of the organization would be so greatly diminished that it would be unable to function effectively.[48] Thus, it would be forced to either abandon its objectives or to shut up shop. This is particularly so when organizations are facing challenging external circumstances. As Peter F. Drucker expressed: "in turbulent times, the first task of management is to make sure of the institution's capacity for survival, to make sure of its structural strength and soundness, of its capacity to survive a blow, to adapt to sudden change, and to avail itself of new opportunities."[49]

[44] Hannan and Freeman, "Structural Inertia and Organizational Change," 150–151; Dutton, "Understanding Strategic Agenda Building," 15.
[45] Etzioni, "Two Approaches to Organizational Analysis," 258.
[46] Ibid., 260.
[47] Ibid., 258.
[48] Ibid., 260.
[49] Drucker, *Managing in Turbulent Times*, 1; Cameron, "Effectiveness as Paradox," 545.

Of course, the disconnect between public goals and actual goals must be hidden from the organization's base. Aaron V. Cicourel has argued that this is achieved by appearing to pursue public goals, while concealing the organization's inner bureaucracy from public scrutiny. Cicourel found that in every organization there are certain members whose job it is to present the organization's "front" to the public. Often, these members are the public's only direct contact with the organization. In a terrorist organization, this would be the political or propaganda wings. According to Cicourel, the "back" of the organization comprises actions and communications that often directly contradict the organization's official line and are carefully fabricated to deceive the persons in the front. Cicourel posits that this structure exists in organizations whether its leaders are aware of the fact or not.[50]

Zald and Ash state that in order to maintain and gain public support, an organization must appear to be capable of fulfilling its promise of achieving its stated goals. Thus, the ideal organization would be "one which over time always seemed to be getting closer to its goal without quite attaining it."[51] As Hannan and Freeman put it, "Being too successful may result in a loss of mission, which results in survival failure."[52] Successful organizations must therefore master the art of redefining objectives and shifting goal posts. A key aspect of organizational maintenance is to present the organization in a way so that it appears to be the most viable vehicle for goal accomplishment, while never actually achieving the ultimate objective. By maintaining a credible front, and hiding their inner bureaucracy from view, terrorists can present their organization as the most viable means of advancing their constituents' cause.[53]

The Organizational Survival Approach: An Explanation for Conflict Persistence

The organizational survival approach provides a compelling explanation for conflict persistence. The key factor is the development of the bureaucracy. This is an element of conflict that has been neglected by terrorism and political violence researchers. This oversight is curious, as the role played

[50] Cicourel, "Front and Back," 55.
[51] Zald and Ash, "Social Movement Organizations," 333.
[52] Hannan and Freeman, "Obstacles to Comparative Studies," 128; Bedeian, *Organizations*, 126.
[53] Cicourel, "Front and Back," 55; Goffman, *Presentation of Self*.

by the bureaucracy has featured prominently in research on organizational decision-making in governments and political parties.[54] Bureaucracies, in essence, are "permanent, goal-oriented open systems."[55] They are built around specific objectives and are therefore goal oriented. However, the nature of the goals can affect the probability of their being realized. Bureaucracies are more prone to engage in goal displacement when they have been formed to pursue intangible goals. W. Keith Warner and A. Eugene Havens explain this principle:

> Intangible goals are expressions of intended states of affairs that do not adequately describe the desired states or the activities that would constitute their achievement. Such intangible goals do not provide adequate guidance for group action, and as a consequence, more tangible substitutes are developed.[56]

This is directly relevant to terrorist and insurgent organizations. The liberation of a people, or freedom from oppression, is an intangible goal. There are good reasons why terrorists or insurgents would choose to adopt intangible goals. This enables them to state their objectives in a grand and dramatic manner, inspiring people to take action. Intangible goals can also be open to interpretation, which can give the movement broad appeal.[57]

A bureaucracy with such an intangible mission is susceptible to goal displacement. Intangible goals are typically substituted for short term tangible goals.[58] Activities that are designed to protect and promote the organization are generally more tangible than those related to its broader overarching mission. As Warner and Havens state, "The activities needed to promote organizational equilibrium, survival, and growth tend to be more tangible and more easily comprehended than the activities necessary for the accomplishment of the ultimate goals professed by the organization."[59] Therefore, goals related to organizational survival are prioritized. In a competitive environment this can mean expanding at the expense of competitors to secure the organization's position in the marketplace, or to maintain its popular

[54] For example, Bendor and Moe, "Adaptive Model of Bureaucratic Politics"; Lebovic, "How Organizations Learn"; Wood, "Principals, Bureaucrats, and Responsiveness."
[55] Meier, "Bureaucracy and Democracy," 195.
[56] Warner and Havens, "Goal Displacement," 540.
[57] Ibid., 544.
[58] Simon, "Strategy and Organizational Evolution," 139.
[59] Warner and Havens, "Goal Displacement," 545.

support and access to resources.[60] Brian J. Phillips made the apparently counterintuitive observation that having adversarial relationships with other terrorist groups helps terrorist organizations survive.[61] This may be partly attributable to bureaucratic permanence. It may be that well-established bureaucracies are more likely to engage in competitive behavior to promote organizational survival. Competition also provides an organization with a tangible goal. Achieving better results than an adversary is the kind of clear, definable goal that could be readily adopted by an established bureaucracy.

Organizations are also open systems, which means that they respond to external pressures.[62] They both adapt to and shape their environment. A terrorist group is like a nonviolent organization with intangible and precarious goals. Burton R. Clark argued that social values are precarious when those responsible for their implementation are not fully legitimized.[63] A terrorist organization is, by definition, an illegitimate organization. The values that they espouse are not those held by the incumbent regime. Clark analyzed the "enrollment economy" of adult education schools in the United States. However, Clark's arguments are equally applicable to terrorist organizations. Clark found that organizations without a firmly legitimized status needed to focus on achieving parity with similar organizations. In the short term, this manifests in prioritizing activity that shows results. Accordingly, the organization focuses resources on attracting enrollments. In the case of the terrorist organization, this equates to recruitment. As Clark notes, unless the organization can maintain and increase its membership, "future support is likely to stagnate, and a major slump in attendance constitutes a serious threat to organizational welfare."[64] In order to attract recruits, the terrorist organization must adapt its message to appeal to a broad range of potential members. The content of this message will depend on prevailing market conditions. It may be moderate if the pool of potential recruits favors a political and/or conciliatory approach. Or it may be more radical if there is a demand for violent action and if the organization is in competition with a hard-lined rival.

According to goal displacement theory, the anticipated trajectory of an organization is that it will become more conservative over time. This is

[60] Porter, *Competitive Strategy*; Gimeno and Woo, "Hypercompetition," 325; Minkoff, "From Service Provision," 965.
[61] Phillips, *How Terrorist Organizations Survive*, 217.
[62] Meier, "Bureaucracy and Democracy," 195.
[63] Clark, "Organizational Adaptation," 328.
[64] Ibid., 332.

because the assumption is that an organization that wants to survive will seek to maintain a harmonious relationship with the society in which it exists. As a terrorist organization becomes established it may seek to expand its influence by branching out into the political sphere or into labor organization. The terrorists may establish an affiliated political party, workers' unions, student organizations, community groups, and other nonviolent organizations. To appeal to a broader proportion of society, it could be expected to soften its message, at least in certain forums. The militants may see it as being in their interest to broaden their base to attract recruits and resources and to secure political influence.[65]

Michels's argument, extracted earlier in this chapter, includes the statement that organizations will find it in their interest to adopt a "defensive and even a reactionary policy when the interests of the working class may dictate a bold and aggressive policy."[66] This notion was developed out of the work of Weber and is a key characteristic of what Zald and Ash call the Weber-Michels approach.[67] I argue that this is equally applicable to terrorist organizations, with one caveat—they may become more radical if their organizational survival is threatened. If the terrorist organization perceives that its survival is under threat, it may shift back to its original radical position or even become more extreme. As an example, if the terrorists find themselves in competition with rival challengers who threaten their survival, they may engage in "outbidding" to protect their position and their access to resources.[68] Outbidding typically manifests as an escalation in violence and brutality.[69] Rival groups may engage in more daring and more brutal attacks to show that they are the true threat to the incumbent regime, as well as to signal to potential recruits that they are the best vehicle for advancing the cause.[70]

A swing back toward radicalism can also be explained by the fact that a terrorist organization will only continue to attract attention and resources if it maintains its position as the most prominent and credible challenger.[71]

[65] In their analysis of the political demands of ethno-political organizations, Vogt et al. detected a phenomenon they referred to as "underbidding," an attempt to raise their profile by adopting a more moderate stance than their rivals: Vogt et al., "From Claims to Violence," 24.

[66] Michels, *Political Parties*, 353.

[67] Zald and Ash, "Social Movement Organizations."

[68] Chenoweth, "Democratic Competition and Terrorist Activity"; Polo and González, "The Power to Resist," 2034.

[69] Biberman and Zahid, "Why Terrorists Target Children."

[70] Nemeth, "The Effect of Competition," 3–5.

[71] Ibid., 28.

If a rival organization were to engage in more brutal attacks, it would be expected to receive more notoriety and media attention, which could in turn make it more attractive to potential recruits. As an escalation of violence will typically attract more repressive counterterrorism responses, the ability to replenish personnel would be crucial to the survival of a terrorist organization. Thus, it can be argued, the more radical group would have better odds of surviving in a competitive environment. Barbara F. Walter has analyzed the instrumental use of extremism by militant groups. She suggests that terrorists may use extremism to overcome the organizational challenges of highly competitive environments. Extremist ideologies enable leaders to offer compelling rewards and punishments, they serve as a signal of dedication to the cause, and they assure the populace that the leaders will not succumb to corruption once in power. Thus, increased radicalism can give terrorist groups a competitive advantage in highly uncertain and information-poor arenas.[72]

Vested Interests

Vested interests is another key aspect of goal displacement theory that can be used to explain conflict persistence. Michels referred to the "universally applicable social law" of vested interests in his elaboration of the concept. He argued that when individuals are given roles within an organization, they develop special interests that are unique to their position within the organization.[73] These incentives may be tangible, such as monetary incentives, or intangible, such as power. Usually, they are a combination of both. Instead of making decisions that would maximize the organization's public goals, members are more likely to act in a way that protects their incentives. When members' financial interests are linked to the survival of the organization, they become less inclined to support actions that could lead to the disbanding of the organization.[74] This is particularly relevant when members are receiving a salary, stipend, living expenses, and other perks or incentives. These vested interests will inevitably conflict with the terrorists' public goals. The ultimate objective of any conflict should be to bring about the political change that would make their own existence redundant. Thus, vested

[72] Walter, "The Extremist's Advantage."
[73] Michels, *Political Parties*, 353.
[74] Tolbert and Hiatt, "On Organizations and Oligarchies."

interests in a perpetual conflict will necessarily conflict with the objectives they formed to pursue.[75]

One difficulty in convincing terrorists to demobilize is that it involves a loss of benefits. The work of Daniel Kahneman and Amos Tversky demonstrates that individuals tend to give greater weight to potential losses than they do to potential gains.[76] Individuals make choices to achieve a desired outcome. The alternative selected, however, is often a function of the way that the various options were framed. The crucial factor is whether alternatives are framed as gains or losses. This influences the individual's willingness to accept or reject risk.[77] According to prospect theory, actors perceive outcomes in terms of losses or gains relative to a reference point.[78] This reference point is the status quo, which is perceived as having a special legitimacy. Research has shown that individuals are more likely to defend the status quo than to seek to improve it.[79] Individuals also tend to recalibrate their reference point quickly after receiving gains but much more slowly after losses.[80] Therefore, political and military victories are unlikely to induce militants to consider disarming because the gains would be quickly assimilated into their perceived reference point, or status quo.[81] Individuals are also understood to place greater value on what they have than on what they do not have, in a phenomenon known as the endowment effect.[82] Accordingly, terrorists would be predicted to place a greater weight on any diminution of their position within the organization, or of the organization itself, than they would on any anticipated gains that could come from leaving the organization, or from the organization's dissolution. This is also explained by the "certainty effect," whereby outcomes that appear certain are weighed more heavily than those that appear uncertain.[83] Accordingly, the status quo would be preferred over any proffered peace agreement, even if the status quo only holds prospects of diminishing returns.[84]

[75] Zald and Ash, "Social Movement Organizations," 332.
[76] Kahneman and Tversky, "Prospect Theory"; Levy, "Prospect Theory," 89; Hancock et al., "Prospect Theory," 185.
[77] Masters, "Support and Nonsupport," 704.
[78] Ibid., 703–704.
[79] Weyland, "Risk Taking," 189.
[80] Schenoni et al., "Malvinas/Falklands a Diversionary War?," 38.
[81] Levy, "Prospect Theory, Rational Choice," 90–91.
[82] Ibid., 89–90.
[83] Trott, "Prospect Theory," Art. 43.
[84] Weyland, "Risk Taking," 189.

According to this framework, resistance to change should be more marked in the leadership.[85] As the recipients of more tangible and intangible benefits, leaders would have more to lose if the organization were dissolved. Michels argued that power inevitably corrupts and that leaders will always act to maintain their positions, even when that means going against the interests of the membership and the base.[86] Thus, leaders should display a strong inclination to continue hostilities even when there are viable options to advance the goals of their constituency by disarming. Vested interests do not just affect individuals. Factions and divisions within organizations can also have special interests that they wish to protect. Organizational changes, including demilitarization and demobilization, are bound to benefit certain organizational subunits at the expense of others.[87] For example, the political and propaganda wings may be elevated to nonviolent political roles, while the military divisions may be sidelined. The subunits that stand to lose from the change would be predicted to oppose it more vehemently than the subunits that would benefit. This would create strong organizational inertia and resistance to change.[88]

Another cause of organizational inertia is concerns about legitimacy. Adapting to changing circumstances, such as new political developments, can affect the legitimacy of an organization. Any factor that causes an organization's legitimacy to be called into question also jeopardizes its position and resources, and potentially its very survival.[89] This concern is particularly salient for a terrorist organization. If legitimacy is understood to mean the level of cultural support for an organization, an organization that originated as a vehicle for violent struggle against an unjust regime may hesitate to lay down arms for fears that this could alienate its base.[90] Such an organization, which has fought against the system, may need to adapt its image if it wants to enter electoral politics. The necessity of rebranding would be a transaction cost that would be opposed by sections of the organization, especially the more militant subgroups that would lose power and influence in the process. The switch from terrorism to legitimate electoral politics

[85] For a discussion of how vested interests cause institutions to become resistant to change, see Olson, *Rise and Decline of Nations*,. 31; Moe, "Vested Interests," 2; Moe, "Mancur Olson and Structural Economic Change"; Gilpin, "Economic Evolution," 413.

[86] Leach, "Iron Law of What Again?," 313; Pearlman, "Spoiling Inside and Out," 83.

[87] Hannan and Freeman, *Organizational Ecology*, 68.

[88] Ibid.

[89] Ibid., 69; Singh et al., "Organizational Legitimacy"; Tokdemir, "Reputation Building," 2–3.

[90] Scott, "Unpacking Institutional Arguments," 169–170.

is an uncertain move. Not only does it put the future of the organization at risk, but it could cause a rearrangement of the organization's internal power balance. Certain leaders who found success in the violent organization may be less suited to legitimate politics, or even to civilian life.[91] This can cause influential individuals within the organization to oppose demilitarization.[92] This in turn can result in the defection of more moderate group members, which can ultimately lead to the organization becoming more radical.[93]

Significance

The implications of the organizational survival approach have considerable significance for the study of civil conflict. The approach asks scholars to rethink certain tenets of orthodox counterterrorism canon. If it were accepted that terrorists do not necessarily want what they say they want, this would shift focus away from the terrorists' demands and enable a deeper exploration of internal organizational dynamics that perpetuate conflicts. It is also significant for counterterrorism theory and practice, which has put great emphasis on addressing terrorist grievances and providing opportunities for demobilization.[94] Disarmament, Demobilization, and Reintegration (DDR) programs focus on facilitating exits for terrorists and providing them with means to reintegrate into civilian life.[95] This work can be enhanced by incorporating more nuanced understandings of the incentives that terrorists receive from their positions within the organization and their potential resistance to relinquishing those benefits.

A successful reintegration program would need to provide terrorists with incentives that would outweigh those they already receive from the conflict. This could include meaningful employment, housing, amnesty, and so forth. Whatever the benefits are, they would need to surpass those the terrorists receive from the organization by a sufficient margin to overcome

[91] Aldrich and Auster, "Even Dwarfs Started Small," 170.

[92] Moe, *Governance, Growth, and Global Leadership*," 16–17; Olson, *Rise and Decline of Nations*"; Moe, "Vested Interests," 2.

[93] Crenshaw, "Theories of Terrorism," 22–23; Phillips, "Enemies with Benefits?," 67.

[94] Berman et al., "Can Hearts and Minds Be Bought?"; Fitzsimmons, "Hard Hearts and Open Minds?," 338.

[95] Knight, "Expanding the DDR Model"; Jennings, "The Struggle to Satisfy," 207.

any status quo bias. The existence of status quo bias has been established by experiments and observational studies, and yet it is remarkably underutilized in demobilization research.[96] Research has shown that in choice situations, individuals disproportionately choose the status quo.[97] This is particularly so when issues of personal principle and reputation are concerned. As Arnold put it: "There is nothing so inelastic as a great organization of any kind because of men's passion for appearing consistent in public."[98] This tendency must be factored into any program that asks individuals to change their course of action.

A potential criticism could be that this theory would not apply to conflict organizations that have a disaggregated cell structure. However, it is argued that this structure is not substantially different from the coalition and subunit conception of organizations adopted by Selznick and by Zald and Ash.[99] Indeed, part of the reason why organizations could be resistant to change is that subunits or cells may compete against each other for prominence and resources. Those units that are in the ascendancy would have less incentive to accept a course of action that could diminish their power. They would also be in a strong position to oppose any such proposal.

Conclusion

In this chapter, I have presented the theoretical framework of this book, entitled the organizational survival approach to terrorism. This is a fused model, which combines insights from organizational theory and rational choice theory to create a hybrid approach to understanding terrorist incentive structures. I have argued that the dominant conflict research streams hold that terrorist organizations exist for the purpose of advancing their goals. These goals may be their stated political objectives, or in the case of certain groups that have moved into organized criminal activity, the pursuit of material benefits. There are also many studies that extrapolate organizational objectives from examining the aims of individual members.

[96] Masatlioglu and Ok, "Rational Choice."
[97] Samuelson and Zeckhauser, "Status Quo Bias"; Fernandez and Rodrik, "Resistance to Reform."
[98] Arnold, *Folklore of Capitalism*, 356.
[99] Zald and Ash, "Social Movement Organizations." See also Carty, "Parties as Franchise Systems," 9–12.

I argue that current understandings of terrorism and counterterrorism neglect a crucial piece of the puzzle. That is, the influence that organizational structure has on terrorists' strategic decision-making and goal-setting processes. In support of this, I draw on the writings of Weber and Michels, who argued that once like-minded people come together to form an organization, they become imbued with special interests that interfere with their willingness and ability to advance the goals that they originally assembled to pursue. In organizational theory, Michels's work formed the basis for the concept known as "goal displacement". According to this theory, the internal dynamics of organizations cause them to shift away from pursuing their stated aims, or "public goals" and instead focus on self-maintenance. One of the reasons for this is that members, and in particular leaders, seek to maintain their positions and the benefits that they receive from the organization.[100]

The goal displacement concept is highly significant for the study of conflict. It means that regimes that wish to encourage terrorists to demobilize must provide sufficient incentives to outweigh the benefits they were receiving from organizational membership, as well as to overcome loss aversion, organizational inertia, and status quo bias. It must also be remembered that certain factions or subgroups within the organization would be anticipated to lose more from any cessation of hostilities. These factions may hold positions of power and influence within the organization. Therefore, their interests and concerns would need to be specifically addressed.

The chapter also contains a discussion of some potential challenges to the organizational survival approach. These are that any organization that strayed from its stated objectives would lose the support of its base and thereby jeopardize its survival. However, it is argued that terrorist organizations manage this dilemma by appearing to be the most appropriate vehicle for advancing the goals of its constituency while disguising an internal bureaucracy focused on self-preservation. I also argue that the approach applies equally to conflicts that comprise disaggregated cells, as this structure is equally recognized in conventional organizational theory. Indeed, competing cells can aggravate organizational inertia by fomenting power struggles among the disparate groups.

The chapter closed with a brief outline of the potential utility of this approach. Insights from organizational theory can assist conflict theorists

[100] Zald and Ash, "Social Movement Organizations."

to develop strategies that consider internal dynamics that may contribute to the perpetuation of conflicts. This approach may help to explain cases in which militants to continue engaging in hostilities beyond the point at which such action can lead to positive political outcomes or generate meaningful material incentives. This may in turn assist in the development of programs that provide militants with commensurate benefits to enable them to demobilize.

4

Background to Assembly VII

In this chapter I provide an overview of the internal and external factors that effected ETA-pm's organizational structure and strategy at the time of Assembly VII in 1976. I first give an overview of the Basque nationalist movement and the development of ETA and then chart the divisions that emerged within ETA during the early 1970s. These internal tensions caused the organization to split into three separate groups in 1974, with the majority adopting the name ETA-político-militar, or ETA-pm. I then discuss how ETA-pm reformulated its strategy and redefined its identity in 1975. Assembly VI of 1975 allowed ETA-pm to refine the political-military strategy. This approach, which would define the organization's trajectory, made armed action subordinate to political action. The chapter will close by setting the scene for Assembly VII, which will be analyzed in the following chapter.

The Genesis of ETA

Euskadi ta Askatasuna, which can be translated as Basque Homeland and Freedom, is an organization that emerged out of the Basque nationalist movement. Basque nationalism was popularized at the end of the nineteenth century by Sabino Arana Goiri. Arana was the author of *Bizkaya por su Independencia*, which set out the principles of the nationalist movement.[1] Joseba Zulaika and William A. Douglass hold that the movement emerged in response to a fear that Basque culture was in danger of extinction. By the nineteenth century the Basques had lost two wars against the Spanish governments in attempts to secure regional autonomy.[2] The defeated region then became a target for industrialization and immigration from the rest of Spain.[3] Juan Díez Medrano states that the rapid social changes

[1] Larrea, "Orígenes del Nacionalismo Vasco," 157.
[2] Zulaika and Douglass, "Interpretation of Terrorist Violence," 243.
[3] Laitin, "'National Revivals and Violence," 7.

Euskadi Ta Askatasuna. Nell Bennett, Oxford University Press. © University of Maryland National Consortium for the Study of Terrorism and Responses to Terrorism (START) (2025). DOI: 10.1093/9780197764268.003.0004

the Basque Country underwent in the late nineteenth century resulted in the disenfranchisement of the preindustrial Basque elite, who formed the support base for the independence movement.[4] The influx of immigrants led to a decrease in the use of the Basque language, Euskera, and expressions of regional culture. In response, Arana called for the deportation of recent arrivals and for the Basque Country to be the exclusive home of ethnic Basques.[5] According to the nationalist movement, the Basque Country comprised seven regions in the north of Spain and south of France. These are Alava, Gipuzkoa, and Bizkaia of the current Basque region, the Spanish autonomous community of Navarra, and three French provinces: Basse Navarre, Labourd, and Soule and the lower Navarrese portions of Pyrénées-Atlantiques.[6]

During the Spanish Civil War of 1936–1939, the Basque Country was divided into those provinces that supported the Francoist rebels and those that supported the Republican forces. Navarra and Alava aligned with the conservative, Catholic rebels. Bizkaia and Gipuzkoa sided with the Republicans. After the defeat of the Republicans, the Franco regime labeled Bizkaia and Gipuzkoa as traitorous provinces. Businesses were closed, property was expropriated, and monks and priests who had opposed the rebel violence were deported, imprisoned, and executed.[7] This generated a sense of relative deprivation among the inhabitants of these provinces—provinces that would serve as valuable recruitment bases for ETA.[8]

The Basque nationalist movement grew in response to General Franco's repressive regime, which lasted from 1939 until 1975.[9] While expressions of Basque identity were prohibited as early as the 1920s, this policy intensified under General Franco. During the dictatorship a wide variety of typical Basque activities were illegalized, including hiking, traditional dance and music, and speaking Euskera. Even the most casual use of Euskera was punishable by imprisonment.[10] This gave the Basque people a sense of grievance and justified the nationalist struggle.[11] The repressive measures were perceived by segments of the Basque population as an attack on their ethnic and

[4] Medrano, *Divided Nations*.
[5] Zulaika and Douglass, "Interpretation of Terrorist Violence," 243.
[6] Alonso, "Spain," 594.
[7] Whitfield, *Endgame for ETA*, 38–40.
[8] Reinares, "Who Are the Terrorists?," 478–479.
[9] Ibid., 593; Hamilton, *Women and ETA*, 134; Woodworth, *Dirty War, Clean Hands*, 34.
[10] Woodworth, *Dirty War, Clean Hands*, 34.
[11] Zulaika, *Basque Violence*"; Anderson, "Separatism and Devolution," 146.
Llera, "ETA, Ejercito Secreto," 184.

cultural identity. This in turn created a perception of injustice and alienation from the central government.[12]

ETA originated out of secret study sessions organized by university students in Bilbao in 1952. These students started meeting to discuss Euskera, but their focus soon shifted to nationalism.[13] This early organization was known as Ekin, which in Euskera means "to do" or "to make."[14] Ekin fused with the youth branch of the Basque Nationalist Party, the PNV. This alliance lasted several years, and when Ekin split from the PNV in 1958, it took many of the more militant PNV youth with it. A year later the new group took the name Euskadi ta Askatasuna (ETA).[15] ETA's approach to Basque nationalism differed from that of Arana. While Arana had been concerned with maintaining the purity of the Basque race, ETA focused on Basque culture, in particular, the use of Euskera. Basque identity therefore became more inclusive. As Diego Muro expressed, "One did not have to be born Basque, it was possible to become one." This could be achieved by speaking Euskera and supporting the nationalist cause.[16] The use of language was significant, as it created a boundary between Basque people and the Spanish, thereby "demarcating group belonging."[17]

During the 1960s and 1970s, ETA consisted of several hundred members, many of whom lived in rural and coastal villages in the south of France, near the Spanish border. This location allowed them to engage in operations in Spain then return to France, which they used as a sanctuary.[18] The organization had a loose hierarchical structure. Volunteers and autonomous cells would operate independently but in accordance with the directives of the organization's leadership.[19] As early as 1962, ETA recognized that propaganda was an organizational priority. Their official magazine, *Zutik*, was prepared in Bayonne, France, then printed and distributed in the Spanish Basque Country. During the Franco years, possession of any ETA materials, including their magazines and pamphlets, was punishable by imprisonment.[20]

[12] Alonso, "'Why Do Terrorists Stop?,'' 696.
[13] Ibid., 35; Muro, "ETA: Basque Nationalist."
[14] Barros, "Intervention Analysis of Terrorism," 402.
[15] Woodworth, *Dirty War, Clean Hands*, 35.
[16] Muro, "Politics of War Memory."
[17] Bray, "Basque Militant Youths.".
[18] Olmeda, "ETA Before and After," 4.
[19] Llera, "ETA, Ejercito secreto," 184–185.
[20] McCreanor, "ETA and the Public," 74–75.

ETA had two kinds of operatives: *legales* and *liberados*. *Legales* were ETA operatives who had not yet been identified by police and were therefore able to go about their normal lives while collaborating with the organization. Their functions would vary from active participation in operations to support roles.[21] *Liberados* were members who were known to law enforcement and were therefore required to operate in a clandestine manner. The *liberados* generally worked in autonomous cells. They were paid a modest stipend and provided with weapons and explosives for operations.[22] ETA had a disaggregated cell structure, which was directed by a leadership committee. By the late 1960s ETA established an overarching policy-making committee, the *Biltzar Nagusia*, or National Assembly. This comprised the Executive Committee and the leaders of the various zones or *herrialdeak*.[23] Below the National Assembly were two subordinate committees, the Small Assembly, which was in France (the *Biltzar Txikia*) and the Tactical Executive Committee in Spain.[24]

The strongest recruitment base for ETA was Gipuzkoa. This region supplied nearly half the group's members, despite the fact that it only contributed less than a quarter of the population of the Basque Country.[25] In 1970 the population of the Basque Country was 1,867,274 whereas that of Gipuzkoa was 424,888.[26] By contrast, the population of Spain was more than thirty-four million.[27] While the exact numbers of ETA members are unknown, Fernando Reinares estimated that from the early 1970s until the early 2000s, they recruited around 1200 active militants, excluding collaborators.[28] Between 1970 and 1982 the membership was approximately 95 percent male. Most members came from towns or cities with more than 10,000 inhabitants. They were generally in their twenties, were single, and had a specialized trade.[29] Around 80 percent of ETA members were ethnic Basques; however, over time an increasing number of recruits came from immigrant parents.[30] The use of Euskera was adopted by the organization as a costly signal of dedication to the nationalist cause.[31]

[21] Llera et al., "ETA: From Secret Army," 124.
[22] Rekarte, *Lo difícil es perdonarse.*
[23] Llera, "ETA, Ejercito Secreto," 184.
[24] Ibid.
[25] Reinares, "Who Are the Terrorists?," 478–479.
[26] Eustat, "1.7. Population by Place of Birth."
[27] Worldometer, Spain Population.
[28] Reinares, "Who Are the Terrorists?," 465.
[29] Ibid.
[30] Ibid., 487.
[31] Joly, "La cause basque."

ETA's first serious terrorist operation occurred in 1961.[32] It was the attempted derailment of several trains carrying Franco supporters to Donostia to celebrate the 25th anniversary of Franco's military coup.[33] The organization went to great lengths to ensure that no one would be injured in the incident. In fact, no one was hurt because the operation failed.[34] In spite of this, the Spanish government responded swiftly by arresting more than one hundred Basque citizens. Many of those detainees reported being tortured while in police custody.[35] This event set in train an action-repression-action sequence between ETA and the Spanish government. ETA took advantage of this dynamic by provoking the Spanish government to engage in a repressive campaign, which would cause the Basque people to rally around ETA.[36]

In 1968, an ETA activist was killed. ETA retaliated by killing an officer of the National Police and a member of the Civil Guard.[37] The Franco government responded by laying siege to the Basque region and instating a "state of exception," which was akin to martial law. Habeas corpus was suspended, and many Basque people reported being detained without charge or access to legal representation.[38] In 1969, most of ETA's leadership were arrested. Sixteen former leaders faced trial in a military tribunal in December 1970. Two of these defendants were priests. These proceedings became known as "the Burgos trial" and provoked demonstrations and strikes across the Basque Country, as well as protests from the Basque clergy.[39] This further consolidated the sense of grievance among the Basque populace and provided justification for the use of violence to defend the Basque nation against Spanish repression.[40]

Intra-organizational Divisions

In the early 1970s tensions emerged within ETA, and divisions widened between its different factions. The main cause of this splintering was disagreement over which organizational structure would best serve the group

[32] Duva, "La primera victima de ETA."
[33] Barros, "'Intervention Analysis of Terrorism," 402.
[34] Murua, *The End of ETA*," 72.
[35] Woodworth, *Dirty War, Clean Hands*, 36.
[36] Mahoney, "End of the Cycle," 923.
[37] Laitin, "'National Revivals and Violence," 24.
[38] Clark, *The Basques*, 170, 182–183; Laitin, "National Revivals and Violence," 24.
[39] Woodworth, *Dirty War, Clean Hands*.
[40] Zernova, "Restorative Justice," 653.

in the new democracy that was predicted to emerge after the death of Franco.[41] The majority faction, ETA-pm, wanted to embrace the opportunities that democracy would provide to the nationalist movement. They argued that the organization should be integrated into unions and institutions and that it should form a mainstream political party that could contest elections.[42] The hard-line militant faction ETA-m, on the other hand, wanted to remain a clandestine organization to avoid government repression.[43] The tensions between the two factions of ETA were revealed in a series of debates that took place in 1971. In that year, ETA organized a meeting of Basque nationalist organizations with the objective of forming a unified Basque National Front. This failed, as the Basque Nationalist Party (the PNV) was not interested in participating.[44] This was because the majority of the PNV leadership viewed ETA as a Marxist, totalitarian organization.[45] ETA published its observations of those meetings in its internal magazine, *Kemen*. Among these they set out their organizational objectives, which began with "the violent destruction of the state."[46] However, not all members of ETA agreed that the total destruction of the state was necessary or even desirable. Some preferred to take a more pragmatic approach to self-determination. These moderate views were denounced in that same issue of *Kemen*:

> . . . it is very suspicious that some of those who maintain the need for the creation of the [Basque National Front] do not say at once that our national freedom requires the destruction of the State. If we do not want to make the Front a useless instrument for the people . . . it is necessary to consider the TOTAL destruction of the old apparatus of the dominant and the imposition of the new power apparatuses in the hands of the workers and the people.[47]

This division within ETA led to increasing political polarization between late 1974 and early 1975. This coincided with the second half of Assembly VI. The two factions took different views on how national liberation was

[41] Domínguez, "El fin de ETA político militar," 2.
[42] Calvo, "Izquierda abertzale," 383–384.
[43] Romero, "El Proceso de Liquidación," 3–4.
[44] Rueda, "Religión y Nacionalismo Vasco," 722; Rivera and Soldevilla, "Frente Nacional Vasco," 28.
[45] Rueda, "Telesforo Monzón," 379.
[46] ETA, *Kemen*, No. 6, 1971.
[47] Ibid.

to be achieved. The political-military faction (or the "*polimilis*") wanted to pursue a combined political and military structure, in which their leaders would oversee both the military and political wings.[48] The military faction (the "*milis*") argued that this approach was unsustainable because it would attract government repression that could destroy both the political and military wings at once. The *milis* therefore opted for a rigid separation between political and violent struggle. These tensions reached a crisis point in 1974. The *milis* executed a bomb attack at a busy Madrid café, Cafetería Rolando. The attack had been intended to target police personnel but ultimately killed thirteen civilians and injured another eighty.[49] ETA debated whether to claim responsibility for the attack. The *milis* argued strongly in favor of declaring themselves responsible for the bombing. Others within the organization were concerned that doing so might backfire on the organization and reduce its popularity among its base. Ultimately, the organization did not admit responsibility.[50]

The resulting crisis caused the group to split into three different organizations. The military front defected and formed ETA-militar (or ETA-m), the workers' front formed an organization called Langile Abertzale Iraultzaileen Alderdia (LAIA), which was a political party dedicated to the advancement of workers' rights. The remaining members took the name ETA-políticomilitar, or ETA-pm.[51] As ETA-pm later put it, they were what remained from two scissions: "that of a group of militants who demanded the liquidation of our armed struggle to devote ourselves entirely to the work of the masses, and that of another group who demanded exactly the opposite: to transform ETA into an exclusively military organization."[52]

ETA-m was led by José Miguel Beñaran Ordeñana and Domingo Iturbe Abasolo.[53] Beñaran, who was better known by his nom de guerre, "Argala," was twenty-seven. Despite having been raised in a pro-Franco household, Argala joined ETA in the late 1960s.[54] He believed that ETA should become the revolutionary vanguard of Basque nationalism and dedicate itself exclusively to armed struggle. According to ETA-m, it was only by force that

[48] Duhart, "Directing Disengagement," 47.
[49] Barragán and Ballesteros, "13 víctimas."
[50] ETA finally claimed responsibility for the Cafetería Rolando attack in 2018, just before announcing that it was dismantling the organization: Gorospe, "ETA asume el asesinato."
[51] Soldevilla, "Agur a las armas. EIA," 57; Iñesta, "Los Que Volvieron A Casa," 31.
[52] ETA-pm, "Euskal Herriari," 302.
[53] Schumacher, "Domingo Iturbe Abasolo."
[54] Real Academia de la Historia, "José Miguel Beñarán Ordeñana."

ETA could protect itself from state repression and from potential contamination from the moderate and reformist elements within the nationalist movement.[55] Iturbe Abasolo, who went by the name "Txomin," joined ETA in 1968 and was thirty-two at the time of Assembly VII. Txomin was a native of Gipuzkoa, ETA's biggest recruitment base. He was also an avid football fan and was the goalkeeper for the Mondragon team. He coined the phrase "*aurrera bolie*," which can be roughly translated as "advance the ball." This became a slogan for radical Basque nationalism.[56]

ETA-m went on to wage a violent campaign against anyone they considered to be a representative of the Spanish government and anyone they labeled a traitor to the Basque cause. In late 1975 they issued a declaration that all government informants in the Basque Country would be shot. On November 24, 1975, an ETA-m operative shot the mayor of the town of Oiartzun, Antonio Echeverría Albisu, at the front door of his home. ETA-m used this as a warning to all other mayors that they were to be either "*with the people or against them, there is now no place for neutrality*" (emphasis in original). ETA-m made it clear that all those who were against the people would meet with the same fate as Echeverría.[57]

ETA-pm, on the other hand, developed strategies that were broader in scope and encompassed nonviolent political activism. Eduardo Moreno Bergaretxe, "Pertur," was the leader of the ETA-pm political office. Pertur was twenty-six and came from a middle-class Spanish-speaking family in Donostia. He studied business at university and joined ETA after assisting defense lawyer Juan María Bandrés at the Burgos trial in 1970. He initially applied to join as a militant, but the leadership instead put him in charge of the cultural front.[58] Pertur was a leading force behind the ETA-pm philosophy that military action should be combined with political action.[59]

ETA-pm was more active in both the military and the political movements than ETA-m. The younger generation of activists joined ETA-pm rather than ETA-m, leading to the perception of ETA-pm as the vanguard of the movement. ETA-pm was more attractive to the new generation of Basques, while ETA-m was viewed as an older and less up to date faction of the organization.[60] This perception made it much more difficult for ETA-m to recruit

[55] Soldevilla, "De las armas al parlamento," 247.
[56] El Diario Vasco, "El portero del 'Mondra.'"
[57] ETA-m, "A Todo el Pueblo Vasco," 300.
[58] Real Academia de la Historia, "Eduardo Moreno Bergaretxe."
[59] Auñamendi Eusko Entziklopedia, "MUGICA ARREGUI, Iñaki."
[60] *Documentos Y*, vol. 18, 54.

new members. To make up for the loss of the military front, ETA-pm created the Komando Bereziak (the special commandos), who were led by Pedro Ignacio Pérez Beotegui, also known as "Wilson." Wilson was twenty-eight and had joined ETA in the 1960s. He was originally a member of ETA-m and had participated in the assassination of Spanish Prime Minister Luis Carrero Blanco in 1973 with ETA-m leaders Argala and Txomin.[61] However, Wilson was also one of the militants who opposed claiming responsibility for the bombing of the Madrid café. As a result, he was expelled from ETA-m and labeled a pacifist by the military front.[62]

In 1974, before the organizational division, ETA was infiltrated by an undercover police officer named Mikel Lejarza Eguía (also known as "Lobo"). When the organization divided into ETA-pm and ETA-m, Lejarza decided to remain with ETA-pm, as this was the larger and stronger group. As a result of this one infiltration, 145 ETA-pm members were arrested. This was the highest number of political arrests in ETA's history. Two of the ETA members who were arrested were subsequently executed.[63] This left ETA-pm in an extremely vulnerable situation. Its top leaders had been imprisoned, and it was left with only one active commando.[64] Pertur devised a plan to help ETA-pm to recover from the arrests of 1974. This was to create a strategic association of diverse Basque nationalist organizations.[65] In 1975, ETA-pm created Koordinadora Abertzale Sozialista, or the KAS Alternative. The coalition was formed around an eight-point program called Herrikoi Batasuna (Popular Unity). These included the establishment of a provisional government in the Basque Country; making Euskera an official language in the Basque Country; the dissolution of the Fuerzas de Orden Público, a law enforcement organization run by the central government; the nationalization of essential industries; amnesty for Basque political prisoners; and democratic rights for the Basque people.[66]

ETA-pm set out these points in their internal magazine, *Hautsi*. They stated that these points represented the level of nationalist consciousness in the Basque Country. Of all the nation-building proposals that were being considered in the Basque Country, these minimum points were "the tactical alternative that most favors the development of the Basque revolutionary

[61] El Mundo, "Pedro I. Pérez Beotegui."
[62] ABC, "La ETA-V Asamblea expulsa."
[63] Soldevilla, "De las armas al parlamento," 248; *Documentos Y*, vol. 18, 49.
[64] Soldevilla, *Historia de una Heterodoxia Abertzale*, 111.
[65] Ibid., 116.
[66] ETA-pm, *Hautsi*, 116; Muro, *Ethnicity and Violence*, 128.

process, and which most faithfully captures the democratic and national aspirations most felt by our people today." Thus, they argued, these were the points that most left-wing organizations could agree to and that would facilitate a unified left-wing nationalist movement.[67]

In 1975, ETA-pm gathered to debate these points and the broader strategic direction of the organization. The leadership saw the need to "take the pulse of the militancy" ahead of the debates. To do so, they distributed a survey to all the cells. The answers were to provide them with a better understanding of the main themes that would be discussed. In the survey, ETA-pm referred to itself as "Y." "Y" is the Spanish translation of the Basque word "eta" (which means "and"). This was presumably adopted for security reasons. In February 1975, ETA-pm emerged from Assembly VI with a redefined strategy. They were going to execute a policy of mass action that would bring together the workers and all the Basque people. They would use armed action to support their strategy in the knowledge that "the more military strength we present, the greater will be our political conquests."[68]

Pertur's plan to revitalize ETA-pm was successful. By 1976 the organization was integrated into the social fabric of the Basque Country. ETA-pm played a large role in the workers' movement and had an important labor union, the Nationalist Workers' Committee (Langile Abertzaleen Batzordeak or LAB). They had also developed a large student movement, known as the Patriotic Students' Movement (Ikasle Abertzaleen Mugimendua or IAM). ETA-pm was also connected to the activist group Hauzo Batzarrak.[69]

However, these successes were undermined by the unauthorized activities of ETA-pm's internal militant faction, the Komando Bereziak. In 1976, unbeknownst to the political-military side of ETA-pm, the Bereziak kidnapped two businessmen for ransom, José Luis Arrasate and Ángel Berazadi Uribe. Arrasate was released on payment of his ransom. However, Berazadi's family was not able to raise the entire ransom. Berazadi had been a Basque nationalist and had promoted Basque schools, called ikastaolas. Despite this, and against the orders of the political-military leadership, the Bereziak killed Berazadi on April 8, 1976.[70] The incident was a public relations disaster for

[67] ETA-pm, *Hautsi*, February 15, 1976, 17.
[68] ETA-pm, "Euskal Herriari," 304.
[69] *Documentos Y*, vol. 16, 293.
[70] Roldán, "La mano que mató a Berazadi."

ETA-pm. The killing sparked outrage and protests in the Basque Country.[71] This event created a divide between the political-military faction of ETA-pm and the militants. The Komando Bereziak began to oppose Pertur's leadership and took the position that his strategic leadership was a betrayal of the organization's original vision.[72] This tension is apparent in the Bereziak's responses to the proposal that ETA-pm presented at Assembly VII.

Conclusion

In this chapter I have provided a summary of the history of ETA, with a focus on their activities in the years 1970–1976. The purpose of this is to equip the reader with sufficient context to understand the arguments and the intra-organizational dynamics that will be explored in the following chapters. I first provided an overview of the origins and genesis of ETA, including the development of the narrative that was used by ETA to justify the use of political violence in defense of the Basque nation. I explained the internal crisis that caused ETA to split into three separate organizations. I then charted the trajectory of ETA-pm as it redefined its strategy and consolidated the political-military approach. In the next chapter, I will examine the debates that took place in 1976. This will include analysis of ETA-pm's political-military strategy and the view that the organization took of its role in the nascent democracy.

[71] RTVE, "Eduardo Moreno Bergareche."
[72] Iñesta, "'Los Que Volvieron A Casa,'" 33.

5

Assembly VII of 1976

The chapter will examine the debates that took place within ETA during 1976, referred to by the organization as the VII Asamblea, or Assembly VII. The significance of Assembly VII is that it shows how ETA-pm made a notable shift toward conservatism. This was a dramatic change in organizational policy and a move that is in line with the predictions of goal displacement theory. At the 1976 debate, ETA-pm took the resolution to create a nonviolent political party, even though they had successfully used violence to exact political concessions from the central government and in the face of opposition from the internal militant faction, the Komando Bereziak. The reason for the shift was strategic. The organization was looking to the future. It foresaw that after the death of Franco, Spain would transition to democracy. Some within the organization were concerned that if ETA-pm continued as a purely militant organization they would run the risk of being marginalized in the new regime. On the other hand, a political party would be able to capitalize on nationalist sentiment in the Basque Country and obtain a position of power and influence. Therefore, by adopting a more moderate stance and by participating in the new democracy, they could safeguard their position in Basque social and political life. Accordingly, ETA chose to alter its trajectory and to take a more moderate approach, thereby ensuring its survival.

This chapter is divided into three sections. I first discuss the Ponencia Otsagabia, or the Otsagabia Proposal. This was a proposal advanced by ETA-pm, which argued in favor of creating a political party that would advance a nationalist agenda. The political objectives of this party would be supported by ETA-pm's military activities. I then look at the plan presented by ETA-m. Although ETA-m was a separate organization, they were invited to present their views on the movement's strategic direction. ETA-m broadly supported ETA-pm's proposal. However, they stressed that the political party must be separate from the military organization to prevent state reprisals. The third proposal to be examined is that presented by the Komando Bereziak, the militant faction of ETA-pm, that argued against the Otsagabia Proposal and

Euskadi Ta Askatasuna. Nell Bennett, Oxford University Press. © University of Maryland National Consortium for the Study of Terrorism and Responses to Terrorism (START) (2025). DOI: 10.1093/9780197764268.003.0005

said that it would lead to the ultimate dissolution of ETA. I then examine the records of the conduct of the debate. These include transcripts of arguments that were presented by leaders from ETA-pm, ETA-m, and the Komando Bereziak. I conclude with a discussion of the significance of this debate and the decision that was made to enact the Otsagabia Proposal. I argue that the decision to branch out and create a nonviolent political party was a deliberate attempt to expand ETA's base and to enable Basque moderates to become affiliated with ETA. This shift towards conservatism is in accordance with the organizational survival approach to terrorism.

The End of Francoism and Assembly VII

The death of General Franco in 1975 marked a pivotal point in Spanish and Basque political history. It signaled the demise of the Francoist regime and the beginning of a transitional period between authoritarianism and democracy, which would culminate in the first general elections in 1977. The end of the Franco era and the advent of democracy also signaled the beginning of a period of modernization for Spain. The regime change would enable Spain to become a modern western democracy and to enter the European Economic Community (EEC) and the North Atlantic Treaty Organization (NATO).[1]

By 1974, the mood in Spain was that of disaffection and concern for the future, yet there was general support for democracy. Although the Franco regime had lasted more than three decades, there was no realistic prospect of its surviving. Survey data from 1974, the year before Franco's death, indicated that only around 15 percent of the Spanish population still identified with the regime. Another 25–30 percent actively opposed the regime, and the remaining majority were uninformed and disinterested in politics.[2] When asked about the kind of regime they favored, most respondents opted for democracy. However, around two thirds of the surveyed population was anxious about the political instability that could accompany the transition.[3] The disinterest and disaffection in the general Spanish population can be contrasted with the increasing mobilization of the Basque population. As discussed in the previous chapter, beginning in 1975 ETA-pm infiltrated

[1] Edles, *Symbol and Ritual*, 57.
[2] Gunther et al., *Democracy in Modern Spain*, 159.
[3] Ibid., 162.

workers' unions and students' groups so as to become an integral part of Basque social life. They were thus able to effectively socialize new generations into supporting ETA as a legitimate and even necessary antirepressive organization.[4]

In May 1976, ETA held a Conferencia de Cuadros or Conference of Cells. This was a predebate meeting of the organization's cells and commando units. The purpose of the gathering was to discuss the future of ETA under a post-Franco democracy. At that meeting a date was set for Assembly VII, which was to be held in September of the same year. It was also decided that in the interim a temporary council would provide direction for the organization. This would be made up of representatives of all factions of the organization, including the Komando Bereziak and the student movement, IAM.[5] While the Assembly concerned the future strategic direction of ETA-pm, ETA-m was also invited to contribute. ETA-m submitted two documents to be considered at the debate. They also sent representatives to advance their position. It is believed they were ETA-m's two leaders, Argala and Txomin.[6]

There were two key issues to be discussed in the debate. First, whether ETA-pm should establish a political party, and second, whether there was still a future for armed struggle. Various proposals were presented. The two most prominent proposals were the Gaurhuts Proposal and the Otsagabia Proposal. Otsagabia was primarily authored by Pertur. It proposed dividing ETA-pm into two organizations. One would be a workers' political party that would participate in elections. The other would be a militant organization that would use violence to advance the aims of the workers' party.[7] The proposal reflected Pertur's view that the parliamentary democratic system that would be implemented in Spain in the post-Franco era would mean that in its current form ETA-pm would be unable to compete with mainstream political parties like the Basque Nationalist Party, the PNV. The Otsagabia Proposal was his attempt at preventing ETA-pm from being sidelined in the new democracy.[8]

This idea was strongly opposed by the Komando Bereziak, who believed that it would lead to the dissolution of ETA. Indeed, the Bereziak were so

[4] Tejerina, "Protest Cycle, Political Violence," 45.
[5] *Documentos Y*, vol. 16, 28.
[6] Egido, *Viaje a la nada* 19.
[7] Soldevilla, "De las armas al parlamento," 249–250.
[8] Soldevilla, *Historia de una Heterodoxia Abertzale*, 113.

opposed to the proposal that in April they kidnapped Pertur to prevent him from attending the conference. The reason given for his detention was that Pertur had sent a letter to a member of the organization who was in prison. The Komando Bereziak claimed that in doing so, Pertur had compromised the safety of the organization and that he should not be entitled to participate in the discussions.[9] However, a vote was held to determine whether Pertur should be present. The majority held that the Komando Bereziak should release him and that he should be permitted to attend the debate.[10] The kidnapping incident is demonstrative of the tensions within ETA-pm. By 1976, the atmosphere within ETA-pm had reached a point that Pertur described the organization as being "a police state where everyone suspects their neighbour. . . ."[11] Pertur disappeared in July 1976, and although there was very little known about his last movements, many believe that he was killed by the Bereziak.[12] This extreme reaction from the Bereziak underscores the importance that they attached to the conduct and outcome of this debate. There was a significant concern that if the wrong decision were taken, it would jeopardize the future of the organization.

The Otsagabia Proposal

The Otsagabia Proposal was the primary proposal that ETA-pm presented for debate. This was a plan to create a socialist political party that would participate in elections. ETA-pm would continue in its role as a militant organization, but its use of violence would be directed toward supporting the party's political objectives.[13] It would therefore make terrorism subordinate to legitimate political activity. ETA-pm representatives argued that it was well equipped to establish a legitimate political party because the organization was already participating in legal political activism. ETA-pm was very active in workers' rights and was the driving force behind the workers' union LAB, which was an important institution in the 1970s. It was also extremely active in the student movement and used the student platform IAM to exercise its influence with Basque youth. ETA-pm was also

[9] La Verdad, "'Antxon' culpa de la desaparición"; RTVE, "Eduardo Moreno Bergareche."
[10] *Documentos Y*, vol. 18, 28.
[11] Soldevilla, "De las armas al parlamenta," 251.
[12] Aizpeolea, "¿Qué fue de Pertur?"
[13] Soldevilla, "De las armas al parlamento,". 249–250.

active within intellectual and artistic spheres in the Basque Country.[14] Thus, ETA-pm had the organizational capacity to create a political party.

The key issue that the proposal explored was whether the existing structure of ETA-pm was best equipped to bring about self-determination for the Basque People. The proposal argued that ETA-pm was already responsible for bringing about significant change within Spanish governance. It claimed that the fascist regime was experiencing a crisis that was in part caused by ETA's actions, in particular, the organization's assassination of President Carrero Blanco in 1974. This event, combined with Franco's terminal illness, signaled a weakening of the dictatorship and led to the emergence of a liberalization movement within the regime.[15] This view has been supported by some historians, including Paul Preston, who argued that ETA's assassination of Carrero Blanco "smashed the myth of Francoist invulnerability."[16] The authors of the Otsagabia Proposal argued that ETA's armed campaign was an important element in precipitating the crisis. As they put it, ETA's use of terrorism was "one of the key factors in the definitive unmasking of Francoism."[17] ETA's "action-repression" strategy succeeded in revealing the true brutality and repressive nature of the dictatorship. As the authors wrote, "action-repression, a dynamic well known in ETA and that has long been one of the fundamental principles of our line of action."[18] By "action-repression" they refer to the strategy of using terrorism to provoke the Spanish government into a disproportionate response, often involving indiscriminate violence against the Basque people.

The proposal argued that the action-repression strategy had yielded positive results. The repression that ETA had provoked from the state had had the effect of awakening the political consciousness of the Basque people. The authors argued that ETA's armed campaign had achieved, "with complete success, one of the fundamental tasks of any revolutionary organization. . .," that of awakening their people to the "manifestations of national oppression and those of social exploitation."[19] However, the proposal also argued that the action-repression strategy had had negative effects on the movement. Namely, it had attracted ruthless state repression that had destroyed

[14] *Documentos Y*, vol. 18, 153.
[15] Soldevilla, *Historia de una Heterodoxia Abertzale*, 107.
[16] Preston, *Triumph of Democracy in Spain*, 68; Lieberman, *Growth and Crisis*; Friend, *Stateless Nations*.
[17] ETA-pm, "El Partido de los Trabajadores Vascos," 9.
[18] Ibid.
[19] Ibid., 10.

the revolutionary vanguard, or at least limited its capabilities to the point where it was unable to keep pace with the people's desire for change. Thus, they argued, the action-repression strategy may provide initial victories but was inherently limited.[20] Indeed, in Juan Aviles's analysis of ETA's use of action-repression he observed that the Francoist response to ETA's activities was so severe that the organization had been virtually dismantled by 1975.[21]

The proposal observed the conundrum the organization had been facing. This was that the popularity and prestige of the nationalist left, and organizations affiliated with ETA-pm, were rising. However, both ETA-pm and ETA-m were struggling to recruit new members to the armed struggle. This was particularly so in the over twenty-five and over thirty age groups. One of the ETA members who was involved in the debate on the proposal expressed the situation in these terms: "The fact is there, and it is indisputable. The number of members of the patriotic mass organizations increases, the number of our militants in them does not, or does in a much slower way: there is something that is not working here."[22] This, they argued, was evidence the people were looking for new structures and institutions within which they could advance the cause. The secrecy required for clandestine armed struggle was antithetical to a mass political movement. Accordingly, the authors argued, ETA-pm needed to adapt so that the organization could better accommodate its constituency and provide them with a legitimate political institution through which they could take an active role in Basque politics.[23]

Before expounding the plan for a radical restructuring of ETA-pm, the Otsagabia Proposal made one key point. ETA-pm, as it was constituted, was not capable of leading a nationalist left political movement. Neither could the nationalist left play a leading role in Basque politics without political leadership.[24] Accordingly, it was time for the political transformation of ETA-pm.[25] Thus, the fundamental argument of the proposal was that the only viable solution to the current situation was for ETA-pm to create a political party that would carry on the political work they had been doing up until that point. The proposal noted that the party they were proposing

[20] Ibid.
[21] Aviles, "Experiencing Terrorism in Spain," 44.
[22] ETA-pm, "El Partido de los Trabajadores Vascos," 11.
[23] Ibid., 11–12.
[24] Ibid., 12.
[25] Ibid.

would still, at that time, be illegal. However, even if the party were illegal, its unarmed and political nature would mean that it would not be subjected to the same degree of repression that the Spanish government was inflicting on ETA-pm, a level of repression that was making it extremely difficult for ETA-pm to continue to operate.[26]

The proposed party's political line was another key issue. The authors argued that if the party adopted a revolutionary position, it could alienate certain sectors of the Basque population. Therefore, they argued, the party should maintain a more moderate political position. This would allow the party to achieve greater electoral success. This moderate approach would not contradict the objectives of ETA-pm. Rather, it would complement them and enable more sectors of the Basque populace to become involved with and show their support for the independence movement.[27] An unarmed political party could set up local committees and conduct meetings in person, which ETA-pm could not do, but "*that other parties are doing, and that are an indispensable condition for an effective mass policy*" [emphasis in original].[28] Thus, the authors noted that other organizations were setting the groundwork for a legitimate political movement that could be launched once democracy was established, the implication being that if ETA-pm did not do the same it ran the risk of being rendered superfluous in the new regime. This restructuring of ETA-pm did not mean that the organization would be renouncing violence. On the contrary, the authors argued that violence would continue to have an important role to play in the democratic system. Indeed, the very success of the independence movement would depend on the use of violence. What it meant was that ETA-pm was seeking a way to incorporate moderate Basques into their political project. In essence, adopt a more conservative approach to broaden their support base.

ETA-m's Contributions to Assembly VII

At the request of ETA-pm, ETA-m submitted two position papers for discussion at Assembly VII.[29] While the authors of the documents are unknown, it is suspected that they were written, at least in part, by the leaders of ETA-m,

[26] Ibid., 13.
[27] Ibid.
[28] Ibid.
[29] ETA-m, "Dos aportaciones de ETAm."

Argala and Txomin.[30] ETA-m broadly agreed with the Otsagabia Proposal, because it recommended a separation between ETA-pm's armed activity and its political activity. However, it made strong recommendations regarding the segregation of the two sectors.[31]

ETA-m perceived that the transition to democracy could derail the nationalist struggle in the Basque Country by subsuming the independence movement within a new "bourgeois democracy." ETA-m argued that the biggest threat to the Basque nationalist movement was the danger that the Basque people would be "led to the path of reformism through an ideological triumph of the bourgeoisie." By this they meant that the Basques could be convinced that the central government's reform agenda would satisfy their desire for autonomy and thus turn away from the revolutionary movement.[32] The risk, as they saw it, was great. The nationalist struggle could be lost by allowing the Basque people to believe the false rhetoric about representative democracy. This, they argued, could distract them from the fact that the old power structures of the Francoist dictatorship were still in place.

ETA-m also argued for a strict separation between the political and military sectors. They did not think it would be possible for ETA-pm to pursue a combined political-military strategy with a porous division between the legitimate political party and the armed organization. This would leave their entire organization vulnerable to state repression. ETA-pm had envisaged a system in which the political leadership could direct the military action. However, ETA-m argued that the only feasible way to continue operating was to maintain the separation between the political movement and the military apparatus. While this was less than ideal, ETA-m argued that it was the only way to safeguard the organization.[33]

Aside from the issue of state repression, ETA-m argued that another reason to separate the political party from the armed organization was that only a minority of Basque people supported armed action. Most Basques did not want political independence. ETA-m argued that even if they were able to bring about political independence for the Basque Country, they would be faced with large sections of the population who would refuse to accept it. They would then be put in a position in which they would be forced to repress their own people, which was completely unfeasible. Therefore,

[30] Ibid.
[31] ETA-pm, ETAren Agiria.
[32] ETA-m, "Dos aportaciones de ETAm."
[33] Ibid.

they argued, any plan that combined armed action with an expanded political agenda was doomed to fail. In using political structures to expand their armed struggle and boost recruits, ETA-m warned, ETA-pm "will lose everything."[34]

ETA-m advocated for a grassroots political front that would emerge out of the KAS Alternative. They argued that this would enable them to combine sufficient forces to isolate the oligarchy from the Basque people "opening the road to a popular revolution."[35] They argued for a political front, rather than an "interclass, heterogeneous party without ideological definition" that would not be able to "carry out a coherent policy or lead a people to their liberation." However, they argued that the military organization should be unitary for reasons of security and efficiency.[36] ETA-m set out their recommendations for how the political party should interact with the armed organization. They said that the military organization would coordinate its activities with the political front and that it could do this by maintaining bilateral relations with each organization that was part of the political front. While noting that there might be difficulties in coordinating the political and the armed struggle, they considered this option to be "the lesser evil."[37] ETA-m argued against members being permitted to belong to both the political and military organizations. Their reason was that this could attract the same degree of repression as a political-military strategy and thus impede the creation of a successful political movement.[38] A strict separation was essential, in their view, because a combined political-military structure would not be "an antidote to the disease" but would accelerate the disintegration of the revolutionary vanguard and lead to the downfall of ETA.[39]

ETA-m argued that there were four necessary features for a successful revolutionary vanguard. These were an independent political existence, an intelligence network that would enable them to engage in independent political analysis, actions that would prevent the bourgeoisie from connecting with the people and bringing them over to the reformist agenda, and a propaganda apparatus that would enable the military to communicate the meaning and objectives of their armed strategy, without the need for political intermediaries. The last two requirements, they argued, would

34 Ibid.
35 ETA-m, "Opcion structural," 76.
36 Ibid.
37 Ibid.
38 Ibid., 79.
39 Ibid., 80.

develop "the conditions that enhance the revolutionary consciousness of the People . . . with a view to preventing them from abandoning the revolutionary line."[40] ETA-m also elaborated on the kind of armed activity that would be needed during the transition to democracy. They anticipated that at a tactical level it would be "fundamentally defensive in nature against the attempts of the oligarchy to impose itself on the People by force." At a strategic level, ETA-m argued that the role of the armed organization would be to provide the Basque people with "direction, organizational channels and material remedies, all of a military nature, which will enable the popular Basque victory over the Spanish oligarchy."[41] Overall, ETA-m approved the proposal to create a political party, on the understanding that this would be an independent organization and segregated from the armed organization.

The Komando Bereziak Contribution

The Komando Bereziak also contributed a proposal to Assembly VII. It was presented on the day that the debate began. Although it was submitted by members of the Bereziak, it did not represent the group's consensus position. The proposal was not discussed at the debate because it was decided that it was not feasible to have a meaningful discussion about a proposal that was provided on the first day of the debate. It was therefore withdrawn from official consideration. It was, however, included in the records of the debate. The Komando Bereziak document argued that the decision to create a political party would be fatal to ETA-pm. They argued that it "contradicts all the previous struggle and lays the foundation for this kind of struggle (the Revolutionary War) to be isolated . . . because it no longer has the massive support of the people."[42] The proposal argued that there was nothing more methodologically removed from ETA-pm than a political party and that this alternative betrayed ETA-pm's trajectory and eliminated its possibilities of waging a revolutionary war.[43]

They argued that the conversion of ETA-pm into a political-military organization with a political-military structure would not bring anything new to the organization. Rather, it would take what had always been one of the

[40] Ibid.
[41] ETA-m, "Dos aportaciones de ETAm."
[42] Komando Bereziak, "Ponencia retirada," 207.
[43] Ibid.

organization's weaknesses and elevate it to an organizing principle. They argued that history had shown that combining political and military leadership enabled their opponents to attack both at once. "The result of the P-M structure has been the complete disorientation and disorganization of ETA . . ." and would ultimately lead to "THE DISAPPEARANCE OF ETA."[44]

This argument was similar in substance to that presented by ETA-m. However, there may have been additional reasons for the Bereziak's opposition to the Otsagabia Proposal. In a 1992 interview with historian José Antonio Egido, a former member of the Bereziak, Jorge Labordeta, discussed the reasons for the faction's position:

> In principle, everyone could agree with the creation of a legal party. But those of us who were living the struggle from the position of illegality did not see the issue clearly, because we perceived the intentions [of the leadership] to send the majority of people from the north and south of the Basque Country to join the political activity. Some of the people who were in Bereziak saw that there was a weakening of the armed struggle. There was fear that what was intended was to liquidate the armed struggle. There was resistance to that approach and distrust of those people. . . .[45]

According to Labordeta, the Komando Bereziak's opposition to the Otsagabia Proposal was based on the fear that it would ultimately compromise the armed struggle and that the ETA-pm leaders were intending to prioritize the new political party at the expense of the militant organization.

The Letamendia Proposal

The proposal written by Francisco Letamendia, also known as "Ortzi", was called "Sobre la necesidad del Partido independentista de los trabajadores vascos" (Regarding the necessity for an independent party for the Basque workers). This proposal was not debated but was substantially similar to the Otsagabia Proposal. Ortzi was not a member of ETA-pm but was a lawyer who had defended various Basque political prisoners. For this reason, his proposal was not debated at Assembly VII. Ortzi advocated for the creation of a Basque nationalist workers' party that would be independent of

[44] Ibid., 208.
[45] Egido, *Viaje a la nada*, 19–20.

ETA-pm. He argued that ETA-pm in its current state could not be this organization because the political party could not be armed and there was still a need for an armed organization. However, he said that the party would not condemn ETA-pm, which he referred to as the "armed nucleus." He said that the party would "neither interfere nor proclaim the need for the subsistence of such a nucleus, nor define its tasks . . . because any statement on these tasks would be qualified by the centralist legislation as 'apology or complicity with violence.'"[46] In this argument, Letamendia did not grapple with the issue of how the political party would respond if pressed by its rivals to express its view on ETA-pm's armed action.

Letamendia was aware that the new political climate would not allow ETA-pm to play the leading role in the next stage of the people's revolution, and that the political party would need to be independent.[47] Letamendia also noted that his proposal was similar to the course that was advocated by ETA-m in their recent writings in that it argued for a separation between the armed organization and a new political party.[48] And indeed, this tension between the political party and ETA-pm would begin to develop under the new democracy, as predicted by ETA-m.

The Debate

Assembly VII took place in September of 1976. Hundreds of ETA members were present at the debate, which took place over a period of six days.[49] Among them were the leaders of ETA-pm, the Komando Bereziak, and representatives of ETA-m, including leaders Argala and Txomin. The deliberations were recorded in an internal document produced by ETA-pm called "Apuntes de un debate sobre el Partido" (Notes of the debate about the Party). The notes record that the debate opened with a discussion of the strategic situation in the Basque Country. The organization stated that the death of Franco had led to "a change in the correlation of forces in the heart of the oligarchy."[50] This, they felt, would open the government up to the people and allow for more popular representation.

[46] Letamendia, "Sobre la necessidad del Partido," 191.
[47] Ibid.
[48] Ibid., 192.
[49] ETA, ETAren Agiria.
[50] ETA-pm, "El Partido de los Trabajadores Vascos," 1.

It was also noted that Franco's death had resulted in a reduction in the level of repression that had been experienced in the Basque Country and that there was more tolerance for nationalist left protests: "There is a notable change in the attitude of the government, with a decrease in repression, permitting certain manifestations, etc. . . . At first this creates a certain amount of confusion at all levels. . . ."[51] However, they were cynical of the true nature of this new democracy.[52] The members took the view that the reform was in name only and that the repressive system would remain intact. They argued that this new democratic government would only permit Basque nationalism to a certain extent. The two movements that would push the democratic government to the limits of its tolerance were the labor movement and the amnesty movement for the Basque political prisoners.[53] Those issues, they believed, would demonstrate that the central government was not genuinely inclined to allow the Basques the right to self-determination. Thus, the transition to democracy would not be sufficient in and of itself to provide the Basque people with the political reform for which ETA had been fighting. Indeed, the organization took a hostile view of the liberalization movement within the central government. This was based on the view that the appearance of reform would lure the Basque people away from the struggle for self-determination with false promises of democracy. They opined that the new democracy would merely be a modified version of Francoism in the guise of representative democracy. However, this apparent liberalization would undermine their attempts to mobilize the Basque people.[54]

The notes record that the organization had a clear view of how they needed to respond to the political situation. They had two objectives. The first was to "denounce and break down" the liberalization movement within the Spanish government and show it for the farce that it was. The second was to provide a framework for the people who were prepared to mobilize. They needed to "give a political cause to all the people who throw themselves into the fight in the Basque Country," with programs, objectives, and institutions to provide structure.[55] However, they noted that their existing organizational structure was not well equipped to advance these two objectives. The political-military structure was already struggling to find roles for

[51] Ibid.
[52] Ibid., 2–3.
[53] Ibid., 1.
[54] Ibid., 2–3.
[55] Ibid., 2.

the people who were disposed to engage in the political process. "It seems that in this new phase, the political-military structure is having difficulties integrating and directing the people who every day are more disposed to intervene directly in political life."[56] Thus, not only were they having difficulties recruiting, but they were also struggling to place the new members who were joining the movement.

The deficiencies were not just in their own organization. They also expressed the view that the Basque nationalist left was showing itself to be incapable of exercising effective political leadership and that the right and centralist groups were using the opportunity to take control of Basque politics.[57] However, it was argued that a change in strategy should not be solely based on external conditions, namely the transition from Francoism to democracy. Rather, they should conduct an internal analysis and "clarify the characteristics that define the genuine process of revolution in Euskadi, because creating a different process presupposes that the solutions at this juncture are also different."[58]

It was argued by one speaker that they should have a political party within the year.[59] This was seconded by another speaker, who said that the problem ETA-pm was facing was not unique to the organization but that the entire nationalist left was facing the same issue. Thus, the party should emerge from the entire nationalist left movement.[60] "The oligarchy is not trying to destroy the Patriotic Left, what it is trying to do is isolate it politically. . . . An immediate response is needed."[61] The issue of legalization was the subject of much discussion. The leaders did not know whether the kind of party they were proposing would in fact be condoned by the new regime. One speaker reasoned that a party which, for example, represented 30 percent of the population could not be made illegal, though it could be held to stricter standards.[62] Another speaker argued that the external change occasioned by the transition to democracy was more "psychological" than actual, noting that the liberalization would not provide the Basque nationalist left with the same freedoms as would be afforded to other political parties and institutions because, regardless of whether or not they were engaging in armed struggle,

[56] Ibid.
[57] Ibid.
[58] Ibid., 3.
[59] Ibid., 5.
[60] Ibid., 6.
[61] Ibid., 5.
[62] Ibid.

their ideology was not compatible with centralist democracy.[63] The accuracy of this prediction was reflected in the fact that, for all ETA-pm's desire to create a legitimate political party, they did not want to lay down arms. Indeed, it was repeatedly emphasized that the gains made by the Basque popular movement needed to be defended by the armed organization. As one speaker put it, "All militants and oligarchs are potential fascists, hence the necessity of militarily guaranteeing the what the people achieve."[64]

One of the main criticisms that was leveled against Otsagabia was that it was overly influenced by ETA-pm's internal situation. Those who held this view, which was strong within the Komando Bereziak, argued that the organization had to move with caution because mistakes made at this critical time in history could prove disastrous.[65] Advocates of this view argued that a rigid compartmentalization between the political party and the military organization, such as would be required for a legal political party, would not be possible without a "super-clandestineness" and without an extraordinary increase in the number of operatives and infrastructure. This would in turn lead to the "ATOMISATION" of the organization, which could have the dangerous effect of leading to a gradual growth in political/ideological divergences and which would in turn undermine the structure of the organization.[66] This could lead to increased factionalism and internal power struggles, ultimately compromising the entire organizational structure.

The Outcome of the Debate

Despite these criticisms, the Otsagabia Proposal was approved. The ETA-pm members who were present at the debate voted to implement this plan, which was supported by the leaders of ETA-m. ETA-pm determined that they would establish a socialist/communist political party. This ultimately took the name Euskal Iraultzarako Alderdia (EIA). It formally announced its creation in the Bizkaian town of Gallarta in 1977. Francisco Letamendia and Goio López Irazuegi oversaw the creation of the new political party. According to its manifesto, EIA was an anticapitalist workers' party that would pursue the objective of advancing the KAS Alternative.[67]

[63] Ibid., 4.
[64] Ibid., 7.
[65] Ibid., 48.
[66] Ibid.
[67] ETA-pm, "Etaren VII Batzarra, 1976."

ETA-m also made a declaration in which they announced their support for the proposal. In a document written in Euskera, ETA-m stated that in the new phase of the Basque revolution there was a need for "a mass struggle and an armed struggle. . . . ETA sees the need to separate these two tasks into two different institutions." As a result, the document stated, ETA-pm was to create "a revolutionary party of the Basque worker, capable of assuming and fulfilling political leadership." ETA-m stressed the fact that the organizations would be entirely separate, in accordance with its submissions to the debate. They clearly stated that "ETA-m, for its part, endorsed the decisions of the polimili [ETA-pm] Congress."[68]

Consideration

Assembly VII is a significant event because it is an example of a terrorist organization shifting toward a more moderate position to expand its membership base and its social influence. This debate shows an organization that had made significant strategic gains through violence voluntarily selecting a nonviolent strategy. The reason for this decision was that most of the ETA-pm membership perceived democratic politics to be the best means of advancing the organization and of preventing its marginalization in the new regime. ETA's perception of its position in the Basque political landscape is critical at this juncture because it provides an explanation for its decision. Susanne Martin and Arie Perliger note that organizations will select tactics based on the perceived attractiveness of those tactics, which is influenced by their environment. They note that in certain environments, terrorist groups have minimal popular support, and therefore, electoral politics is an unappealing course of action. In others, the terrorists can appeal to a broad part of the populace if they engage in electoral politics. While the former is the more common scenario, in this instance, ETA conforms to the latter.[69] It is a prime example of a terrorist organization that can see that electoral politics will provide it with an opportunity to expand. In order to expand, they must take a more moderate political position.

While this is a shift toward conservatism, it is important to note that ETA-pm did not renounce violence in Assembly VII. In fact, they emphasized that armed action would be necessary to defend any gains made through

[68] ETA-pm, ETAren Agiria.
[69] Martin and Perliger, "Turning to and from Terror," 35–36.

nonviolent activism. It is also noteworthy that the organization chose to engage in a democratic process in which they had little confidence. The members predicted that the Francoist leaders would use the guise of democracy to legitimize centralist oppression, but they still argued that it was necessary for the organization to be part of the system and to have a political wing that would be able to represent their interests in the new democracy. It was a calculated, strategic move that was not entirely consistent with the organization's ideological position. Although ETA-pm decried what they called the fascist democracy, the group still made the choice to radically alter its organizational structure to participate in this new system. This is even more remarkable because the result of this decision was that the organization would voluntarily limit its own power and relinquish some of its strategic decision making to a new nonviolent organization. The issue of control is critical, and indeed ETA-m and the Komando Bereziak argued that ETA-pm could not have control over a political party because interconnected leadership of the two groups would attract a repressive response from the central government and make it easier for the government to dismantle the party, and ETA-pm itself.[70]

In addition to this, the debate is significant because all the factions that were represented argued that membership of the political party should be open to anyone who adhered to their *minimum* ideological and strategic points, what they referred to as the Herrikoi Batasuna. This suggests that ETA-pm was not concerned with holding power to the exclusion of their more moderate rivals but was prepared to unite with them and give them power, provided they were prepared to prioritize self-determination for the Basque people. Thus, ETA-pm's priority was expansion, even if this resulted in an influx of new members who did not share their commitment to violent revolution. They also wished to create organizations and structures that would provide roles for all Basques who wanted to participate in the movement, regardless of their degree of commitment. In effect, the organization was choosing to dilute the ideological purity of the organization to ensure its broad appeal.

The outcome of this debate is contrary to the general prediction of outbidding theory that competitive political environments are more conducive to terrorist violence. At the time of the debate, ETA-pm's structure had been weakened by the antiterror efforts of the Spanish central government, and

[70] Komando Bereziak, "Ponencia retirada," 200.

it was struggling to attract recruits.[71] It should therefore be predicted to engage in terrorist attacks to attract new militants.[72] Justin Conrad and Kevin Greene applied the logic of nonviolent organizations in competitive markets to terrorist organizations, arguing "the use of extreme violence primarily benefits the organization in short-term recruitment and 'shoring up' of support, despite the fact that it may harm their long-term strategic goals."[73] However, external influences are also significant. ETA had suffered negative publicity prior to this debate, due to several attacks and killings that were poorly received by its Basque constituency. Thus, the environment influenced the attractiveness of the tactics, as predicted by Martin and Perliger.[74] Rather than using violence to re-establish its political position and attract new recruits, ETA-pm decided to begin the transition to nonviolent activism. Indeed, it is notable that there are no records of any discussion of recruitment by coercion. The anonymized notes from the debate record that in their deliberations several ETA-pm leaders argued that by creating a legitimate political party and affiliated labor unions they would allow the Basque people to freely participate in the nationalist cause.

It is also noted that this proposal was made, and later adopted, at a time when ETA-pm had no pressing strategic or practical need to cede power to another organization.[75] While they had suffered strategic and organizational setbacks, the discussions focused less on damage control and more on how to optimize the nationalist movement to best fit within the nascent democratic regime. Another important feature of this proposal is that it was made and endorsed during a transitional period between dictatorship and democracy. This was a time at which there were numerous parties vying to secure positions of power in the new regime. Under these conditions, a terrorist group would be predicted to use violence to secure its position in the new democracy. This is because new democracies are less likely to provide violent groups with access to political systems, thereby depriving them of social and economic goods.[76] However, rather than using violence to secure a prominent position within the democratic system, ETA-pm adopted an inclusive and predominantly political plan. This was despite persuasive

[71] Iñesta, "'Los Que Volvieron a Casa,'" 38.
[72] Conrad and Greene, "Competition, Differentiation," 556.
[73] Ibid., 547.
[74] Martin and Perliger, "Turning to and from Terror," 35.
[75] Aviles, "Experiencing Terrorism in Spain," 44.
[76] Kingma et al., "Regime Type and Terrorist Attacks," 4.

arguments that this would signify the end of ETA-pm.[77] ETA-pm endorsed the Otsagabia Proposal because they were worried that an armed organization would become marginalized in the new democracy and would lose its support and influence. The environment was the deciding factor. ETA-pm did not select violence as the default option. It assessed the likely outcomes of violent and nonviolent actions and selected the option that was most expedient, even though this did not align with its ideological principles.

Another significant aspect of this debate is the way the terrorists factored state repression into their decision-making. ETA-m and the Komando Bereziak were worried that creating a political party that was affiliated to ETA-pm would render both the terrorist organization and the political party vulnerable to state repression. In effect, they would be creating an easy target for the government. This indicates that terrorist organizations can be deterred from engaging in violence even when state repression is not at the high end of the scale. The very fact that they would lose members through routine counterterrorism measures was a factor that weighed in the balance. Many studies have argued that repression is effective against terrorism, but only when it is extreme.[78] However, as Gregory Saxton and Michelle Benson note, there are complex and context-dependent factors that influence the kinds of tactics that terrorist groups adopt.[79] In this case, it is possible to see the ameliorative effects of the elections. ETA-pm found a nonviolent means of expanding their reach and advancing their organizational objectives.

It is also important to note that the parties to the debate emphasized organizational survival in their arguments. ETA-pm wanted to expand their base to counteract the loss of members due to recent counterterrorism actions. The Komando Bereziak were concerned that the increased security requirements would lead to the atomization of the organization, which could result in factional in-fighting. ETA-m was worried that the new structure would make the organization as a whole more vulnerable. Thus, it is arguable that the primary concern of the debaters was protecting the organization from internal and external threats. Overall, the debate evidences a radical organization shifting toward conservativism to ensure its organizational survival. ETA-pm resolved to create a legitimate political party as a way of mitigating the risk that they would lose relevancy in the nascent democracy. While

[77] Soldevilla, "De las armas al parlamento," 250.
[78] Zhukov, "Repression Works"; Gaibulloev et al., "Regime Types and Terrorism."
[79] Saxton and Benson, "Means, Motives and Opportunities," 73.

they would not renounce violence, the political party would set the objectives, and violence would only be used in support. This debate shows that a change in external conditions prompted the organization to alter its trajectory and compromise its militant identity to maintain its position in the political sphere and increase its influence.

Conclusion

In this chapter, I examined how ETA-pm shifted toward conservatism when presented with the opportunity of engaging in electoral politics. This supports the predictions of the theoretical approach adopted in this book. I first set out the pre-existing tensions between ETA-pm's different wings, namely between ETA-pm and ETA-m, and between ETA-pm and its militant faction, the Komando Bereziak. In doing so, I explained the different views that each group had of the strategic landscape and how the nationalist agenda should be advanced. I then presented the proposals that the three groups submitted at the assembly. The Otsagabia Proposal was presented as representing the majority position of ETA-pm. This proposal was for the development of a political party that adhered to the minimum political agenda set by ETA-pm. The proposed party would be nonviolent, but it would be supported by the armed organization. ETA-m's documents argued that any political party that was aligned with a terrorist group would attract the repressive forces of the state. Thus, a rigid separation would be needed between ETA-pm and any nationalist political party.[80] The Komando Bereziak supported ETA-m's position. They argued that a party perceived to have ties to ETA-pm would either be dismantled by the central government or forced to publicly denounce ETA-pm's activities. Either course, they argued, could signal the demise of ETA-pm.[81] The Bereziak were also worried that the restructuring could result in increased factionalism and in-fighting, which could ultimately compromise the entire organization.

I concluded with a discussion of the significance of proposals that were advanced at the debate and the decision to endorse the Otsagabia Proposal. The decision is remarkable because it is an example of a terrorist organization selecting a nonviolent strategy because most of its members took the view that this would be the best way to advance their organization and cause

[80] ETA-m, "Dos aportaciones de ETAm."
[81] Komando Bereziak, "Ponencia retirada," 200.

and to expand their influence. The decision shows a clear shift toward conservatism. The records of the debate clearly demonstrate that the members adopted this position because they wanted to broaden the organization's base and allow more moderate Basques to participate in the movement. Thus, the terrorists chose to expand their organization and their social and political influence at the expense of ideological purity.

In making this decision, ETA-pm also ceded part of its autonomy and strategic decision-making capacity to a new nonviolent organization. Although this organization would be linked to ETA-pm through ideology and personnel, it was to be an independent political party. Thus, in a highly uncertain transitional period, this terrorist group selected an alternative that hampered their ability to engage in violence. This decision was taken because the members took the view that this was the best way to protect the future of ETA-pm in the new democratic regime. This decision point is an illustration of goal displacement. ETA-pm chose to prioritize a tangible goal, namely organizational expansion, over the more nebulous goal of national liberation. Even the dissenters were preoccupied with organizational survival and argued against the proposal on the grounds that it would compromise the organization and render it more vulnerable to counterterrorism efforts. Accordingly, I argue that ETA-pm chose to create a political party and engage in electoral politics with the objective of preserving and expanding its organization. In the next chapter, ETA-pm will face the prospect of the first democratic elections. The organization will need to determine how it will respond to this development and whether participation will ultimately strengthen the organization, or whether it will in fact signal tactic acceptance of the legitimacy of central governance.

6
The Elections of 1977

According to the organizational survival approach, the paramount concern for an established organization should be self-preservation. In a changing environment, an organization needs to adapt to survive.[1] In 1977, ETA-pm was faced with a crucial decision: whether they would support the first general election under the new democracy and call a ceasefire. One of the key concerns raised by the members was that this would signify ETA-pm's implicit acceptance of the democratic process—a process that many members considered to be a front for the continuation of fascist central governance. To determine whether the organization would support the elections, ETA-pm presented a proposal to their members. This was that they would support the left-wing nationalist candidates who would stand for election and that they would call a ceasefire until after the elections. The ceasefire would allow a peaceful political campaign. Despite vocal internal opposition, most ETA-pm members approved the plan to halt all violence and both support and participate in the democratic elections.

Before taking a decision, the leadership of ETA-pm put the proposal to the militancy and asked for their views. Six cells wrote position papers, which were distributed among the members. These papers reveal a divide within the organization between those who agreed with the leadership's proposal for a nonviolent political campaign, and those who saw such a course as a betrayal of the fundamental ideals of ETA. Ultimately, the more radical elements within the organization attempted to stage a coup to take control of ETA-pm and oust the leadership. This failed attempt ultimately resulted in the defection of the more radical faction, the Komando Bereziak. The year 1977 was crucial in ETA-pm's transition from violent political activism to peaceful politics. Despite their reservations about the ultimate utility of representative governance under a bourgeois democracy, most of the members of ETA-pm supported their leaders' proposal to cease armed action and engage in the democratic process. Most of the rank-and-file members saw

[1] Ansell et al., "Dynamic Conservatism," 94.

Euskadi Ta Askatasuna. Nell Bennett, Oxford University Press. © University of Maryland National Consortium for the Study of Terrorism and Responses to Terrorism (START) (2025). DOI: 10.1093/9780197764268.003.0006

more benefit in attempting to adapt to the new democracy than in boycotting the elections or using violence to disrupt the political process. This chapter will show that the reason for this was that ETA-pm believed that this approach best accorded with the desires and expectations of the Basque people and would therefore be the best way of ensuring their continued relevancy in the political process.

The General Elections of 1977

The year 1977 presented the organization with a new decision point. When the central government, under the leadership of Adolfo Suárez González, announced that there would be a national election, ETA-pm needed to determine what stance it would take.[2] Assembly VII of the previous year had resulted in ETA-pm taking the decision that they would alter the trajectory of their revolutionary struggle and form a political party that would participate in the new democracy. This was a markedly different approach to that of ETA-m, which boycotted the elections and used violence to dissuade the Basque people from voting. ETA-pm discussed the election in their internal bulletin *Kemen* number 10. They outlined the advantages and disadvantages of participating. Among the points in favor was that it would be to their advantage to have a representative in the national legislature who could advocate for their political goals. They thought it would benefit them to be able to influence the legislative process and to have politicians who could inform the Basque people of political developments as they were taking place in the capital. The disadvantages included the negligible impact that any Basque representative would be able to have over laws that were passed in Madrid.[3]

However, in their view, the most significant point was the high voter turnout they had witnessed in the recent referendum. On December 15, 1976, the central Spanish government held a referendum to assess public support for the Political Reform Act. The purpose of this act was to transform Spain from a Francoist dictatorship into a constitutional monarchy with a system of representative democracy.[4] Voter turnout in the Basque Country was estimated at 53.86 percent with 96.47 percent of voters saying "Yes"

[2] Meisler, "Spain's New Democracy."
[3] ETA-pm, *Kemen*, no. 10, 3.
[4] Sánchez-Navarro and Vale, "Political Transition," 8.

to the proposed political reforms.[5] ETA-pm opined that this turnout, along with the high "Yes" vote, indicated that there was a strong desire among the Basque people to participate in electoral politics.[6] Accordingly, they were concerned that if they were to boycott the first general election, they would run the risk of being marginalized. As ETA-pm stated in *Kemen*, "It can be seen . . . that the percentage of participation in the Basque Country is going to be high. Consequently, one can see the dangers of maintaining an abstentionist position if it is going to be followed by a small minority."[7] In particular, ETA-pm expressed their concern that if they were to boycott the election they could cause a widening in the divide between the moderate and the more radical sectors of Basque society.[8] They said, "Of course, it is about making a policy that will be valid for the entirety of Euskadi, not just for the most radicalized sectors."[9] In consequence of the resolution passed at Assembly VII, ETA-pm had created a political party, EIA. The party was made up of leaders selected by ETA-pm's Executive Committee. All appointed EIA leaders had been prominent members of ETA, though most had little connection with armed action.[10] The creation of the political party placed ETA-pm in a good position to use the elections to gain support from both radical and moderate Basques.

ETA-pm were concerned that participation in the elections could be interpreted as their legitimation of the new democratic regime. The leadership expressed a cynical view of the new democracy. Their opinion was that it was little more than a front to allow the fascist forces to maintain their power in the post-Franco era.[11] However, they were awake to the fact that a democratically elected government, regardless of its political inclinations, would be recognized by the people as the legitimate leader. "From that moment, all political proposals change; one phase of the revolution has finished and another begins; and we have to change our approaches very thoroughly if we really want the revolution to advance."[12] On balance they took the view that there was a greater risk of alienating the Basque people by adopting a position at too great a variance from their own.[13] They said

[5] Gobierno de España, Consulta de Resultado Electorales.
[6] Sullivan, *ETA and Basque Nationalism*, 186.
[7] ETA-pm, *Kemen*, no. 10, 3.
[8] Ibid., 4.
[9] Ibid.
[10] Soldevilla, *Historia de una Heterodoxia Abertzale*, 143.
[11] Ibid., 3.
[12] ETA-pm, "Sobre la problemática electoral," 297.
[13] Ibid., 300.

that the Basque people may have unrealistic expectations of the new democracy. The best way to show them the limited utility of engaging would be by demonstrating that elected Basque officials would not be able to make a difference to the national political agenda.[14] As one member expressed, the Basque people were not aware of the "uselessness" of the Spanish Parliament; "it is necessary to demonstrate this exact uselessness from the inside."[15] The ETA-pm leadership also observed that the fact that they were participating in the elections did not mean that they were accepting elections as the sole or even the primary means of bringing about political change. Rather, the elections would be one more instrument that they could use to mobilize the Basque people, to initiate debate, and to offer solutions to the problems that the people were facing.[16] Thus, they placed electoral politics on one end of a spectrum of political action. At the other end would be armed action. Ultimately, they concluded that they could not "walk in the opposite direction to that of the popular will."[17] Failure to heed the Basque people's desire to engage in the democratic process would jeopardize their survival. The pragmatic approach, therefore, was to put forward their own representatives.

ETA-pm Proposes a Ceasefire

The most significant part of ETA-pm's proposal was the initiation of a complete ceasefire for the duration of the elections. The reason for this was that the leadership believed a cessation of hostilities was needed to allow for a peaceful election campaign. They communicated their proposal to the militancy through their internal bulletin, *Kemen*. In an article titled "Analysis of the Situation in Euskadi Today," ETA-pm stated that in the preceding weeks events had taken place that required the leadership to exercise its responsibility as a revolutionary organization. One of these was what they referred to as "a change in the attitude of the government with respect to Euskadi."[18] In essence, they argued there were concrete signs that the central government was taking a more permissive approach to Basque nationalism. The policy change was signaled by the legalization of the ikurrina, the Basque

[14] Ibid., 303.
[15] Ibid., 305.
[16] Ibid.
[17] Ibid., 299.
[18] ETA-pm, *Kemen*, no. 11, 1.

flag. There was also a decrease in reports of state repression in the region of Gipuzkoa, a historic ETA stronghold.[19]

The second significant development that ETA-pm discussed was the spontaneous protests that were triggered by the deaths of two ETA militants, Sebastian Goikoetxea and Nicholas Mendizabal (also known as "Zaharra"). The two militants were killed by Civil Guard officers at a roadblock in the province of Gipuzkoa on March 9, 1977. News of the killings was received with outrage across the region. There were widespread strikes, reported to have affected a minimum of 1,372 businesses comprising around 32,901 workers.[20] Approximately 8,000 people marched in protest between the towns of Ordizia and Beasain, and around 4,000 marched from Tolosa to Ibarra, in Gipuzkoa. There were also protests in the towns of Zumarraga and Ondaretta and in Donostia. It was reported in the newspaper *El Pais* that around 4,000 people attended Mendizabal's funeral.[21] In response to the killing of the two militants, on March 13 ETA-pm operatives killed Civil Guard officer Constantino Gómez Barcia. The twenty-one-year-old police officer was shot after leaving a nightclub in the town of Arrasate in the early hours of the morning by two ETA militants in a stolen car.[22] In *Kemen* number 11 ETA-pm described this attack and expressed their satisfaction with its execution, "the most positive aspect of which has been the speed with which it has been carried out, giving the people an image that we are fully capable of responding instantaneously."[23]

The ETA-pm leadership argued that the explosion of popular sentiment provoked by these killings confirmed three important facts. First, "If the people want peace, they will not allow the false peace born of repression."[24] Second, "The people distinguish between the violence of the police and the violence of ETA. This does not mean . . . that we have *carte blanche* for any stupidity, but that the people of Euskadi do not see us as the disturbers of democracy."[25] The third fact was that the nationalist and leftist political forces used the opportunity to condemn ETA. This revealed to ETA-pm the "latent division" between their organization and the political parties of the nationalist left. However, ETA-pm noted that while this was unfortunate,

[19] Ibid.
[20] Genoveva Gastaminza, "Duelo en Guipúzcoa."
[21] Ibid.
[22] RTVE, "Constantino Gómez Barcia."
[23] ETA-pm, *Kemen*, no. 11, 3.
[24] Ibid., 4.
[25] Ibid.

they could not allow this division to form a permanent rift. They stated that in the new democracy ETA would need the support of these political parties. ETA-pm needed to take a pragmatic approach and court the more moderate left if they were to have electoral success. Their objective, as they put it, was to consolidate the nationalist left bloc, which "with its active participation and its backing, has been supporting us and has identified with our struggle."[26]

ETA-pm was not going to allow the fact that various left-wing organizations had condemned their reprisal to affect their strategic calculations. They were aware that their nation building program would require them to ally themselves with these groups. What this event had shown them was that they may have some allies who were unreliable and who may not support their actions. The important thing was to maintain the unity of the nationalist left bloc.[27] ETA-pm said that the public response to the killings of Goikoetxea and Mendizabal demonstrated that the Basque people, in particular the people of Gipuzkoa, supported ETA-pm and were ready and willing to mobilize. The organization must capitalize on this momentum to consolidate their political position. This was particularly pressing because during the transition to democracy the political landscape was changing "at an impressive speed" and "he who arrives last of all will be left with the crumbs."[28] The external environment was changing, and ETA-pm needed to adapt if was to survive.

It was therefore necessary to act fast and capitalize on the public sentiment. The key card that ETA-pm had to play was violence. The document stated that it was the authors' opinion that it was time to play this card in support of the nationalist left. However, it clarified, this did not necessarily mean that they should engage in acts of violence. Rather, they should demonstrate their capacity to control violence. The ability to influence political action lay in control.[29] Not using violence, under the right circumstances, could be as if not more effective as terrorism. The leadership believed that the time was right to make a declaration to the Basque people explaining the conditions under which they would stop using violence. These would be free elections, the legalization of ETA-pm's political party and "some means of freedom for

[26] Ibid., 7.
[27] Ibid., 6.
[28] Ibid., 7.
[29] Ibid.

the prisoners."[30] The key aspect of this declaration would be that they would be stating very clearly that it would be the government and not ETA-pm that would be responsible for disrupting the Basque political process with violence. In that way, the government would be forced to either "grant those demands, or to engage in a repressive escalation."[31] In effect, they would be putting the government in the position of being the party that disturbed the peace. ETA-pm expressed the view that they could make substantial political gains by being the initiators of this détente with the central government. The move would allow them to appeal to a more moderate segment of the Basque populace, thereby expanding their appeal. It would also put the government in a position in which they had to choose to either respond positively to ETA-pm's demands or invite a return to violence.[32]

There was also a more practical reason for making the declaration. Ceasing violence would give ETA-pm the time and resources it needed to rebuild the organization.[33] ETA-pm had suffered under recent counterterrorism measures and was depleted in both personnel and finances. Thus, they could present the ceasefire as an altruistic action to promote peace and democratic participation, while using the time to reformulate their strategic direction and gather resources for the next phase of the revolutionary struggle. As they put it, a period of organization stability was needed to restructure. A ceasefire would provide them with the time they needed to build a strong and secure apparatus.[34]

ETA-pm Call for Submissions

The ETA-pm leadership presented their proposal to the broader militancy in *Kemen* number 12. In that bulletin they asked the members to debate the issues and to send in their views on the proposed ceasefire and the general elections.[35] To facilitate this, they proposed that discussions take place within the cells. Those operatives who were already grouped into cells for active militancy should debate the ideas among themselves. Those who were not already in cells, such as ex-prisoners, would be put into groups

30 Ibid.
31 Ibid.
32 Ibid.
33 Ibid., 8.
34 Ibid.
35 Ibid.

specifically for the purpose of the debate. ETA-pm requested that each cell put their views in writing and submit them to the leadership to be published in the next issue of *Kemen*. This bulletin would then be distributed among the members so that all could read and discuss the ideas that had been submitted. They wrote that it was extremely important that each cell share its views with the entire organization. Active participation in the debate was presented as a positive duty for the militants.[36]

ETA-pm noted in the document that being a secret organization they were forced to maintain a compartmentalized structure. However, given the importance of the matters under debate, they argued that it was necessary for all militants to try to consider the issues and contribute to the discussion. Their concern with the representative nature of the debates was expressed in their exhortation to the militants: "The organization's leadership has made a special effort during the last few weeks to inform the militancy as much as possible, but this is not enough . . . it is necessary that we all express our opinions on the issues that we are discussing."[37] They asked the militants to consider three factors. The first was the legal-political structure of the central government at the national level, including the anticipated structure of the new regime, the distribution of power, and legal and political processes. The second was the legal-political structure that would come into effect in the Basque Country, including state and municipal elections and the distribution of power. The third was the process of class struggle within the Basque Country, including the development of a strategy of popular power, the forces that would support this strategy, the forces that would be involved in electoral politics, and the institution of anti-system structures.[38] These three factors would determine the parameters within which ETA-pm would develop a new strategy for achieving its objective, which was: "The achievement of self-government for Euskadi, which is to say, the institutionalization of the relationship between the Basque forces and the Central Power [and] the consolidation of the organisms of popular power."[39] Through the achievement of these objectives ETA-pm would seek to create a unified Basque national policy, in which the people would play a leading role.[40]

[36] ETA-pm, *Kemen*, no. 12, 1.
[37] Ibid.
[38] Ibid., 2.
[39] Ibid.
[40] Ibid.

The Cells' Responses

The responses from six cells were published in the following issue of *Kemen*. All the cells were anonymized, and their responses ranged in length from one paragraph to several pages.

1. Taldeak

The first published response was signed Taldeak and was dated Aberri Eguna 1977.[41] The cell agreed with the analysis presented by the leadership of ETA-pm that the ruling classes were seeking to consolidate their interests in the new regime and that the new democracy would be a front for the same bourgeois repression that had existed under Franco. However, they disagreed with ETA-pm's view that the new government was taking a more tolerant approach to Basque nationalism.[42] They argued that the presence of the repressive forces was still strong in the region and that to say otherwise showed the authors' ignorance of the socio-political realities of life in Gipuzkoa.[43] The cell also attacked the document written by members of the ETA-pm leadership, "Analysis of the Situation in Euskadi today," for the way it had discussed the deaths of Goikoetxea and Zaharra. It took issue with the organization's response to the killings, saying that it was a weaker response than had been expected and that this was in part due to the organization's weakened capabilities.[44]

The cell took a strong stand against the ceasefire that had been proposed by the leadership. They argued that a ceasefire would only benefit the central government. They said that a ceasefire would allow Suárez to "maintain and increase his 'democratizing' halo." Whereas ETA-pm, "lacking unity, economic resources and logistics, in other words, disorganised," would end up disconnected from concrete action.[45] They argued that the only way a ceasefire could be negotiated would be if the central government positively guaranteed the Basque people the democratic and national liberties set out in the KAS Alternative.[46] The cell stated that the proposal for the ceasefire would

[41] Aberri Eguna is a Basque nationalist holiday celebrated on Easter Sunday.
[42] Ibid., 3.
[43] ETA-pm, *Kemen*, no. 13, 4.
[44] Ibid., 4–5.
[45] Ibid., 6.
[46] Ibid., 6.

remain "absolutely IN SUSPENSE" until the entire militancy had been given the opportunity to express their opinions on the issue. If the leadership decided to proceed with the announcement of the ceasefire the proposal would be "automatically DESTROYED," and they called for an immediate meeting of the cells to discuss the proposal and the future of the armed struggle.[47] The submission ended with this startling declaration: "Treachery is not immaterial . . . and is practiced in many cases by those who we least suspect. Hopefully ETA will one day be able to escape from its web."[48] The cell that wrote the document thereby accused the ETA-pm leadership of betraying the nationalist cause by proposing a ceasefire and participating in the elections. Despite these inflammatory comments, this submission was distributed to the broader membership, with the following response from the leaders.

One anonymous member of the leadership of ETA-pm wrote a response to the critique submitted by Taldeak. The response said that it would not reply to each of the criticisms that had been made in Taldeak's letter. However, it did state that the document was written in inappropriate terms and that its descent into personal attacks signified a refusal to "resolve the debate in the terms in which it was originally planted, in this case, political."[49] The author reaffirmed ETA-pm's position that the shift away from armed activity and toward politics was due to the regime change from fascist dictatorship to democracy and that an alternative strategy was needed for these new conditions. The decision to cease using violence would be based on the fact that under certain circumstances, namely, the absence of violent coercion from the state forces, a political approach would be capable of achieving a series of objectives.[50] However, just as the central government would maintain its armed forces to protect the oligarchy, so too would ETA-pm maintain its militancy in defense of its interests.[51] The leader directly acknowledged that ETA-pm's strategy had changed from the 1974 declaration in *Kemen* number 6 that the "total destruction" of the state was a necessary part of the nationalist struggle.[52] ETA-pm was now prepared to work within the system to seek political reform. This was a significant shift in the direction of conservatism.

[47] Ibid., 7.
[48] Ibid.
[49] Ibid., 15.
[50] Ibid., 16.
[51] Ibid., 19.
[52] ETA, *Kemen*, no. 6.

2. Talde Bateak

The second response was from another anonymous cell that signed its document Talde Bateak. This response was much shorter and stated that in general the cell agreed with the statements made by the leadership. However, they did raise a simple economic question: How would ETA-pm finance its operations during a ceasefire? According to the declaration made by the leadership, they observed, the ceasefire would provide a period in which the organization could strengthen its structures. However, they noted that it was not possible to wage any kind of armed struggle without money, money that the organization did not have. The cell said: "To obtain this money we see feasible: Tax, Robberies and Kidnappings." If these options would not be possible under a ceasefire, the organization would need to consider how it would continue to finance its operations.[53]

3. Un militante. S

The third response to the ETA-pm position paper was signed Un militante. S. The response opened with a request for further information about the ETA-pm ceasefire proposal. It then asked to know whether the proposal was that of one militant, or whether it came from the entire leadership. If the proposal was not from the entire leadership, or if the proposal was presented at a meeting of the leadership at which not all attendees agreed, the cell requested to know who was responsible for presenting this proposal as though it were the result of a consensus decision of the leadership. The response demanded to know who was responsible for manipulating agreements and going against the interests of ETA-pm and the point of view of most of the members of the organization. They stated that ETA-pm's base did not want a ceasefire. "We are a revolutionary organization that has a responsibility within Euskadi and our revolutionary strategy is armed struggle. . . ."[54]

The author conceded that there may come a time when ETA-pm would need to stop using violence; however, that would not come through a ceasefire with the government. The Suárez government was fully aware of what ETA-pm was demanding for the elections: amnesty, legalization of political

[53] ETA-pm, *Kemen*, no. 13, 9.
[54] Ibid.

parties without exception, democratic freedom, equal conditions for all electoral campaigns, and press freedom.[55] The author observed that only days had passed since the deaths of Zaharra and Goikoetxea and the killing of two other Basques at the hands of the police. "In little time 4 deaths, by the brilliant actions of the forces of public order. . . . It seems we soon forget the deaths of these companions who died for some ideals. Because in a few days we want to sign a ceasefire, it's a disgrace."[56] This submission reveals that despite the scission of the military front, hard-line militarist components persisted in the organization. These members were strongly opposed to any disarmament and not afraid to say so.

4. GEA GES

The fourth response was signed GEA GES. This document agreed in broad terms with the proposal made by the leadership. However, it argued that it was important to consider what kind of democracy they would be living in after the elections. Issues such as amnesty and the legalization of political parties were not the only issues that ETA-pm needed to be concerned with. They also needed to consider their long-term objectives and what role armed struggle would play in achieving those objectives. However, they agreed with the proposal to cease their activities until after the elections.[57] This cell also raised one semantic point: "We do not think it correct that in our language and to signify our tasks we use the word VIOLENCE, particularly because at this time this is the vocabulary that is being used by the forces who wish to deceive with their democratic game. A simple question of aesthetics."[58] Although they were not averse to using terrorist tactics, this cell thought it in bad taste to describe ETA-pm's armed activities as "violence."

5. Comando "Andoni"

The Comando "Andoni" submitted two responses. The first was a strongly worded reply to the leadership's proposal. They disagreed with the analysis presented by the leadership that the central government was showing more

[55] Ibid., 10.
[56] Ibid.
[57] Ibid.
[58] Ibid.

tolerance in the Basque Country. Rather, they argued that the government was responding to the people's demands with repression, as they always had.[59] The Comando "Andoni" presented the view that ETA's focus should be on strengthening the patriotic left movement and providing it with armed support. The patriotic left had stipulated certain minimum conditions be met before they would agree to participate in the general elections. The cell stated that if these conditions were not met and if there was not a climate of de-escalation and good faith, ETA should use all the means it had at its disposal to oppose the elections.[60] Therefore, they argued, ETA-pm should not make a public announcement of a ceasefire. "We cannot announce that it will not be us who will break the political process that is being created in Euskadi with violence."[61] Equally, they said, ETA-pm could not publicly state that it would renounce the only weapon it had to obtain and defend its objectives. This, they believed, would paint the organization into a corner and leave it without tactical options.

The cell further argued that ETA-pm should not support the upcoming elections. To do so would be to legitimize the new political process and signify that they accepted the validity of the new government, "accept that it is no longer fascist, that it is not the same that has killed, tortured and massacred the people and our militants." Their response closed with a note stating that all members of the Comando "Andoni" agreed with this position paper. However, one member wanted to add that despite agreeing with the arguments presented, he would accept that it was valid for the political party to present itself at the elections. The other members of the cell disagreed with this point.[62]

In their second response, dated April 5, 1977, the cell presented their criticisms of ETA-pm's strategic vision. They wrote that the leadership comprised a small number of people who did not represent the organization's base and did not think like its members.[63] They argued that the membership should be responsible for determining the strategic direction of the organization, not the leadership. The leadership's role should be putting into action the strategy that the members decide upon. They argued that it was not the fault of the base that they had not taken a more active role in the

[59] Ibid., 12.
[60] Ibid.
[61] Ibid.
[62] Ibid.
[63] Ibid.

development of the strategic direction. "We think that specific people have been much to blame. We believe that these people have been the ones who have created a 'leading' class. . . ."[64]

The Ex-Prisoners Weigh In

The position papers summarized above show a division of opinion within ETA-pm regarding the proposed ceasefire and participation in the general elections. On one side were the members who considered the ceasefire and participation in the elections to be appropriate, on the condition that amnesty be granted to the political prisoners and that Basque nationalist parties be granted the same liberties as other political parties. On the other side were the militants who viewed the proposed ceasefire as a betrayal of the principles of the revolutionary struggle and who saw participation in the elections as legitimizing the pseudo-democracy of the Suárez government. These divisions were exacerbated by a series of responses that representatives of the ETA-pm leadership wrote to the authors of the Taldeak document in which they restated and justified their position.[65]

A group of fifteen ex-prisoners reacted to this division by issuing two letters to the militancy calling for an internal debate to resolve their differences. In their first letter, titled Carta a toda la militancia (Letter to all the militancy), the ex-prisoners warned that the division within the organization could jeopardize its very existence. In a second letter, dated May 12, 1977, the ex-prisoners repeated their call for an internal debate.[66] The ex-prisoners wrote that since the distribution of their first letter they had maintained contact with the members of the two blocs within the militancy. They did this in the hope of preventing a scission of the group, which they considered to be the biggest political error the organization could make at that time. They opined that if the group were to splinter it could put the future of the entire organization at risk and could provoke a crisis within the nationalist left movement.[67] They observed that it was highly unusual for a group of ex-prisoners to call for a debate on the future of ETA-pm. However, the organization was being presented with a series of questions, and they would

[64] Ibid., 13.
[65] ETA-pm, *Kemen,* no. 14.
[66] ETA-pm, "Convocatorio a toda la militancia," 483–484.
[67] Ibid.

not be able to continue their political or military activities until they had answered these questions. Therefore, they called on all members of ETA-pm to participate in the debate.[68]

The Komando Bereziak Break from ETA-pm

In May 1977 the Komando Bereziak issued a declaration in which they stated their intention to break with the leadership of ETA-pm. The reasons that they gave for this decision were in line with the criticisms that were made in the Taldeak letter and by the Comando "Andoni." That is, they disagreed with the leadership's decision to negotiate with the Suárez government, their willingness to institute a ceasefire, and their decision to participate in the general elections. The Bereziak argued that the Basque people were at a point at which they had to choose between continuing with the revolutionary project without compromising, or "integrating themselves into the reformist agenda."[69] They took a cynical view of the transition to democracy, saying that the Suárez government was taking "the first step toward guaranteeing the continuation of [the oligarchy's] Power assuring itself of popular legality through universal suffrage. . . ."[70] The Bereziak criticized Basque groups that were engaging with the democratization project and accused them of playing a "double game" with the Basque people, on the one hand, presenting democratic projects to advance the nationalist movement, and on the other hand promoting policies that showed that they had given up on self-determination and were now supporting a system that was contrary to their own interests.[71]

Even though the practical outcome of this declaration was that the Komando Bereziak would leave ETA-pm, in this document they referred to themselves as ETA-pm. They elaborated their strategic vision for the organization: "ETA (p-m) as a Basque Socialist Revolutionary Organization maintains the right to form its own autonomous policy based on the tactical principles and strategies of Socialist Revolution. . . ." They stated their intention to follow the decisions taken in Assembly VII to form a political party, as well as their desire to reunite with ETA-m. The Bereziak were

[68] Ibid.
[69] Komando Bereziak, "Comunicado Denuncia de ETA," 487.
[70] Ibid.
[71] Ibid., 488–489.

not hesitant to present themselves as the real ETA-pm to the Basque people. In June, the leader of the Bereziak gave an interview to the Basque magazine *Punto y Hora*. When asked what he thought of the discrepancies in the organization's approach, he replied, "I don't think one can talk about discrepancies, rather the expulsion of the majority of the leadership by the majority of the militants of the base. . . ." He also stated that he thought there should be just one armed organization fighting for the socialist revolution in the Basque Country and that it should be democratic, "that is to say, committed to the Basque Working People. . . ."[72] Thus, he publicly positioned the Bereziak as the true ETA-pm, free of the elitist leadership structures of the old organization.

ETA-pm Regroup

ETA-pm responded to the scission within its ranks by prioritizing organizational restructuring. They set up teams and committees tasked with assessing their existing personnel and infrastructure and identifying areas that needed reinforcement. They also established a group that would be dedicated to propaganda.[73] They communicated to their membership by way of an internal letter to the militancy the need to maintain a united front. "The biggest political error that we can commit is to remain in a vacillating position. That is what the Government has been looking for and that would be our ruin. . . ."[74]

ETA-pm also issued a letter to the Basque people, explaining the split within the organization. Discussing their approach to the revolutionary struggle, ETA-pm wrote that they considered "armed intervention to be the maximum form of political struggle." They wrote that in the existing political circumstances political violence should be "entwined in the general process of the Basque Revolution." Therefore, they argued, its role would be significantly different to that which it played in the times of Franco.[75] The leadership of ETA-pm also contributed a statement to the Basque weekly magazine, *Punto y Hora*, in which they wrote that ETA-pm were "the first to want the violence to end and for their people to be able to freely create their destinies." Accordingly, they publicly demonstrated their good faith by

[72] *Punto y Hora*, "No estoy implicado," 10.
[73] ETA-pm, "Carta a la militancia," 504–505.
[74] Ibid., 504.
[75] ETA-pm, "Comunicado de ETA," 524.

proclaiming: "we will not carry out any armed action before the elections if the Government convokes them under the minimum conditions we have stipulated: total amnesty and legalization of all political parties."[76]

The Conference of the Cells

In May 1977, a faction within ETA-pm who called themselves the "ex-prisoners" organized an internal debate among the cells. The ex-prisoners drafted a paper that was distributed to the militancy in which they set out the objectives of the debate along with their analysis of the internal crisis that had led to the defection of the Komando Bereziak. The ex-prisoners noted that the Bereziak had been invited to take part in the debate but had declined the offer.[77] The first issue for discussion was the recent scission. The ex-prisoners expressed their view that the Bereziak did not leave ETA-pm for the reasons they gave. Rather, they said that "the reasons for this crisis must be sought elsewhere and that they predate these events. The issue of the truce would be nothing more than the excuse that Bereziak has taken to initiate the split based on the discontent that exists in the militancy."[78] However, the ex-prisoners also thought that the ETA-pm leadership was partially responsible for the crisis. They opined that the leadership had not engaged in sufficient discussions with the militancy. The result of this was that when they presented the proposed ceasefire to the militancy, they found that they had lost touch with the base. "The price paid for this is very clear and it is thought that it is for this reason that we are in the current situation."[79]

They also said that this lack of debate had been a historic problem for ETA and that there had been times in the past when militants had submitted protests, orally or in writing, to the leadership about the direction the organization was going in and that the leaders had not made any reply to these submissions. This, they said, had generated discontent that could be used to divide the organization.[80] But above this, the biggest problem with ETA, according to the ex-prisoners, was that the idea of what a political-military

[76] ETA-m, "Declaracion del Biltzar Tripia," 9.
[77] ETA-pm, "Informe sobre la Conferencia. 3
[78] Ibid.
[79] Ibid., 4.
[80] Ibid.

organization was had never been properly defined. "Nobody, neither the Leadership nor the Bereziak has developed a theory of armed struggle."[81]

Setting the issue of the scission to one side, the ex-prisoners discussed the organizational problems facing ETA-pm in broader terms. From their perspective, the advent of democracy meant that ETA-pm could not continue to operate as it had under Franco. The new conditions would require a more active militancy that would pose a real challenge to the central democratic government and show the Basque people that the same powers that held control under Franco were in operation.[82] The ex-prisoners argued that ETA-pm's primary difficulty would be developing the military capacity and coordinated direction that they would need to be able to support the people's political advancement against the aggressions of the central government and the repressive forces.[83] However, this was not ETA-pm's only difficulty. "We are aware that political struggle is dirty," they wrote. The central power would not only rely on laws but also on their army and police. "If we want to win, ETA will have to outweigh the disadvantage . . . with selective attacks. . . ."

Notes from the Debate

ETA-pm produced a summary of the discussions that took place at the conference. One of the key topics for debate was "The Function of Armed Struggle in a Bourgeois Democracy: Strategic Characteristics and Tactical Characteristics." In this discussion the organization debated their changing role under the new regime: "The armed Organization must keep in mind that already . . . the principal role in the fight will pass to the masses."[84] Thus, their new role would be to facilitate mass uprisings. ETA's role would be to create conditions favorable to such popular revolt. The armed struggle was to be "constantly creating revolutionary conditions; maintaining those that exist today and creating new ones."[85] One way it would do this would be by teaching the Basque people that armed struggle was an essential element of the fight for self-determination.

This discussion differed from the arguments advanced by the ex-prisoners. The ex-prisoners had advocated for more high-profile attacks,

[81] Ibid., 5.
[82] Ibid., 5.
[83] Ibid., 5.
[84] ETA-pm, "Informe de una Reunion."
[85] Ibid.

like the killing of the former prime minister, Carrero Blanco. However, it was argued that while such attacks were valuable in that they could be used to show the Basque people that the central government was vulnerable, there was more to be gained from teaching the people to conduct their own revolutionary warfare. The ex-prisoners argued that in the next phase of revolutionary struggle, the nationalist cause should be advanced by popularizing violence and by encouraging the Basque people to take the fight to the streets. "The mission of ETA is, therefore, in this sense, like that of other political organizations. Organize the people for their own self-defense. Except that ETA's military experience should be used in the technical aspects of the armed struggle at this popular level."[86]

The Results of the 1977 Elections

In the lead-up to the elections, ETA-m perpetrated thirty-four minor attacks but incurred no fatalities. Despite ETA-m's efforts to dissuade the Basque people from voting, the abstention rate in the Basque Country was only 22.6 percent. This was only slightly above the rate in the rest of Spain, which was 21.17 percent.[87] The Basque Nationalist Party (PNV) and the Socialist Party (PSOE) received the most votes: 296,193 votes were cast for the PNV and 267,897 for the PSOE. ETA-pm's party, EE, received 61,417 and 67,978 for the senate. With these results, EE representative Francisco Letamendia was elected a deputy. and the party had two members of parliament for Gipuzkoa.[88] Reflecting on the election results, ETA-pm acknowledged that the Basque people had legitimized the electoral process, and had, for the most part, ignored ETA-m's called for a boycott. This, they recognized, would require the organization to rethink its strategic direction.[89]

Consideration

This chapter provides a unique view inside a terrorist organization at a crucial decision point. There were two key questions for debate: whether the organization should support the elections, and whether they should call a

[86] Ibid.
[87] Soldevilla, "Ya no es todo blanco," 417.
[88] Ibid., 418.
[89] Ibid.

ceasefire for the duration of the process. These questions are simple, yet they go to the very basis of a terrorist group's reason for existing. Terrorist groups typically form because they do not believe that they can make meaningful change through the electoral process, and their principal instrument is violence. Thus, supporting elections and halting the hostilities is a definite and possibly irrevocable move away from radicalism and toward the center left.

ETA-pm put these two questions up for internal debate because they were confronting a changing environment. The death of Franco at the end of 1975 and the advent of democracy had brought with it a sense of optimism in the populace. The leaders of ETA-pm recognized that a substantial proportion of Basque people wanted to participate in the democratic process. ETA-pm's leadership were aware that they could no longer continue to operate in the same way that they had under the dictatorship. To do so would be to risk marginalizing the organization. Their response was to shift toward the center. This is as predicted by the theoretical model. As Kees Huizinga and Martin de Bree expressed, goal displacement "is the phenomenon by which the original and often radical or idealistic goals of an organization are displaced by the inferior goals required to maintain the organization and keep its leadership in power."[90] At this point in ETA-pm's history, the leadership reoriented the organization's goals from revolutionary warfare to nonviolent electoral participation for the express reason that they believed this was what the Basque people wanted. Without the support of the people, the organization's resources would be diminished, which would hinder its ability to operate. This in turn, would jeopardize the positions of the leaders themselves.

According to goal displacement, an organization with intangible goals is likely to become more moderate in response to change. An organization like ETA-pm, formed around the idea of rebellion and national liberation, has what Young Han Chun and Hal G. Rainey refer to as "directive goal ambiguity," that is, there is a substantial degree of "interpretive leeway available in translating an organization's mission or general goals into directives and guidelines for specific actions to be taken to accomplish the mission."[91] In effect, ETA-pm's overarching objective was the abstract idea of liberation for the Basque people. This does not immediately translate into clear, actionable steps, and any measures employed to achieve the overall objective must be

[90] Huizinga and de Bree, "Exploring the Risk of Goal Displacement," 868.
[91] Chun and Rainey, "Goal Ambiguity," 532.

informed by external conditions. As William E. Barber and John N. Taylor explain, members of organizations with ambiguous objectives will attempt to make intangible goals tangible and actionable. In doing so, they will construct goals to which they can orient their efforts.[92] In this case, the leaders of ETA-pm developed new, tangible goals to match the altered environment. These new goals included supporting Basque left-wing nationalist candidates in the upcoming election, advancing their own political party, and consolidating the leftist bloc. None of these were part of ETA-pm's original objectives, a fact that was noted by many of the militants.

The defection of the Komando Bereziak is highly significant from a theoretical perspective because it provides a clear illustration of the paradox expounded by Ethan Bueno de Mesquita, which is that as terrorist groups become more moderate, there is an increased risk that radical splinter groups will form. In effect, "Policies such as strengthening the economy or outlets for nonviolent expression of grievances reduce mobilization but also make terrorist factions more extreme."[93] De Mesquita warned that liberalization and concessional policies can have the unintended effect of creating more extreme groups while at the same time decreasing overall mobilization. This may not result in a net decrease in violence.[94] In this case, there was a clear disagreement over the best means of advancing the organization's overarching goals in the new democracy. The more radical faction, the Bereziak, strongly opposed the ceasefire, and as a result, a more extreme splinter group was formed.

Conclusion

This chapter has examined the debate of 1977. In this year, ETA-pm found itself in a changing environment. The advent of democracy and the Basque people's desire to participate in the first general election signaled to the leadership that they needed to adapt if they were to survive. In response, the leadership proposed a strategy that better suited the new democracy, namely, to support the democratic elections and call a ceasefire. This proposal was approved by the majority of members. However, it was far from unanimous. The suggestions provoked outrage in the more radical faction of

[92] Barber and Taylor, "Importance of Goals," 369.
[93] Bueno de Mesquita, "Terrorist Factions," 411.
[94] Ibid.

the organization. The Komando Bereziak took the opportunity to denounce the ETA-pm leadership and present the members with an alternative course of action. However, the Bereziak's proposal to boycott the elections and continue with violent activism did not attract many ETA-pm members, and ultimately, the Bereziak split from ETA-pm. Although they adopted the name "ETA-pm," the greater part of the members stayed with the original organization.

Despite the division that emerged within ETA-pm, there was minimal divergence in the ways the two factions perceived the existing political landscape. Both took a dim view of the central government and the transition to democracy. Both sides opined that the new regime was merely a new front for the old forces that were in power under fascism. Both the ETA-pm leadership and the Komando Bereziak expressed concern that participating in the general elections would cause the organization to run the risk of signaling to their constituency that they supported the new regime. Both worried that they could be seen to be legitimizing a political process that they did not believe would provide substantial benefit to the nationalist movement.[95]

What differed between the two factions was not their view of the strategic situation but their opinions on how to best advance the organization. ETA-pm emphasized the voter turnout that they had witnessed across the Basque Country in the referendum. They argued that this indicated that the Basque people wanted to be involved in the political process.[96] If the organization was to remain relevant, it needed to serve the Basque people. If the people wanted to vote, ETA-pm needed to provide them with candidates. Violence was not off the table, but it would only be used when necessary to support the people's political struggle. While the leaders agreed that they ran the risk of legitimizing the new regime through their participation in the election, the greater risk was that by boycotting the election they would lose the support of a large proportion of the Basque people.[97]

The Komando Bereziak, on the other hand, took the view that the position advanced by ETA-pm was a betrayal of the organization's history and ideology. They argued that as an armed organization it was their responsibility to use violence to advance the interests of the Basque people and retaliate against the aggressions of the forces of the central government.[98]

[95] ETA-pm, *Kemen*, no. 10, 3; Komando Bereziak, "Comunicado Denuncia," 491.

[96] ETA-pm, *Kemen*, no. 10, 3.

[97] Ibid., 4.

[98] Komando Bereziak, "Comunicado Denuncia," 491.

In making their case, the Bereziak used highly emotive arguments. They said that declaring a ceasefire was a betrayal of all those who had died in the struggle against Spanish oppression. They accused the ETA-pm leadership of advancing their own self-interest at the expense of the broader militancy and that the leadership did not properly represent the views of the militancy. Their position was that the ETA-pm leadership was attempting to bring about the ultimate dissolution of ETA-pm.[99] These arguments were presented in a plausible and persuasive manner. They were accompanied by an alternative course for the militancy. They called for the expulsion of the leadership who supported the ceasefire and for the remaining members to reintegrate with ETA-m. Yet, most of the ETA-pm militants chose to support the ETA-pm leadership and the proposal for a ceasefire and participation in the elections.[100]

It is not possible to understand the decision-making process of each militant who chose to support the leadership and those who defected. What can be inferred from the position papers advanced, and the resultant scission, is that the arguments presented by ETA-pm were accepted by the majority of the militancy over those advanced by the Komando Bereziak. Thus, the ETA-pm leadership's arguments that the role of the organization was to support the people's revolutionary process by providing them with their preferred means of enacting political change was more persuasive than the Bereziak's call to arms. The result was that in 1977, ETA-pm made a significant shift to conservativism. They ordered a ceasefire and turned their focus to making political gains within the democratic system. They did this because they believed that this was what the Basque people wanted. Unless they served the people, the future of the organization would be at risk. In the next chapter, ETA-pm takes a further step toward conservativism. In 1981, the organization took the decision to halt all terrorist violence. As revealed in the internal documents, this decision was prompted by waning popular support and a need to reevaluate the organization's strategic direction and relevance in the new democracy. Terrorism was not advancing ETA-pm's goals, and the leadership called for a thorough reimagining of its role in Basque social and political life.

[99] Ibid.
[100] Ibid.

7

Admissions of Failure and the 1981 Ceasefire

In this chapter, I explore ETA-pm's decision to pause all terrorist violence. ETA-pm's internal records show that this decision was taken because the members believed that the very survival of the organization was at risk. Recent violent attacks had met with approbation from their constituents and their affiliated political party. Thus, ETA-pm risked being marginalized and rendered irrelevant in the new Basque democracy. This is a clear example of a terrorist organization tempering its actions to align itself with the desires and expectations of its constituents. In calling the 1981 ceasefire, ETA-pm was not just motivated to maintain popular support. The organization was also under pressure from unexpected political competition. In all its strategical calculations, ETA-pm had envisaged itself at the helm of the Basque nationalist movement. However, by 1981, it found itself eclipsed by the Basque Nationalist Party (PNV). This moderate nationalist party had captured most of the Basque nationalist constituency. ETA-pm faced additional competition from the radical side of politics. ETA-m's political party, Herri Batasuna, had encroached on the more militant segments of the Basque populace. ETA-pm's activities were also being condemned by its own political party, EIA. The tipping point may have been the failed coup d'état of 1981. A section of the Spanish military attempted to seize control of the Spanish government with the express intention of reinstating an authoritarian right-wing government that would put down Basque separatism. This incident demonstrated the fragility of the new democracy and convinced ETA-pm to work within the system.

In this chapter, I analyze internal documents produced by ETA-pm in 1980 and 1981. These candid reflections reveal the organization's self-criticism. Members discussed their strategical and political failures, including their inability to fully realize the strategy developed in the Otsagabia Proposal. These documents are significant because they show a terrorist organization admitting its own shortcomings. They also show the internal

Euskadi Ta Askatasuna. Nell Bennett, Oxford University Press. © University of Maryland National Consortium for the Study of Terrorism and Responses to Terrorism (START) (2025). DOI: 10.1093/9780197764268.003.0007

deliberations of an organization deciding to halt their armed strategy and commit to a complete ceasefire. The chapter begins with a discussion of the political developments that took place between 1976 and 1981. ETA-pm held another Conference of the Cells in the second half of 1980. The transcripts of this debate were published in an internal bulletin in September 1980. They then published a second bulletin in November. In both documents, ETA-pm acknowledged the weakened position of both their organization and the EE coalition. This, they argued, was largely due to the rise of the PNV and ETA-m's creation of their own political coalition, Herri Batasuna. I then discuss the attempted military coup of 1981 and ETA-pm's decision to set aside their arms. I conclude with a discussion of the significance of these documents. The key points highlighted are ETA-pm's frank admission of their own errors and their willingness to halt all armed activity and instead engage in political negotiation to advance the Basque cause. It was in ETA-pm's best interest to adopt this position, because continuing to use violence when the people wanted peace would cause them to be sidelined in the new democracy. In addition, their actions provided a justification for a return to military rule, which would put their very existence under threat.

Unexpected Political Competition

Perhaps the most salient political issue that ETA-pm faced in the early 1980s was the unforeseen popularity of the Basque Nationalist Party, the PNV. While a minority of Basques supported ETA-pm's party, EIA, the majority supported the PNV. Part of the PNV's success lay in its moderate approach to Basque nationalism. The PNV promoted nonviolent and pragmatic autonomy.[1] As one ETA-pm leader wrote, in the years since 1976 they had gone from being a political party of little moment to "the principal force in politics with an unforeseen public following."[2]

One of ETA-pm's primary concerns in 1980 was what they perceived to be their failure to create a strong political party. The party they had created, EIA, had joined a Basque nationalist coalition called Euskadiko Ezkerra (EE). Despite this, EIA and EE were unable to attract the support of ETA-pm's historic base.[3] This failure is demonstrated by the results from the 1979

[1] Soldevilla, "El Compañero Ausente," 79.
[2] ETA-pm, Boletin Interno, November 1980, 12.
[3] Ibid.

election. The PNV won seven seats in the national Congress of Deputies, whereas EE only obtained one.[4] The leader opined that it was impossible for ETA-pm to strategize about bringing about the workers' revolution that had been envisaged in the Otsagabia Proposal until they had defeated the PNV. The leader argued that they were now entering a new phase in which their principal objective would be to achieve ideological hegemony and to "tear our class from the hands of the nationalist bourgeoisie and the petty bourgeoisie." Thus, they must direct their attacks against the Basque bourgeoisie before they could effectively challenge the central government.[5]

ETA-pm also faced competition from the radical front. By 1978, ETA-m had launched their own political wing, which supported their hard-line militaristic agenda. While ETA-m had originally boycotted the democratic elections, the high voter turnout in the general election of 1977 forced them to change their plans.[6] Their political coalition, Herri Batasuna, was created out of four Basque nationalist organizations (HASI, LAIA, ANV, and ESB).[7] Herri Batasuna had also established a youth organization called Jarrai, which was used to attract young recruits and encourage urban street fighting and vandalism, known as *kale borroka*.[8] An internal bulletin noted that ETA-pm was facing competition it had not foreseen at the time of the Otsagabia Proposal. Its biggest problem was the challenge posed by Herri Batasuna.[9] According to the bulletin, ETA-pm had thought back in 1976 that either they would lead the nationalist left movement, or the whole movement would fail. They had not foreseen a situation in which ETA-m would challenge their position as the leader of the revolutionary movement.[10] Or worse still, that the actions of ETA-m would destabilize the entire nationalist left movement.[11] The success of Herri Batasuna was noted in a CIA report on the 1979 elections:

> The big gainers were not the relatively moderate Basque Nationalist Party—which has traditionally spoken for the vast majority of ethnic Basques—but the more extremist separatists who won close to 20 percent of the vote in the two most volatile provinces of the region. The Herri

[4] National Foreign Assessment Center, "Western Europe Review," 2.
[5] ETA-pm, Boletin Interno, November 1980, 12.
[6] Soldevilla, "El Compañero Ausente," 71.
[7] Ibid.; Atkins, *Encyclopedia of Modern Worldwide Extremists*, 129; Rueda, "Telesforo Monzón," 269; Bourne, "Political Parties and Terrorism," 4.
[8] Sarabia, "Violencia adolescente," 2.
[9] ETA-pm, Boletin Interno, November 1980, 1–2.
[10] Ibid., 2.
[11] Ibid., 28.

> Batasuna coalition, many of whose leaders spent the electoral campaign in jail and which openly supports the most violent wing of the terrorist ETA organization, won nearly 200,000 votes—enough to elect three deputies.[12]

The CIA report failed to even note the presence of EE, providing further evidence of its desultory electoral performance. ETA-pm was aware of the damage that Herri Batasuna was doing to its political campaign. Leaders opined that ETA-m's militaristic strategy was pushing more moderate left-wing parties to align themselves with the right. This provided the right with the ability to launch an attack on the left and prevent ETA-pm and EE from organizing a cohesive working-class movement.[13]

ETA-pm argued that the weakness and lack of organization in the left was the primary obstacle to fulfilling their political objectives.[14] They also stated that the weak and divided nature of the left constrained their own strategic choices. In particular, it precluded a frontal attack on the Spanish state and any kind of "scorched earth policy," because this kind of approach would enable the oligarchy to "decimate" the revolutionaries, and to do so with the acquiescence of the Spanish Socialist Party and the Basque Communist Party.[15] Furthermore, the author expressed concern that the strategy that was developed in the Otsagabia Proposal was designed to be carried out by one armed organization. They had not planned for a competitive environment: "Pluralism of parties is admissible in the political game but pluralism of armed organisations theoretically representing the same group is not possible. Different organisations can exist, but either they align or they attack each other, and long term only one can remain."[16] The author considered this competitive environment a threat to their efficacy and to their organizational longevity. However, another member disagreed, arguing that multiple armed organizations had been able to coexist in conflicts in Rhodesia, Angola, Argentina, Palestine, Eritrea, and El Salvador. ETA-pm and ETA-m could reunite if it were not for their ideological differences regarding the use of violence. However, in this member's view, these differences were not enough for them to attack each other.[17]

[12] National Foreign Assessment Center, "Western Europe Review 4.
[13] ETA-pm, Boletin Interno, November 1980, 28.
[14] Ibid.
[15] Ibid., 30.
[16] Ibid.
[17] Ibid.,21.

More concerning, however, was the prospect of how the central government would respond to ETA-m's provocations. ETA-pm were also worried the ETA-m's actions, supported by Herri Batasuna, could cause a repressive response from the central government. As they said in the internal bulletin of September 1980, "the action-repression-action dynamic of the 'milis' and [Herri Batasuna] . . . could qualitatively rise, provoking a 'forceful response' from the Central State that would endanger the democratising process in Euskadi" (emphasis in original).[18] Despite these issues, ETA-pm did not consider it necessary to relinquish armed action. On the contrary, they argued that it was necessary to combine the "mass and institutional struggle . . . with the armed struggle to guarantee the victories that we are making on the road to independence and socialism, and to prevent any setback."[19] Thus, armed action would continue to be used in defense of the rights obtained under the Statute of Autonomy, and to encourage further reforms.

ETA-pm's Strained Relationship with EE

By 1980 ETA-pm was also reaching a crisis point in its relationship with its affiliated political party, EIA, and the EE coalition. Even though the party had been created by ETA-pm and was led by several former ETA-pm members, by the 1980s EIA had adopted a more pragmatic approach to Basque nationalism than its armed counterpart.[20] EIA and EE were trying to appeal to a broader section of Basque society than just the hard-line nationalists. This put them in a difficult political situation when ETA-pm executed unpopular attacks. ETA-pm engaged in one such unpopular campaign in 1979. The organization executed a series of bombings in popular tourist destinations on the Mediterranean coast. While they did not intend to cause any casualties, two Belgium nationals were injured in one attack.[21] The secretary general of EE, Mario Onaindia, spoke out publicly against the bombings, saying, "One thing is what ETA-pm does, and for that only ETA-pm is responsible, another thing is what Euskadiko Ezkerra does. We do not take responsibility for their policies, only ours. Our policy is in complete

[18] ETA-pm, Boletin Interno, September 1980, 18.
[19] ETA-pm, Boletin Interno, November 1980, 31.
[20] Fernandez, "Between Francoism and Democracy," 30–31.
[21] Ibid.

solidarity with the rest of the people, and we have demonstrated this. . . ."[22] This statement clearly positioned ETA-pm's own political party with the Basque people and against the armed organization.

The purpose of the bombing campaign had been to force the Spanish government to concede general amnesty to Basque political prisoners and to transfer prisoners who were residing in jails outside the Basque Country back home. EIA had acted as mediator between ETA-pm and the central government, and while the government acceded to most of the organization's demands, they did not follow through with their promises.[23] ETA-pm had called an end to the bombing campaign, but in spite of this one cell acted of its own accord and executed a coordinated bombing at an airport and two train stations in Madrid.[24] Seven people were killed, and hundreds were wounded in the attack.[25] This attack caused EE to publicly denounce ETA-pm.[26] When the leader of EE, Juan María Bandrés, was informed that the attack was unfolding by the president of the Basque General Council and leader of the PNV, Bandrés's response was that it could not be true. When he was later asked by journalists for a comment he was quoted as saying, "As the news became more credible, my initial surprise turned to deep consternation. . . . Dismay. . . because, apart from any other consideration, this action is politically inexplicable. . . . With these attacks . . . expectations and well-founded hopes for peace opened up by the Statute of Autonomy have been disappointed."[27]

ETA-pm's relationship with EE was further strained by a series of attacks against political figures that they executed in 1980. In February they launched a grenade at the Spanish prime minister's residence. In April they fired another at the civil governor of Navarra. They also made attempts on officials in Bilbao and Donostia. On September 29 ETA-pm assassinated José Ignacio Ustarán, a leadership candidate from Spain's ruling party, the Unión de Centro Democrático (UCD).[28] In November 1980 they also killed another UCD member, law professor Juan de Dios Daval.[29] These attacks were conducted without consulting with EE. Javier Marquiegui, who was

[22] La Vanguardia, "Carta del obispo de Malaga," 6.
[23] Fernandez, "Between Francoism and Democracy," 30–31.
[24] Markham, "4 Killed by Bombs at Madrid Airport and Rail Terminals."
[25] Mira, "El 11-M de la Transición."
[26] León, "Un Árbol En Tierra Yerma," 123.
[27] *El Pais*, "J. M. Bandrés"; *El Pais*, "ETA (p-m) reivindica."
[28] Abasolo, "ETApm reivindica la muerte."
[29] Egido, *Viaje a la nada*, 68.

the EE spokesperson in the Basque parliament recalled, "[t]he truth is that we were very surprised when they started to attack people from the UCD."[30]

The relationship with EE was further discussed in the internal bulletin of November 1980. One ETA-m leader stated that EIA had taken the right course of action by appealing to moderate Basques. By forming the EE coalition and aligning itself with less radical parties and interest groups, EIA had deliberately allied itself with the institutions in which the Basque people would place their trust. EIA's one defect (a defect for which ETA-pm was also responsible) was that the party they created out of Assembly VII was not an appropriate instrument for challenging the hegemony of the PNV. "The party that was born in Assembly VII was not designed, nor did it serve, for the fight in this other field. That was our biggest calculation error, perhaps it was impossible to foresee. . . ."[31] Despite ETA-pm's doubts about the efficacy of EIA and EE in the struggle against the Basque bourgeoise nationalists, they still declared them to be the only appropriate force for uniting the Basque left. ETA-pm concluded the internal bulletin by declaring: "ETA considers Euskadiko Ezkerra the central force for achieving the unity of all the Basque left . . . as much for the progressive development of the Statute of Autonomy as for the advancement of the Basque process toward National Independence and the realization of the Socialist Revolution in Euskadi."[32] As ETA-pm viewed EE as the most appropriate instrument for advancing the nationalist program, it was essential that they repair their relationship with the coalition. This meant that they needed to reassess their use of violence.

ETA-pm Declares a Ceasefire

An event took place in early 1981 that forced ETA-pm to re-evaluate its strategic direction. On February 23, members of the Spanish military attempted a coup d'état.[33] Under the leadership of Lieutenant-Colonel Tejero, around 200 civil guards stormed the parliament and took the government and all 350 deputies hostage. The coup was put down after the rest of the military failed to join the attempt.[34] The failed coup demonstrated the

[30] Ibid., 87; Unzueta, "Euskadiko Ezquerra rechaza la acusación."
[31] ETA-pm, Boletin Interno, November 1980, 15.
[32] Ibid., 32.
[33] Egido, *Viaje a la nda,*. 87.
[34] Powell, "The 1981 Coup d'État," 11–13; Divins, *Four Days that Transformed Spain*, 63.

fragility of the new Spanish democracy.[35] It was also particularly significant for ETA-pm because it was partially motivated by a desire to eradicate left-wing terrorism. The military leaders who were responsible for the attempt had wanted to take control of the government so that they could wage a "dirty war" against ETA.[36] ETA-pm viewed a return of military dictatorship as being against its long-term interests. Thus, they realized that their use of violence could be counterproductive. They took the view that it was important to strengthen Basque democratic institutions to prevent such an attempt from recurring.[37]

As a result of the coup, and to salvage its relationship with EE, ETA-pm declared a unilateral and unconditional ceasefire on February 27, 1981.[38] They released a document in which they explained their reasons for this decision. In essence, their ability to access democratic institutions meant that armed action would take a subordinate position to political action. However, they observed that they had failed to use the early years of the transition to democracy to establish a strong political party. As a result, they had been eclipsed by the PNV. Indeed, by 1981, popular support for ETA in the Basque Country was estimated to be no more than 12 percent.[39] The document admitted, "ETA committed mistakes. . . . However, the biggest mistakes were political: the inability to generate a stable mass organization, the lack of vision when capitalizing on the support of the masses to create a workers' party."[40]

ETA-pm was quick to note its own shortcomings but maintained that their use of violence had been positive overall. However, they did observe that armed struggle has its limitations. Armed action, they argued, was not sufficient to overcome the deficiencies in the left-wing nationalist political organizations. Any attempt to "replace these deficiencies of political struggle by armed struggle leads inexorably to militarism."[41] ETA-pm also observed that political and public approval for violence was waning and that a "consensus against the armed struggle has been unleashed from the right and from sectors of the left." They further argued that their political-military strategy was not dependent on armed action and that "the impact of the

[35] Soldevilla, *Historia de una Heterodoxia Abertzale*, 305.
[36] McLaren, *Constructing Democracy*, 206.
[37] Soldevilla, *Historia de una Heterodoxia Abertzale*, 305–306.
[38] León, "Un Árbol En Tierra Yerma," 126.
[39] Cála, "Is the End Near?"
[40] ETA-pm, "Adios as las Armas," 22.
[41] Ibid., 24–25.

armed struggle at any point in the process does not rest exclusively on the actions that are carried out. On many occasions, [armed] action can be counterproductive and negative for the development of the mass struggle." Thus, they reasoned, it was as important to know when not to act as it was to know when to act. This period was one in which it was best to refrain from engaging in violence to enable the development of political solutions.[42] ETA-pm therefore called an end to all current and planned armed activities and called upon ETA-m to also refrain from engaging in any violence.

The hard-line ETA-m declined ETA-pm's invitation to participate in the ceasefire. While ETA-pm had reasoned that the coup attempt made it imperative that the nationalist left work together to strengthen democratic institutions, ETA-m argued that the very fact of the coup revealed the true nature of the new democracy and the "new and subtle forms of domination and oppression." In a published response to ETA-pm's declaration, ETA-m argued that it was more than ever necessary to continue the fight against the central government.[43] ETA-m warned the Spanish government that they would only lay down their arms once the Basque Country was established as a self-governing regime:

> Only through this framework of national freedoms and rights . . . will we be able to speak of a democratic break with the harsh military dictatorship. Amnesty, the legalisation of pro-independence parties, the withdrawal of the Spanish repressive forces and a statutory regime based on the prioritisation of our national language and the territorial unity of the four historical regions of South Euskadi, as well as the recognition of the right of self-determination, are the central axes . . . offered by ETA to decide the ceasefire.[44]

ETA-m declared in no uncertain terms that for as long as the Spanish Government refused to give in to their demands, they would continue their armed campaign, "attacking those enemy targets that can most influence and favor the conquest of democracy, of self-government for the Basque people."[45]

[42] Ibid., 25.
[43] ETA-m, "La Lucha Continua," 26.
[44] Ibid.
[45] Ibid., 25.

Consideration

This chapter shows ETA-pm make a dramatic strategic about-face in response to external pressures. The organization was facing stiff and unanticipated competition from both ends of the spectrum of Basque nationalist politics, the PNV and Herri Batasuna. In addition to this, ETA-pm's affiliated political party was publicly condemning their activities and seeking to distance themselves from the armed organization. If this were not enough, the attempted military coup demonstrated the fragility of the new democracy and the real risk that the permissive central government could be replaced by a hard-line military dictatorship. ETA-pm responded to these threats to its survival by convoking a debate to discuss the organization's future and declaring an unconditional ceasefire.

From a theoretical perspective, the events described in this chapter raise an interesting question about terrorism escalation and de-escalation. As Crenshaw has observed, "terrorists engage in a process of constant adaptation to the strategic environment."[46] I argue that both the internal conditions and external circumstances influence the direction of that adaptation. One way of understanding this process is to view the adaptation process as a form of isomorphism. That is, "a constraining process that forces one unit in a population to resemble other units that face the same set of environmental conditions."[47] ETA-pm's ceasefire can be understood as being the result of what Paul J. DiMaggio and Walter W. Powell refer to as a "coercive isomorphism." Coercive isomorphism, they explain, "results from both formal and informal pressures exerted on organizations by other organizations upon which they are dependent and by cultural expectations in the society within which organizations function."[48] ETA-pm was dependent on its affiliated political party to maintain its position in the Basque nationalist movement. It was also influenced by the expectations of the Basque people who were tired of violence. For ETA-pm, therefore, the path of least resistance was to relinquish armed action.

Another significant aspect of the documents discussed in this chapter is that they evidence a terrorist organization admitting their own faults, both

[46] Crenshaw, "Theories of Terrorism," 16.
[47] DiMaggio and Powell, "The Iron Cage Revisited," 149.
[48] Ibid., 150.

internally and publicly.[49] ETA-pm's acknowledgment of their errors was sufficiently genuine that it caused them to pause their military strategy and engage in negotiations with the Basque government and the Spanish government, two forces they had identified as their enemies. In the documents, ETA-pm warned against the indiscriminate use of violence, stating that it could lead to "militarism," which had already done enough harm to the left.[50] This indicates that the leadership of ETA-pm saw themselves as more than just an armed organization. They had grander aspirations to be the leading political force in the Basque Country. The armed strategy was not advancing this objective.

Had the military coup d'état been successful, ETA-pm would have faced a real threat to their very existence. A new military dictatorship would have removed the liberties afforded to the Basque Country under the Statute of Autonomy and taken all possible measures to eradicate ETA. ETA-pm was able to recognize that their actions contributed to the coup by providing Tejero and his associates with justification for taking such a drastic step.[51] Thus, by stepping back from armed action and engaging in collaborative discussions with the regional and central government, ETA-pm was seeking to support the democratic system and thereby safeguard its own survival.

Conclusion

In this chapter I have examined internal documents produced in 1980 in which members of ETA-pm presented candid discussions of their failure to realize the strategic vision that they developed in the Otsagabia Proposal. I began by explaining the ways that Basque political life developed in the years since Assembly VII, including the rise of the PNV. Another significant challenge to ETA-pm was ETA-m's political wing, Herri Batasuna, which promoted a militant agenda to destabilize the Basque democratic system. I also examined the internal bulletin of 1980, in which members of ETA-pm openly discussed their failure to unite the left under the EE coalition and EE's inability to successfully challenge the PNV. While warning of the dangers of "militarism," ETA-pm still maintained that armed action was needed to protect the Basque people's political freedoms. It was not until after the

[49] ETA-pm, Boletin Interno, November 1980, 9; ETA-pm, "Adios as las Armas," 21.
[50] ETA-pm, Boletin Interno, November 1980, 19–20.
[51] McLaren, *Constructing Democracy*, 206.

failed coup attempt of February 23, 1981, that ETA-pm declared a ceasefire. In doing this, they acknowledged the importance of protecting the Basque Country's democratic freedom. As one of Tejero's key objectives in seeking to impose a military dictatorship was the eradication of left-wing terrorism, it can also be inferred that ETA-pm was motivated by the desire for self-preservation. ETA-pm had not yet succeeded in building a unified left-wing movement. However, their goals would never be realized under a military dictatorship.

In this chapter, I explained ETA-pm's decision to call a ceasefire through the theory of goal displacement. The organization responded to external pressures and expectations. It was dependent on the EE coalition for political relevancy, and it needed the support of the Basque people. ETA-pm reacted to EE's denouncements of its violent acts by declaring a ceasefire. The members could see that the more moderate Basque political parties, in particular the PNV, were more in line with the expectations of the Basque people. The Basques were tired of violence. Accordingly, ETA-pm moderated its actions to avoid being sidelined in the new democracy. In the next chapter, I examine the records from the first of three debates that would ultimately determine the future course of ETA-pm. By 1981, the organization was beginning to divide into two factions, one that supported the idea of terrorist violence and one that believed that it no longer had any utility. Those who advocated for violence argued that an inactive terrorist organization could not survive. Those who opposed violence argued that in the existing social and political climate there was no place for armed struggle. While each side of the debate took a different position on the utility of violence, the overarching objective was to safeguard the organization.

8

The First Debate of 1981

This chapter examines the first of three debates on the future of ETA-pm that took place in the early 1980s. The discussions reveal that ETA-pm found itself in a difficult strategic position. Political violence was losing favor with the Basque people, and its own political party, EIA, was publicly denouncing its activities. ETA-pm was therefore in a situation in which it perceived the potential demise of the organization. This debate reveals ETA-pm's preoccupation with Basque public opinion and their concern that breaking the ceasefire could cause a rupture in their relationship with EIA. The debate shows two broad schools of thought emerging in the organization. The first acknowledged that in the existing circumstances, violence was counterproductive for both the Basque nationalist movement and for ETA. The second was that violence still had a role to play in the nationalist struggle and that ETA, being an armed organization, could not survive unless it engaged in armed action.

The chapter begins with an outline of the political and social background to the debates. This included new federal legislation designed to take back some of the autonomy given to the Basque Country under the 1979 Statute of Autonomy. This discussion is followed by a summary of the positions that were advanced by the members of ETA-pm. There are seventy pages of notes from the debate, which consist of a position paper from one cell and transcripts of the oral arguments that were made. The chapter concludes with a brief discussion of the significance of the arguments that were advanced by the members. Both sides of the debate were concerned with the survival of the organization; however, each interpreted the internal and external situation in a different way. While one side saw terrorism as a liability, the other side of the debate was that inaction would lead to the weakening and ultimate dissolution of the organization.

Euskadi Ta Askatasuna. Nell Bennett, Oxford University Press. © University of Maryland National Consortium for the Study of Terrorism and Responses to Terrorism (START) (2025). DOI: 10.1093/9780197764268.003.0008

Background to the 1981 Debates

The debates of 1981 took place during a time in which ETA-pm was facing growing opposition from the Basque people and from its own political party. This was largely because 1980 had been ETA's most brutal year. The two branches of the organization were responsible for more than 200 attacks and 98 killings, the majority of which were perpetrated by ETA-m.[1] By 1981 there was mounting evidence that most Basque people no longer supported ETA's tactics. Indeed, a report conducted by the CIA found that in 1980 ETA was losing popular support.[2] The loss of support was not only the result of ETA's brutality. It was also due to the broader social and political changes that were occurring with the Basque Country. ETA had positioned itself as a necessary and legitimate response to the repressive policies of the Francoist regime. However, under democracy, its utility was no longer readily apparent. One example of this was the establishment of a Basque police force. In 1981, the Basque government initiated the creation of a new police force, which would be known as the Ertzaintza. This would limit the role of the Spanish Civil Guard in the Basque Country.[3] Since the 1960s, allegation of Civil Guard brutality had provided ETA with grievances to justify its activities. The creation of an indigenous police force undermined this narrative.

One clear example of the change in public opinion was the reaction to the killing of José María Ryan, the chief engineer of a nuclear power plant in the town of Lemoiz. Ryan was kidnapped by ETA-m on January 29, 1981. The condition for his release was the demolition of the partially constructed plant.[4] He was held for seven days before he was executed. Ryan was targeted by ETA-m because both branches of ETA were protesting against the power plant.[5] However, ETA-pm joined other major Basque and Spanish political parties in demanding Ryan's release.[6] In a statement, ETA-m said that Ryan "has appeared before a revolutionary council that has found him guilty of being a co-author to the maximum degree of the decisions and enforcement actions carried out by Iberduero, SA, at the Lemoiz nuclear power plant and, therefore . . . can be executed at any time. . .". The statement went on to threaten all managers responsible for the Lemoiz plant and

[1] Iglesias, "El pueblo que alimentó a ETA."
[2] *El Pais*, "ETA fracasa en su objetivo."
[3] *El Pais*, "El Gobierno de Euskadi."
[4] Surio, "El fantasma de Lemóniz." Unzueta, "ETAm asesinó ayer."
[5] UPI, "Killing of Engineer Sparks Uproar."
[6] Giacopucci, *ETA pm: el otro camino*, 214.

warned that "the execution of the chief operating engineer is not an isolated event, but rather the opening of a new front of action that affects all of them."[7] In response to his death, the major Basque political parties and labor unions, including the PSOE, PNV and ETA-pm's affiliated EE coalition, called for a strike to protest the killing. Approximately 90 percent of the Basque workforce participated in the strike.[8] The killing also provoked a demonstration. Despite rainy conditions, more than 100,000 people took to the streets of Bilbao on February 10, 1981. The local government and police estimated the protestors to be closer to 200,000 in number. Protestors carried banners with the slogan "Euskadi: peace and freedom."[9] EE deputy Juan María Bandrés responded to the killing saying that "ETA military has reached its highest level of discredit." Ryan's funeral was attended by more than 10,000 people.[10]

The death of Ryan was just one example of EE's public criticism of ETA. By the early 1980s EE had become increasingly vocal in its objections to the use of violence to resolve issues within the Basque Country.[11] EIA, the leading members of the EE coalition, passed a formal resolution rejecting the use of violence at its Congress III on June 18 and 20, 1981. Two proposals were presented at that meeting. One, presented by the more radical members of the party who called themselves the New Left, proposed that the purpose of EIA was to achieve an independent Basque socialist state that could only occur through a revolution. The second proposal, titled "Aketegi," argued that the party should rely exclusively on parliamentary democracy to achieve autonomy.[12] In essence, the first proposal supported the political-military strategy of ETA-pm, the second rejected this approach and advocated the use of legal, democratic means. The nonviolent Aketegi proposal was approved with a 62 percent majority.[13]

Another important issue was the growing peace movement in the Basque Country. Various speakers at the debate referred to the "Peace Front." This was a movement that would later become known as *Gesto por la Paz,* or Gesture for Peace. This movement had its origins in a series of protests that took place in the late 1970s and early 1980s. One of the first major demonstrations

[7] Ibid.
[8] Burns, "Massive Basque Protests."
[9] *El Pais,* "'Huelga general y grandes manifestaciones."
[10] Martinez, "Treinta años del febrero."
[11] Giacopucci, *ETA pm: El otro camino,* 214.
[12] Soldevilla, "Agur a las armas," 86.
[13] Soldevilla, *Historia de una Heterodoxia Abertzale,* 259.

against ETA and political violence occurred in 1978. The protest movement was supported by the PNV, the PSOE, and the EPK, along with the two main unions in the Basque Country, the CCOO and UGT.[14]

ETA-pm also faced opposition from the cultural front. On May 26, 1980, a group of thirty-three Basque intellectuals wrote a manifesto against the use of political violence. The signatories were notable for their prestige within the Basque Country and for their contributions to the fight against the Francoist dictatorship. Indeed, the Basque newspaper *Deia* called them "the most conspicuous personalities that the Basque cultural world had in the 20th century."[15] They included the artists Eduardo Chilliada and Nestor Basterretxea, the poet Gabriel Celaya, anthropologists Jose Migel Barandiaran and Julio Caro Baroja, and writer Martin Ugalde.[16] The letter stated that the authors were aware that violence was being directed against the Basque Country from the outside but that the violence that most concerned them was the violence that "is born and nests among us because it is only that which can turn us into soulless executioners, complicit cowards, or servile accessories." The letter took direct aim at ETA, saying that they were acting without the support of the Basque people: "No one has the right to set themselves up . . . as representatives of a people that already have their political and union organizations that they support with their membership, militancy and vote." It went on to accuse ETA of leading the Basque Country to destruction: "Despite the possibility of being vilified, the time has come to defend ourselves from ruin and annihilation to which we are being led by those who say they love the Country like no one else."[17]

Notes from the First Debate

Prior to the commencement of the debate, one cell submitted a position paper in which they analyzed the future of armed struggle from the perspective of their group. They stated that they had created the document in the hope that it would encourage other militants to write down and distribute their views for consideration by the rest of the organization.[18] This cell analyzed the social and political situation in the Basque country and presented

[14] Bibiloni, "Movilizaciones pacifistas," 229–230; *El Correo Español, El Pueblo Vasco*, "Impresionante Manifestacion."
[15] Rekondo and Lizarralde, "40 años del 'Manifiesto.'"
[16] Gonzalez, "Treinta y tres personalidades."
[17] *El Correo Español, El Pueblo Vasco*, "Intellectuales Vascos," 11.
[18] ETA-pm, "Debate desde la Base," 1.

a strong argument against terrorism. The cell opened their discussion with a question: was ETA's armed struggle really helping the Basque working class? They wrote that Basque society was divided between two moderate parties: the bourgeois PNV and the centralist PSOE. The best way for ETA-pm to advance the nationalist movement was to bring the Basque people together under one banner. The apparatus for this should be the EE coalition.

The cell observed that popular opinion in the Basque Country favored nonviolent activism. This was evidenced by public demonstrations against ETA that had been taking place around the Basque Country in 1980 and 1981. Many of these demonstrations were orchestrated by moderate political parties such as the PNV and the PSOE to enable themselves to present their parties as the guarantors of peace and democracy.[19] The cell did not consider the Basque people's rejection of violence to be negative. Rather, they wrote, it could be used to their advantage: ". . . legal political struggle is gaining credit among the people . . . it is necessary to promote it so that it is the revolutionary left that takes credit from the people and is permitted to exert hegemony ahead of the bourgeoisie."[20] They also affirmed that ETA-pm's role in the nationalist struggle had changed since the Franco era: "Our fight is no longer resistance, but the consolidation of some freedoms and a strategy to make the working class hegemonic."[21]

Discussing the ceasefire, they wrote that it should not be understood as a "sword of Damocles" ready to fall at the first upset. Rather, the truce had created a "different social dynamic. . . . In political and social processes, we should not only consider whether objectives are achieved, but . . . the social transformations they provoke."[22] Rather than hurrying to break the truce, they argued that ETA-pm should learn how to use it as an instrument to help it to achieve its goals. They warned that breaking the ceasefire would set the organization back to the strategic position they had been in a year previously in that it would isolate them from EE. Losing EE would cost ETA the ability to take a leadership role in Basque politics: "We cannot bind ourselves solely to the path of illegality as the only solution."[23] They closed their arguments with a strong affirmation of their support for EE and maintaining the truce: "We see EE as a political alternative in the strategy to socialism . . . we think that a tactical break of the ceasefire could generate strategic divergences

[19] Bibiloni, "Movilizaciones pacifistas," 230.
[20] ETA-pm, "Debate desde la Base," 5.
[21] Ibid.
[22] Ibid., 11.
[23] Ibid., 12.

which would destroy this new strategy which we believe to be the only path to socialism in Euskadi."[24]

The arguments advanced in this position paper are significant because they evidence a terrorist cell arguing *against* terrorism. The cell understood the objectives that ETA-pm formed to pursue—cultural and political freedom for the Basque people. They carefully considered the social and political context and concluded that terrorism would not bring ETA-pm closer to its goals. In fact, it was likely to damage both the organization and the nationalist movement. This paper broadly encapsulates the arguments presented by one side of the subsequent debate, those that advocated an end to terrorist violence.

Transcripts of the First Debate

The records of the first debate include typed minutes that record the oral arguments made by the assembled members. The records begin with a note from the Political Office that reads: "The debate which is presented here is the beginning of a process in which a deepening of the issues of the future of the armed struggle will be generated. As much as in the type of armed struggle and the type of Organization that will need to be created." The Political Office explained that there were two primary positions within the party about the future of armed struggle, which were the subject of the debate.[25] They then explained the format of the transcriptions. They wrote that the urgency of the debate had caused them to prioritize the immediate publication of the minutes of the meetings, and as a result the transcription had been made in "record time. . . . This explains the imperfect and often literal drafting of what was said. . . ."[26]

A Discussion of the Strategic Landscape

The notes from the debate began with an analysis of the social and political situation in the Basque Country. They commenced with a lengthy discussion of new federal legislation called the *Ley Orgánica de Armonización del Proceso Autonómico* (Law of Harmonization of the Autonomous Process).

[24] Ibid., 13.
[25] ETA-pm, "Debate I," 1.
[26] Ibid.

These laws, commonly referred to by the acronym LOAPA, were designed to regulate the process of granting autonomy to the Spanish regions, including the Basque Country.[27] The LOAPA was created out of a concern that the demands of the Basques and the Catalans would encourage other regions to make more demands for autonomy. The LOAPA was the result of a pact between the ruling party, the UCD, and the main national opposition party, the PSOE. Their effect was to strengthen the central government at the expense of regional autonomy.[28] The Basque Government, led by the PNV, passed a resolution against the laws in the Basque parliament and organized protests, which were supported by the EE coalition and Basque Communist Party (EPK). One protest in October 1981 in Bilbao gathered between 100,000 and 200,000 people.[29]

ETA-pm saw the LOAPA as an attack on the Basque Country. However, the ceasefire prevented them from retaliating with violence. There was a concern was that breaking the ceasefire could have the unwanted consequences of bolstering the PSOE. The PSOE had positioned itself as a moderate left-wing party and a guarantor of peace. Armed action could give credibility to this narrative.[30] ETA-pm was also acutely conscious that an attack could provoke condemnation from EE. One important issue for discussion was how best to combat these laws and whether violence was an appropriate tool. As one member said, it was not about whether to use violence, but rather, "about putting the armed action in . . . its most effective context, so that it has a multiplying effect of the political struggle on all fronts in which the LOAPA and LOFCA are fought."[31] While the speaker did not think that ETA's old strategy would be applicable in these new circumstances, they also said that "it cannot be held that armed practice in this context cannot make a positive contribution. . . . What should be determined is the moment and the conditions in which we are going to use it. . . ."[32] Thus, terrorism should not be off the table. Equally, it could not be used in the same way that it had been used under the dictatorship. A more nuanced approach was needed.

Another member entered the discussion and agreed that the strategic situation had changed over the past two or three years. ETA-pm, with the

[27] Caballero, "Los Nacionalistas Vascos," 66.

[28] Ibid; Parra, "PSOE y PSC-PSOE," 81.

[29] Soldevilla, *Historia de una Heterodoxia Abertzale*, 245.

[30] Parra, *Nación Española y Estado Autonómico*, 103–107.

[31] The LOFCA was the *Ley Orgánica de Financiación de las Comunidades Autónomas*, or the Law of the Financing of Autonomous Communities.

[32] ETA-pm, "Debate I," 17.

EE coalition, wanted to be the predominant leftwing political party in the Basque County. In effect, take the position that was being occupied by the PSOE. This was a markedly different objective from those that ETA-pm were pursuing under the dictatorship. "In this context the criteria with which we practiced armed struggle two years ago are no longer valid."[33] This speaker did not discount the utility of violence but instead said that the organization needed to reconceptualize armed struggle so that it could take a "qualitative leap" after the truce ended.[34] As the first speaker had argued, terrorism was still a viable tactic, but it could not be used in the same way that it had been employed under Franco. The use of violence needed to be adapted to the new democratic society.

The next speaker argued that it was necessary to exhaust all available civil and mass actions before resorting to violence. Armed action should not be brought in as "a kicking" but as additional pressure on the political campaign. If correctly developed, armed action could strengthen the Basque left. They observed that within ETA-pm there were currently two views regarding the use of violence. One was a political-military strategy that saw the use of violence within the context of class struggle, alongside political and mass struggle. The other perspective was one that "does not see the possibility of armed action in this phase, and it could be a long phase."[35] In essence, the speaker distinguished the two schools of thought within the organization: those that favored the continued use of selective violence and those that thought violence was no longer an appropriate instrument.

Violence as a Negotiating Tool

A notable aspect of the debate was the instrumentalist view that most of the speakers took of the use of violence. Violence and the control of violence by way of the truce were assessed in terms of whether they were bringing the organization closer to achieving its objectives. As one speaker put it, "The truce has had many positive things for the Organization's militancy. . . it has allowed new sectors to approach [the organization]." But, in this speaker's opinion, the value of the truce was inherently limited because ultimately,

[33] Ibid., 18.
[34] Ibid., 18–19.
[35] Ibid., 20.

"armed struggle is necessary to advance the political process."[36] The speaker explained that all revolutionary movements are processes of negotiation between the rebels and the incumbent, ETA-pm was maintaining the truce as part of a negotiating process, and "as soon as it is no longer useful, it is broken and we continue that negotiating process in another way."[37] They argued that while the truce had created new possibilities for action and negotiation, ETA-pm could also choose to return to armed action. This would bring about a new phase of negotiations and position armed action as an element of political action. "If there is mass political action, armed struggle has a role to play, as does the general strike, as does parliament or as does civil disobedience."[38]

The next speaker argued that there was little utility in discussing armed action in the abstract. Rather, it was necessary to analyze "concrete actions" that affect the organization in "concrete situations." Breaking the truce would diminish the credibility of the organization. Raising and lowering the sword of Damocles would not benefit the organization's image or gravitas.[39] This speaker warned that a large section of Basque society was against armed struggle. This was due in part to the fact that violence had been forced on the Basque people because of circumstances beyond their control. It was argued that there was no subjective radicalization of the Basque people and that engaging in armed action would not convince them that such practice was an appropriate tool for solving problems.[40] Therefore, there was no need to use armed action to continue the resistance. The Basque Country had passed that era. They were now in a phase in which nationalism had become mainstream.[41] Neither was it desirable for ETA-pm to create a dynamic of eternal revolution, because this would require the organization to be constantly provoking violence to justify their actions.

The next speaker entered the debate by saying that resistance and coercion were not moral categories. Armed action could serve a useful function in the context of civil disobedience and other forms of nonviolent resistance. Indeed, it could augment their chances in succeeding against the LOAPA. "Armed struggle is an instrument of class struggle and when it influences

36 Ibid.
37 Ibid.
38 Ibid., 38.
39 Ibid.
40 Ibid., 39.
41 Ibid., 41.

specific conflicts it can be an advancing factor."[42] Thus, terrorist violence was not to be viewed as an end in and of itself. Terrorism was just one method by which ETA-pm could use to advance their objectives at specific times. This speaker warned that that the actions of ETA-m were damaging the image of armed action in the eyes of the Basque people. "The things that they are doing are burning the image of ETA. . . . We must avoid contributing to this dynamic."[43] ETA-m's actions and their general unpopularity, evidenced by the popular revolt against the killing of Ryan, constrained ETA-pm's tactical choices. They found themselves in a situation in which they were being viewed by the Basque people as an equally undesirable and destabilizing organization. The view expressed was that ETA-pm's loss of public support was largely due to ETA-m's ill-conceived acts.

ETA-pm's analysis of the utility of armed action was also influenced by the way they themselves perceived their use of violence. One speaker suggested that armed struggle could be viewed in two broader categories: offensive and defensive action. In the bourgeois democracy, ETA-pm was waging a defensive struggle in support of the platforms that the Basque people had taken over through democratic means. The speaker conceded that ETA-pm had made mistakes but that their actions had been necessary and had been "selective and pedagogical."[44] In arguing along this line, the ETA-pm leaders were seeking to distinguish themselves from ETA-m on the grounds that their actions had been more discriminate. While this is certainly arguable, as the attacks on the train stations and airport in Madrid demonstrated, ETA-pm's attacks were not always well received.[45]

The speakers appeared to agree that armed action was an element of political action and a tool that could be used when it was appropriate to do so. Of course, the question of when it was appropriate had yet to be determined. One speaker distinguished armed action and political action by saying that armed action was a tactic of last resort, or the last card to be played.[46] This could be understood as an argument that violence should only be used when the organization was left with no other viable alternative. However, the speaker then went on to argue that armed action could be successful when integrated into the political strategy. "[A]rmed action is like

[42] Ibid., 41–42.
[43] Ibid., 43.
[44] Ibid., 45.
[45] Zuloaga, "El drama de los atentados."
[46] ETA-pm, "Debate I," 46.

any other political action, and it is used or not used."[47] Thus, the debate did not advance further from the initial position that violence was but one more instrument of political struggle and was to be used when the organization deemed it appropriate to do so.

Popular Support

Many of the speakers at the debate urged caution about using armed action because it was not being met with approval by most of the Basque people. Public dissatisfaction with violence had led to the strengthening of the peace movement in the early 1980s. This was being exploited by the PSOE and the PNV, who were organizing marches against ETA.[48] As one speaker argued, the Basque people's opinions of armed action had changed substantially in the years since the advent of democracy. "Armed actions can now have a completely different result than what is sought and it is necessary to be extremely cautious."[49] One thing that the attempted coup d'état had shown the organization was that their use of violence could work against them by giving the right side of politics justification for repressive actions. It could also shift popular support away from EE and toward either the centrist PSOE or the PNV. One speaker raised this prospect, warning that, "Under no circumstances should we do anything that politically could lead us to a possible right-wing victory. . . ."[50] The inference was that poorly devised attacks could cause a right-wing backlash that would ultimately prove to be against ETA-pm's long term interests.

Therefore, the ceasefire could only be broken if the organization were confident that the net outcome would not damage the left-wing nationalist movement. One debater warned that breaking the ceasefire would put EE between a rock and a hard place: "The problem is that if the truce were to be broken, the party [EIA] would be forced to defend [the break] and of course that would be to its own detriment, or it would have to condemn it, which would not benefit the party or the Organization."[51] In the event that the ceasefire were broken, EIA and the EE coalition would be put in a position in which they could either defend the violence, at the expense

47 Ibid., 47.
48 Bibiloni, "Movilizaciones pacifistas," 230.
49 ETA-pm, "Debate I," 45.
50 Ibid., 23.
51 Ibid., 32.

of their political standing, or denounce ETA-pm, putting further strain on the relationship between the party and the organization. The party would be expected to decry any terrorist acts, which would damage ETA-pm's political credibility.

Another speaker said that they were currently living in a new social climate in which the political order had been inverted. While in the past the Basque people did not trust the political process, politics had regained credibility. Armed action, on the other hand, had at least partially lost credibility. "[A]rmed struggle would have a specific place if it were clear that the political struggle could not resolve those problems. Today armed struggle would not do more than substitute an anaemic political struggle."[52] In essence, the Basque people had received what they had been asking for—parliamentary democracy. Using terrorism at this time would make ETA-pm the spoilers of the hard-won peace. Another speaker supported this view, stating that violence was no longer necessary because ETA-pm had legal means of enacting political change at their disposal. Equally, the Basque people were not supportive of violence: "the masses are not disposed to a very active struggle . . . at least at the moment."[53] On the other side of the argument, another debater claimed that the utility of armed action should not be judged by its popularity. The organization should avoid looking at "the feasibility of armed action by the number of people who applaud the action."[54] Instead, they should examine whether such action would enhance the revolution, noting that ETA-pm's base was still in the minority in the Basque Country and could be expected to continue to be so for a long time.[55] Therefore, there was no point in selecting tactics based on what the majority of Basque people wanted.

The decline in popular support and the rise of the peace movement were concerning for the organization for two reasons: because they threatened ETA-pm's ability to generate resources to continue as an armed organization and because they jeopardized ETA-pm's political project by giving credibility to their main political rivals, the PNV and the PSOE. Despite this, several speakers argued in favor of selective and what they termed "pedagogical" violence.[56] This kind of discriminate violence was the cornerstone

[52] Ibid.
[53] Ibid., 57.
[54] Ibid., 43.
[55] Ibid., 44.
[56] Ibid., 44–47.

of the political-military strategy, as developed in the Otsagabia Proposal and in the strategic directions of 1977. Thus, despite growing public opposition to armed action, ETA-pm was not yet prepared to abandon the political-military approach.

The Future of Terrorism

The second part of the first debate was directly concerned with the future of terrorism in the Basque Country. ETA-pm wanted to determine whether there was in fact a viable future for what they called "armed action" in the Basque Country. One of the key questions that hung over the organization was whether the tide of public opinion had irrevocably shifted away from approval of political violence. The first speaker set the parameters of the discussion: "Two things need to be seen, the role of violence in the political struggle . . . and the relationship between clandestine political struggle and legal political struggle."[57] Clandestine political struggle referred to the illegal activities of the armed organization, including terrorism.

The first speaker went on to say that although the truce had been positive in general terms, "measured, selective, controlled" armed action still had a role to play in the political future of the Basque Country. However, in keeping with the political-military strategy and the Otsagabia Proposal, the role of armed action would have to be subordinate to the political process: "the political parties have to negotiate, and the armed organization has to be prepared to add fuel at times and stop when it is necessary."[58] Adding fuel referred to using violence to put pressure on the Spanish government as part of their negotiation tactics. While this had been ETA-pm's stated approach since Assembly VII, they did not believe that it had been properly assimilated by the organization. Successful execution of a true political-military strategy would require a "maturation of the organization and a new consciousness of revolutionary militancy . . ." that would take time and work.[59]

The second speaker objected to this line of argument, arguing that it was "contradictory to say that the truce has been positive and break it." Instead, the ceasefire should be broken when it ceased to deliver positive results. ETA-pm were justified in resuming armed action because the central government

[57] Ibid., 49.
[58] Ibid.
[59] Ibid.

was attempting to reduce the freedoms given to the Basque Country under the 1979 Statute of Autonomy.[60] However, even though the speaker felt that ETA-pm was justified in breaking the ceasefire, doing so would hurt their longer-term interests, including building a unified left and negotiating a political solution to the issue of Basque self-determination.

On the other side of the argument were those who took a more militant approach. One member argued that there was no contradiction in saying that the truce had been positive and in breaking the truce. This was because, while the truce had brought about positive things, it had not achieved what it was intended to achieve. In fact, the Basque cause had experienced setbacks since the ceasefire had been declared. This speaker disagreed that breaking the ceasefire would hurt EE, saying that there was enough of a separation between ETA-pm and EE so that ETA-pm's actions would not automatically reflect on EE.[61] Another speaker argued that breaking the truce would not necessarily be construed as a sanction of ETA-m and the policies of their political party, Herri Batasuna. ETA-pm had always said that it would support the development of the Statute of Autonomy. The implications of the speaker's argument were that breaking the truce in response to the LOAPA would be justified within the political-military strategy.[62] The key would be the arguments that would be used to explain the actions. The speaker also distinguished a careful and considered attack from sudden indiscriminate violence. According to this line of argument, the determinative factor was whether ETA-pm broke the ceasefire with selective or with indiscriminate violence. While the former would be justifiable and in keeping with the political-military strategy, the latter would be construed as "militarism" and would lend credibility to ETA-m's position.

Another debater observed that there was no "evident need for violence" in the existing political situation in the Basque Country and that, "If at this moment ETA did not exist, there would be no need to create it." The speaker discussed the issues around the breaking of the ceasefire, "the fact that there is no evident need for violence is not to say the opposite, that is that any kind of violence will be negative. . . ." However, the distinction needed to be made between selective violence and indiscriminate violence. Acts of violence that were poorly received would put EE in the position of being forced to publicly

[60] Ibid.
[61] Ibid., 50.
[62] Ibid., 52.

condemn ETA-pm, which would have the effect of breaking down ETA-pm's political apparatus.[63]

The final reported contribution came from a debater who supported the argument that the organization needed to be transformed and that the result of that transformation would have to be an organization with a political-military methodology and the capacity for political intervention.[64] However, they warned that ETA-pm was in a situation in which any use of violence could be of more political benefit to its rivals than to itself. The implications of this statement are that choosing nonviolence could safeguard the future of ETA-pm by avoiding backlash. This, however, did not address the question of how an armed revolutionary organization could continue to maintain itself as a relevant political force if it relinquished armed action.

In summary, this debate shows ETA-pm facing a difficult dilemma. How could they maintain an active terrorist organization in a social and political environment that was unfavorable for terrorism? The arguments made at this debate can be broadly divided between those who argued that ETA-pm was justified in breaking the ceasefire but acknowledged that doing so could have negative ramifications, and those who argued against breaking the ceasefire but recognized the utility of maintaining the armed organization. Neither side was able to formulate a persuasive answer to the question of how a terrorist organization could thrive when terrorism was no longer desirable. The speakers continued to debate the issue from these two broad perspectives, but no resolution was reached.[65]

The Political Apparatus

A key issue in the debate was how to reconcile ETA-pm's legal and illegal campaigns. ETA-pm's relationship with EE was vital to the organization. EE gave ETA-pm both political cover and infrastructure. EE leaders negotiated with the Spanish government on behalf of ETA-pm. Their lawyers would act as intermediaries in ETA-pm kidnappings and would defend any militants who were arrested. EIA were also responsible for laundering ETA-pm money

[63] Ibid., 54–5.
[64] Ibid., 69.
[65] Ibid.

and distributing their propaganda.[66] As one speaker put it: "The ideal relationship would be that in which the legal struggle does not need to condemn the armed struggle."[67] This is to say that a perfect scenario would be one in which EE would not feel it necessary to publicly denounce terrorism. Of course, this would not have been politically expedient for EE. Another member expressed the view that both ETA-pm and EE were caught in a mousetrap and that this situation was "impeding the very development of this bloc."[68]

In this section of the debate, the speakers repeated the concern that breaking the ceasefire would have negative political ramifications and could put the very existence of the left-wing movement at risk. Thus, resuming hostilities would be a strategic error, because ETA-pm's long-term objective was to position EE as an alternative to the PNV and make EE a "hegemonic force in the Basque left."[69] Another argument advanced against breaking the truce was that doing so would cause political damage to EE. The reason for this was that the PSOE was capitalizing on EE's connection with terrorism to prevent EE from encroaching on its base. The speaker argued that since the truce, "the PSOE has been left without dialectic weapons against EE." If they were to break the truce, they would prejudice the EE's chances of taking a dominant position in the Basque left because "armed struggle is not what the masses are asking for now."[70]

One member argued that the ceasefire should not be broken, saying: "If the truce is broken, EE will have to condemn it and in this situation that condemnation would be different from other condemnations because it will mean the rupture of the bloc. . . . That leaves ETA without political cover."[71] Another member argued that the need to preserve ETA-pm's political cover through its affiliation with EE was going to be a continuous issue for the organization and one that could threaten its very future. Indeed, they argued that if the organization had to always consider whether EE would support or condemn their use of violence, "one must question the viability of armed struggle in the future . . . [and] if it is worth continuing with the Organization."[72] According to the next speaker, the issue was primarily one of popular

66 Fernandez, "Between Francoism and Democracy," 179.
67 ETA-pm, "Debate I," 51.
68 Ibid.
69 Ibid., 56.
70 Ibid., 58.
71 Ibid., 59–60.
72 Ibid., 62.

support. "There is a direct relationship between the popular acceptance that ETA has and the political cover of EE."[73] Therefore, if EE were to condemn ETA-pm's actions, ETA-pm would stand to lose an important sector of its base.[74]

Internal dynamics were also relevant to the decision of whether to break the ceasefire. As one speaker noted, ETA-pm could not remain inactive indefinitely. The militants simply would not accept that. "You can't say to these people from one day to the next that they can't intervene in the political reality indefinitely. . . ."[75] The speaker argued that most ETA-pm members thought the organization should intervene in the political process. Therefore, EE should be persuaded of the utility of armed action. "The sector of the party that today does not believe in coercive practice can only be convinced with an effective coercive practice in the political process."[76] The suggestion that ETA-pm could convince EE of the utility of violence by executing a politically successful armed attack was not supported by any explanation of what would constitute an "effective" attack. It may be assumed that the speaker thought this would be one that would exact concessions from the Spanish government. However, this would appear to be disconnected from the reality that was perceived by the other debaters. There would be no reason for the Spanish government to accede to ETA-pm's demands when their use of violence, and increasingly their very existence, was opposed by most Basque people.

The next speaker took issue with this argument, saying that the problem with this course would be that, as the speakers had observed before, it would cause a rupture in the relationship between EE and ETA-pm. EE had been able to maintain the equilibrium between the different sectors within the nationalist left bloc. This balance could be broken if it were put under pressure.[77] "ETA is facing a historical dilemma. Either armed struggle or mass struggle. So far this has been synthesized well, but now if EE goes to one side and ETA to the other at the political level, it becomes internally uncontrollable." The speaker warned that "breaking the truce can have the same effect as putting a bomb on the railway line to see what happens."[78]

[73] Ibid.
[74] Ibid.
[75] Ibid., 65.
[76] Ibid., 66.
[77] Ibid.
[78] Ibid., 67.

Three rough positions emerged on this issue. There were members who argued against breaking the ceasefire because to do so would damage the relationship with EE and put their political strategy at risk. There were those who argued that the ceasefire should be broken because ETA-pm needed to put pressure on the government to protect the Statute of Autonomy and to exact further concessions. The third group of speakers, and the minority, argued that times had changed and there was no longer any need to maintain ETA-pm. While no resolution was reached in this debate, most speakers supported the view that breaking the ceasefire would damage the relationship with EE. Any resumption of hostilities should therefore be approached with great caution or avoided altogether. The transcription of the debate ended abruptly with this comment: "From here the debate is enormously repetitive without new arguments."[79]

Consideration

The notes and transcripts of the first debate of 1981 reveal several significant tendencies in ETA-pm's deliberations on the use of violence. These include their concern with the negative view that the Basque people had begun to take of violence and their worry that by engaging in violence they could damage their image. ETA-pm was aware that its survival depended on its ability to remain relevant and exert influence on Basque politics. In the new representative democracy, their ability to maintain their position depended on the support of the Basque people. Therefore, they found themselves in a situation in which their use of violence was damaging their reputation. Yet failing to act would render them irrelevant.

The reality was that by the early 1980s, ETA-pm had become an organization that was out of step with the social and political life of the Basque Country. It was a terrorist organization operating on behalf of a people that did not want terrorism. The political gains that ETA-pm had formed to pursue had not been wholly obtained; however, there was sufficient democratic freedom in the Basque Country to enable the nationalists to pursue their cause through legal and nonviolent means. The Basque people were weary from decades of violence, and any actor that engaged in terrorism would be viewed as a spoiler. ETA-pm was therefore in a difficult situation. It needed

[79] Ibid., 70.

to find a way to continue to operate and to justify its existence as an armed organization in a society that was opposed to violence. One way around this was to subordinate their own organization to that of EIA and the EE coalition. In the democratic system, ETA-pm considered their political apparatus to be the most effective instruments through which the Basque people could gain autonomy. However, ETA-pm were also being publicly criticized by EE and put under pressure from their supposed political allies to cease using violence. This situation led several members to suggest that there may be no future for the armed organization.

While it may be obvious that a terrorist group in a society opposed to terrorism serves no purpose, only a few members suggested that there may not be a future for ETA-pm as an armed organization. There were no explicit discussions of the possibility of dissolving the organization. These conversations may have taken place informally but were not recorded as part of the official transcript of the debate. Instead, the members repeated their justifications for discriminate, selective attacks that were directly linked to strategic objectives. The arguments in support of this were that if their use of violence was justified to the Basque people, this could limit backlash and may even garner support for their activities. However, these arguments could be viewed as disingenuous given the strong opposition to political violence in Basque society.

The discussions that took place at this debate are also significant for what they do not include. Aside from one brief comment that armed action and coercion should not be put into moral categories, there is no other mention of the morality of violence. While much of the debate was devoted to discussing whether the ceasefire should be maintained or broken, violence was only ever evaluated in terms of utility and expediency. The success and failure of attacks were judged only by whether they assisted the organization to generate political capital and popular support or to damage their rivals. There was no discussion of whether violence was right or wrong, or whether the loss of life was desirable or should be avoided. Violence was only discussed in terms of whether it could assist the organization to consolidate and expand its presence in Basque politics. Neither was there any discussion of the need for revenge or other emotive justifications for action. This was despite the fact that police brutality continued to be a live issue for the Basque people.[80] ETA-pm discusses the use of selective violence, meaning

[80] Tejerina, "Protest Cycle, Political Violence," 49; Reuters, "Around the World."

violence in retaliation for what they consider to be assaults on the Basque people.[81] However, this was to advance their own position and image by exacting concessions. There is no discussion of revenge in the transcripts.

The issue of popular support also featured heavily in the discussions. The most cited argument against breaking the ceasefire was the fear that this would put EIA and EE in a position in which they would be forced to condemn ETA-pm's actions to ensure their own political survival. EE's opprobrium was not in and of itself a cause for concern. Rather, ETA-pm was worried that a rift in their relationship with EE would cost them their "political cover" and they could lose the support of large segments of moderate Basques.[82] This could lead to ETA-pm's alienation from the Basque populace, political irrelevancy, and inevitable dissolution. ETA-pm clearly recognized that without the support of the Basque people the organization could not continue to exist. This point was accepted as a fundamental premise of the debate and was not a point of argument. Rather than referring to specific examples of the Basque public's dissatisfaction with political violence, the arguments typically cited intangibles like changing social dynamics and the social and political climate.[83] This could suggest that the leaders of ETA-pm were in tune with shifts in public opinion and that they saw the value in responding to such changes.

Another point of significance is ETA-pm's strategic vision for the Basque nationalist movement. Their ultimate objective, according to the arguments presented in this debate, was to position EE as the main left-wing nationalist party in the Basque Country.[84] ETA-pm's role would be to support their affiliated political party. This was because it anticipated a future in which autonomy would be achieved through political negotiation. Indeed, ETA-pm's dependence on EE and EIA for political cover put the organization in a difficult position. While it viewed its own purpose as being the coercive apparatus that would support the nationalist coalition, the extant political environment had little tolerance for violence. Thus, ETA-pm was in the position of being the armed affiliate of a party that could not be seen to condone armed action. ETA-pm was therefore forced to consider how or indeed whether it could continue to operate in this new environment. These questions were not resolved at this debate.

[81] ETA-pm, "Debate I," 45.
[82] Ibid., 59–60
[83] Ibid.
[84] Ibid., 11 and 56.

Conclusion

In this chapter I examined the discussions that took place within ETA-pm at the first debate of 1981. At this debate, the members of ETA-pm had to contend with the fact that public opinion had turned against their activities. Most Basque people no longer wanted an active terrorist organization. Instead, they wanted to pursue the nationalist cause through democratic means. ETA-pm therefore needed to determine whether it would break the ceasefire. Committing an act of terrorism would risk further alienating the people for whom they claimed to be fighting. Failing to act would cause the organization to stagnate and eventually dissolve due to inactivity.

I began this chapter with a brief overview of the political background to the debates. The political issue that featured most strongly in the debate was the new federal legislation known as the LOAPA, which was seen as an assault on the Basque Statute of Autonomy. I went on to analyze seventy pages of original notes and transcripts from the debate. These discussions centered on the feasibility of breaking the ceasefire in the existing social and political environment. Two main and interconnected arguments were made against breaking the ceasefire. These were that any attack would in all probability be publicly denounced by ETA-pm's political party, EIA, and the Basque nationalist coalition, EE. This in turn could sever ETA-pm's relationship with its political partners, rendering it irrelevant and ineffective in the new democracy. The second argument, which is strongly connected to the first, was that there was limited public support for violence in the Basque Country. Nonviolent political solutions were gaining popularity and credibility. Therefore, if ETA-pm were to execute an attack that was badly received, it could lose a substantial proportion of its supporters. Public condemnation from EIA and EE would also damage its popularity and credibility in the eyes of the Basque people. This could jeopardize the survival of the organization.

The debate continued with a more general discussion of the future of armed struggle. Several leaders openly expressed their concern that ETA-pm may no longer serve a purpose in the Basque nationalist movement. There was an acknowledgment that ETA-pm was in an untenable position if it could only initiate attacks with the approval of a political coalition that was increasingly opposed to violence. ETA-pm was at a crossroads. It could dissolve, with certain members being absorbed into the political party, or it could break the ceasefire and continue engaging in terrorism despite the risks this entailed. These issues were not resolved at the first debate, and discussions continued. In the next chapter, I examine the second debate of 1981. In that debate, the positions became more entrenched and the organizational divisions more apparent. Although members on each side of the debate gathered to find a way to maintain the organization, the members appeared to be moving farther away from consensus on the future of the organization.

9
The Second Debate of 1981

This chapter examines the arguments that were expounded at the second debate of 1981. Two primary positions were advanced at this debate. Roughly, they were arguments in favor of and in opposition to breaking the ceasefire. In the first debate of 1981, the leaders on the whole appeared to acknowledge both the benefits and disadvantages of breaking the ceasefire. However, in the second debate a division began to form between the two schools of thought. Debaters on either side of the argument appeared to be equally concerned that ETA-pm was facing serious threats to its survival. The difference between the two was what they perceived to be the best way of safeguarding the organization's integrity.

The speakers who argued that the organization should break the ceasefire maintained that the left needed an armed organization and either supported the view that a break from EE could be beneficial to ETA-pm or else downplayed the risk that breaking the ceasefire would lead to a rupture with their political allies. Those who supported maintaining the ceasefire argued that the political-military strategy, established at Assembly VII, was based on ETA-pm's collaboration with a legitimate political party. Re-engaging in armed action would jeopardize this relationship and put their long-term strategy at risk. Those who opposed the move argued that it would be fatal to ETA-pm's relationship with EE and that this relationship was fundamental to their long-term objectives. Those who were in favor of reinitiating hostilities argued in general that these fears were over exaggerated. Some argued that a little distance between ETA-pm and EE was natural and even desirable. Others argued that the only way to convince those within EE who opposed violence that it could be a useful tool would be by executing a series of successful attacks.[1]

In this chapter I will examine the main arguments that were advanced at the debate. The arguments in favor of violence included the need to provide the Basque people with a coercive apparatus to protect them from bourgeois

[1] ETA-pm, "Debate II," 1.

Euskadi Ta Askatasuna. Nell Bennett, Oxford University Press. © University of Maryland National Consortium for the Study of Terrorism and Responses to Terrorism (START) (2025). DOI: 10.1093/9780197764268.003.0009

repression and the desirability of committing attacks to re-establish their presence in the Basque political debate. Those who argued against violence discussed the increased public opposition to terrorism, EIA and EE's unwillingness to support violence, and the fact that armed action was falling into disrepute within the Basque Country and across Europe in general. Despite clear evidence in opposition to the political-military approach, many of the speakers at the second debate advanced arguments in favor of the resumption of armed action. The arguments adopted by those who were in favor of breaking the truce suggest that there was a disconnection between their perceptions of sentiments of the Basque people and EE and the reality. That, or these were disingenuous arguments that were made to provoke violence in the knowledge that it would cause a rupture with EE and could alienate a substantial section of the populace.

The Need for a Coercive Instrument

The first speaker opened the second debate with a call on the leaders of ETA-pm to break the ceasefire and re-engage in armed action. The reason given was that the Basque nationalists needed a "coercive instrument." The speaker argued that although the left was gaining strength in the Basque Country, the military was still strongly Francoist. This posed a potential threat to the nationalist movement: "If the political process develops in phases and the left and the national left obtain a series of advances, there will be a confrontation."[2] This concern may well have been engendered by the attempted military coup that took place earlier the same year. The speaker elaborated on this argument by saying that in the new democracy the repressive forces of the bourgeoisie were using different methods for controlling the populace than those they had used under Franco. Under the new system they were using the instruments of democracy to dominate by consensus. However, when the left in the Basque Country reached a degree of strength that threatened the right, the bourgeoisie would use repression to protect their interests. Hence, the need for an armed organization in the Basque Country.[3]

The speaker acknowledged that ETA-pm's image in the Basque Country was suffering. It was observed that over the past four or five years there had been two armed organizations in the Basque Country: ETA-pm and

[2] Ibid., 3.
[3] Ibid.

ETA-m. During that time, ETA-pm had engaged in "selective activity, pedagogic activity."[4] In spite of this, the predominate image of armed action in the Basque Country was that of the indiscriminate violence of ETA-m. This had resulted in a "terrible decrease in the capacity for mobilization."[5] The speaker compared 1977, in which ETA-pm had been able to mobilize hundreds of thousands of people, with 1981, in which "not only did [the people] not mobilize in favor, but they have managed to mobilize against armed activity itself, including a general strike and quite large demonstrations."[6] The strike and demonstrations referred to were the popular revolt against ETA-m's killing of José María Ryan earlier that year.[7] "I think the circumstances have changed from the year 77 to today, they have changed in a negative way I think especially for the image of armed struggle and for the support that this generates . . . and therefore I think a global revision of Assembly VII is needed."[8]

The speaker concluded with the observation that a major difficulty facing ETA-pm was that the left-wing parties in the Basque Country felt the need to separate themselves from armed action so that they would not be labeled as terrorist supporters by their opponents. This limited ETA-pm's ability to operate in the political sphere.[9] This was particularly so for EE. Not only was the party being branded a terrorist affiliated party by the PNV, the PSOE was also capitalizing on EE's connection with ETA-pm to prevent EE from encroaching on its base.[10] However, they expressed the view that the majority of members within EE agreed with the need for a "coercive instrument" in the Basque Country. This opinion is directly contradicted by the fact that 62 percent of EE had approved the Aketegi proposal in June of the same year. This proposal, discussed in the preceding chapter, rejected all violence in favor of legal democratic means of advancing the cause.[11] It was also contradicted by EE's public criticism of terrorism and calls for peace. On March 22, 1981, EE's secretary general, Mario Onaindia, said that ETA-m's continued use of violence and refusal to join the ceasefire ran the risk of condemning the Basque people "to the return of fascism."[12]

[4] Ibid.
[5] Ibid.
[6] Ibid., 4.
[7] Burns, "Massive Basque Protests Reject,"; *El Pais*, "Huelga general y grandes."
[8] ETA-pm, "Debate II." 4.
[9] Ibid., 4–5.
[10] Soldevilla, *Historia de una Heterodoxia Abertzale*, 293–294.
[11] Ibid., 259.
[12] *El Pais*, "El terrorismo va a condenar."

Another speaker supported the call for a resumption of armed struggle. They rejected the notion that ETA-pm needed to change its approach because of the new democracy, arguing that even under the democracy there was repression and that it existed at all levels of society. So long as there was repression there would be a place for armed struggle.[13] The key to a successful attack was not that it favored EE but that it strengthened the political cause ETA-pm was seeking to advance. "Therefore, it isn't necessary that the party or the left say amen to everything we do . . . what is important is that we know how to maximize the political struggles that have to be maximized."[14] Furthermore, this speaker argued that EE would need armed action and that the party "will have to decide what type of action or instruments to use to coerce, because it is also necessary to coerce in the class struggle."[15]

For this to happen, the speaker argued, the party would have to maintain the political-military strategy, which had yielded many advances for the Basque Country, including the Statute of Autonomy. "[W]e have to arrive at a point at which the Organization and the party are the same thing, that all the left of Euskadi bets on a p-m strategy."[16] However, again here, the member was arguing for a state of affairs that was not plausible. EE had formalized years of private and public criticism of ETA with a resolution to only use parliamentary means to advance the nationalist cause. The argument that ETA-pm should work toward a situation in which not only EE but the entire Basque left were to adopt a political-military strategy was not based in objective reality.[17]

Breaking Away from EE

The first speaker argued that the tensions existing between ETA-pm and its political apparatus could be solved by loosening the tie between the two organizations. A distinction could be made between ETA-pm's relationship with EE and that which ETA-m maintained with its political party, Herri Batasuna. The speaker argued that Herri Batasuna, along with a proportion of ETA-m's supporters, were "unconditional," meaning that they supported ETA-m regardless of their actions. "The milis don't give a damn that 90%

[13] ETA-pm, "Debate II," 9.
[14] Ibid., 10.
[15] Ibid.
[16] Ibid.
[17] Soldevilla, *Historia de una Heterodoxia Abertzale,* 259.

of the population of Euskadi is against what they do, if they have a group of people, 100,000 or 150,000 people who are unconditional no matter what they do."[18] Instead of a relationship of unconditional support, the speaker argued that ETA-pm should accept that they would be criticized by EE and they may indeed criticize EE. This would be a valid dynamic between two affiliated organizations with different strategies, and it would be necessary to explain this to the Basque people.[19] However, the differences between ETA-pm and EE should not reach the level of ideological differences that could result in strategic differences, and a ceasefire and any type of political action should be carried out in parallel with the party.[20] This, however, completely contradicted the speaker's earlier argument that the ceasefire needed to be broken, because EE as it was constituted would not approve of a resumption of hostilities.

The argument that ETA-pm should separate itself from EE and re-establish its own political priorities was met with approval by several members. As one put it, "For me a p-m organization has to be independent of the party, which is not the armed wing, which has its own [Political Office], its own propaganda apparatuses, its own possibilities for public expression. . . ."[21] Another observed that if the organization has to always be dependent on the party's approval before acting, then ETA-pm "begins to have another meaning and it begins to be the armed wing of the party. If the party, based on its tactical needs, begins to say then now you act, now you don't act . . . the meaning of the organisation changes completely."[22] This argument, however, overlooked the fact that the party's condemnation was damaging to the organization's image and would cost them popular support.

The speaker went on to say that the Basque left was a weak force incapable of confronting the right-wing shift taking place in the political landscape. For this reason, armed struggle was an important weapon and should be performed by an independent organization.[23] In making this argument, the speaker did not address the view advanced in the first debate that ETA-pm's use of violence was in part responsible for the strengthening of the Basque right. Mario Onaindia's comments about a "return to fascism"

[18] ETA-pm, "Debate II," 2.
[19] Ibid.
[20] Ibid., 4.
[21] Ibid., 14.
[22] Ibid., 5.
[23] Ibid., 26.

indicated that EE shared this concern.[24] However, not all the members present agreed with the idea of acting against the party. The discussions showed two clear lines of thought: one that held that breaking the truce would have no serious negative effect on ETA-pm's relationship with EE and the left more broadly, another, which believed such an action would cause an irrevocable division between the two organizations, which would damage ETA-pm.

One problem that the organization did recognize was that new people were entering EE who had not previously been part of an armed organization. As these new members had no background in armed action, it would be impossible to integrate them into a political-military bloc. Thus, despite the organization's failure to appreciate the full significance of Aketegi and EE's resolution to only employ nonviolent means of political change, they did understand that broadening the EE coalition would make it more difficult for them to unite the left under a political-military strategy.

Violence to Maintain the Strategy

One interesting aspect of this second debate is that for the first time, speakers advocated for the use of violence for the sake of violence. As an example, one speaker argued that a political-military strategy could only succeed if ETA-pm continued to execute armed action. The argument was that if ETA-pm were to become the armed wing of EE, the effect would be that they would cease to exist as an organization. The speaker stated of the political-military strategy: "If it is not demonstrated in practice, it does not exist."[25] Another member agreed that it was necessary to break the truce. This member claimed to be planning a series of attacks because in their view it was necessary to attack the LOAPA legislation and all the restrictions on freedom of expression that were taking place in the Basque Country. The member argued that armed struggle "agitates" and "we are not agitating. The party isn't agitating. . . ."[26] Another speaker put it this way: "With doubt, we do nothing. This is the problem. This is a regressive position, this is not how history is written."[27]

[24] *El Pais*, "El terrorismo va a condenar."
[25] ETA-pm, "Debate II," 29–30.
[26] Ibid., 38.
[27] Ibid., 30.

One member who was against breaking the truce responded to these arguments by asking, "what type of intervention do we have? Types of interventions like the one of Navarre: a thousand kilos and doesn't solve anything. . . ." This question was referring to an operation that took place in March 1979 in which five ETA-pm members stole 985 kilos of explosives from a warehouse outside Pamplona.[28] ETA-pm claimed responsibility for the robbery and attributed the blame to the central government's refusal to allow a referendum in Navarre for its incorporation into the Basque Country. They stated that the incorporation of Navarre into the Basque Country was not negotiable, and they guaranteed "consistent armed intervention" until this was achieved.[29] However, by 1981 Navarre was no closer to integrating into the Basque region.

Several speakers who argued in favor of continuing with armed action and breaking the truce stated that the LOAPA was providing them with the ideal motivation and opportunity: ". . . there will be a debate in the parliament and . . . the function of armed struggle is that in this debate the balance is inclined towards those who think this law should not go ahead. That is where it is necessary to intervene."[30] One argued that the truce should be broken as soon as possible for the simple reason that without armed action ETA-pm was becoming irrelevant. "Today in Euskadi there are many people who doubt that we exist, who doubt our capacity enormously, who believe that we are dissolving. . . ."[31] One of the reasons why the Basque people may have thought that ETA-pm no longer existed was that the nationalist Basque magazine *Punto y Hora* had reported that the organization had dissolved.[32] Hence the idea that ETA-pm should break the ceasefire to prove its existence as an organization.[33]

The Decline in Popular Support

On the other side of the debate were those members who were opposed to breaking the ceasefire. One of the main reasons they advanced was that armed action was losing popularity in the Basque Country. They said that

[28] Goñi, "Cinco miembros de ETA (p-m)."
[29] Goñi, "Multa de dos millones."
[30] ETA-pm, "Debate II," 32.
[31] Ibid., 41.
[32] ETA-pm, "Adios as las Armas," 21–26.
[33] ETA-pm, "Debate II," 29–30.

as a result, ETA was falling out of favor with the people. Several speakers observed that the lack of popular support for armed action was becoming a trend both within Euskadi and across Europe. One speaker observed that while terrorism had been a viable tactic in the past, those days were ending, and this was influenced by broader international trends. "Indicators that this is ending for us . . . [are] the global discredit that armed struggle is having."[34]

They went on to argue that this loss of support would lead to ETA-pm's eventual decline. The organization was struggling, and it did not have the same capacity for mobilization and regeneration that it used to have. They argued that part of the reason for this was that the organization was inhibited in its actions because it was trying to incorporate new sectors to bolster its ranks. However, by failing to act they were also damaging their ability to recruit new members.[35] The speaker compared ETA to the Red Brigades, an organization that emerged out of a period of mass mobilizations in Italy. However, once the political situation stabilized, the Red Brigades lost their influence and popular support and armed action fell into disrepute. The speaker said that the Red Brigades, a vastly superior organization to ETA-pm, should be viewed as a cautionary tale. Even though they were executing terrorist acts that were "nice, agreeable, the results have been negative, and I think that's what can happen to us in the future."[36]

The next speaker intervened and accused this speaker of being defeatist. "The panorama presented in the last intervention is a black panorama in which there are no possibilities at all." The speaker argued that this was not accurate because "there's an organisation, there are some militants dedicated to the fight, there's a party which also says that it is p-m and which is for maintaining the organisation."[37] Again here, the argument completely disregarded the significance of EE's implementation of the Aketegi resolution.

Another member entered the debate in favor of maintaining the ceasefire. There was no sense in continuing with terrorism when it was opposed by the people. The increased opposition to armed struggle was "fundamentally due to the actions of the milis," meaning ETA-m, and that this was taking place

[34] Ibid., 7.
[35] Ibid., 7–8.
[36] Ibid., 9.
[37] Ibid., 10.

despite "four years of pedagogical struggle, of sectorial struggle, of struggle perfectly carried out by us."[38] This decline in popular support was, in turn, causing a reduction in new recruits and diminishing the capacity of ETA-pm. As one member expressed: "Everyone accepts that the very image of armed struggle has been significantly damaged, and this has generated a decline in the capacity for political action by way of military action . . . our capacity for intervention has declined by approximately 20 per cent of what it was before. . . ."[39] One member explained ETA-pm's waning support and recruitment problems in simple terms: "Before, being from ETA was to be an important individual, however now it has lost a lot of value, because we are losing importance." This leader opined that ETA-pm's capacity to intervene militarily had decreased and that they were losing their ability to regenerate the organization. This was largely because the Basque people had settled into a new way of conducting politics, and the trend was against armed action.[40]

Another member argued that the Basque people no longer wanted to be represented by an armed organization. In the past, ETA-pm's action had been more impactful because they had been an external manifestation of the subjective experience of the Basque people. However, the people no longer accepted this form of action because "they see themselves represented in other forms of political struggle."[41] This was another acknowledgment of the fact that the Basque people had democratic representation and were no longer reliant on a terrorist organization to defend their interests.

Several ETA-pm members attributed the decline in the popularity of armed struggle to the actions of ETA-m, who they said were engaging in indiscriminate violence. Selective violence, on the other hand, would be acceptable to the Basque people.[42] As one member put it, the organization could consider breaking the ceasefire, but any attacks that they would execute would have to be two things. First, "very selective, so that the result will be very positive, and will benefit EE and strengthen EE. . . . And second, provoke in the government the need for negotiation."[43] Interestingly,

[38] Ibid., 22.
[39] Ibid., 13.
[40] Ibid., 61.
[41] Ibid., 62.
[42] Ibid., 39.
[43] Ibid., 43.

ETA-pm did not explain why they considered their use of violence to be selective and ETA-m's violence to be indiscriminate and "militaristic." Both organizations targeted law enforcement and government sites and personnel. Beyond the vague claim that ETA-pm's attacks were pedagogical and retaliatory, no additional distinction was made.

Consideration

The records from this debate show that it was reasonably clear to a substantial proportion of the members of ETA-pm that their organization no longer had a role to play in Basque social or political life. ETA was formed under the dictatorship, a time of political, cultural, and social repression. In the late 1950s and early 1960s, under the rule of General Franco, terrorism provided the Basque people with a means of protesting the harsh, authoritarian regime and the suppression of their national culture. By 1981, the Basque people had won the democratic freedoms for which they had fought. There were still substantial gains to be made, however, and political parties and coalitions such as the PNV and EE offered the people a way of achieving greater independence through electoral politics and by ending the cycle of violence.

I have argued that terrorist groups do not form with the intention of being permanent organizations. They form to address a specific situation at a concrete point in time. The assumption is that once the terrorist group exacts sufficient concessions to enable the political campaign to be conducted through legal means, the terrorist group should dissolve. However, this is not always the case. In 1981, ETA-pm was beginning to understand that it was no longer wanted and no longer needed by the Basque people. This realization is recorded in the notes from this second debate of 1981. A proportion of the members accepted this reality and raised the prospect of dissolution. However, these suggestions were met with strident opposition. For the first time, a clear division is apparent among the members of ETA-pm, a division between those who recognized that terrorism no longer served a purpose, and those who maintained it was necessary, either to advance the nationalist movement, conserve their gains, or quite simply, maintain the organization.

This shows that ETA-pm was at a crucial decision point. The members were debating the very future of the organization and whether there was still a place for political violence in the Basque Country. The members were aware that most Basques opposed violence. They knew that the political party they had created from their own membership opposed violence. However, to relinquish violence would be tantamount to dissolving the organization. On one side of the debate, members argued that it would not be politically expedient to break the ceasefire, because it would damage their image and their relationship with EE. On the other side, members argued that the ceasefire had to be broken because without action, the organization would become irrelevant. The proponents of both arguments were equally concerned with the survival of ETA-pm. The difference was what they perceived to be the best way forward.

This debate is also notable because several members expressed the view that the organization needed to engage in violence simply because they were an armed organization, and an armed organization without action may as well not exist. Prior to this debate, discussions about the expediency of violence had always been framed in terms of political utility and the effect on popular support for the organization. In this debate, there is a clear argument in favor of violence purely for the purpose of maintaining the organization and keeping the militancy happy. Another interesting element in this debate is the atmosphere of tension that is discernible in the transcripts. There are more interruptions and disagreements recorded in these transcripts than in the those of the earlier debate. The positions advanced are existential in nature: either the organization will fail because it breaks the ceasefire or it will dissolve because it fails to act. Both sides of the argument predicted the demise of the organization if the wrong course of action were adopted.

There is also extensive discussion of selective violence. The advocates for breaking the truce emphasized that it should only be done with selective attacks. Their logic was that the public and EE would appreciate the strategic logic of these attacks and support ETA-pm. However, this argument was not subjected to serious analysis. The killing of power plant engineer José María Ryan, discussed in the previous chapter, was a highly selective attack, and yet it provoked protests across the Basque Country and a general strike.[44] Overall, the argument that selective violence would succeed in revitalizing the organization appears to have little basis in objective fact.

[44] Burns, "Massive Basque Protests Reject."

Conclusion

This chapter has examined the records from ETA-pm's second debate of 1981. The notes from this debate show ETA-pm at a crossroads. The people no longer wanted violence, their party no longer wanted violence, yet they were constituted as a violent protest group. ETA-pm was therefore faced with the real prospect that it might have to dissolve the organization. The immediate question was whether the ceasefire should be maintained. The members present at the debate were divided on this point. Those who argued in favor of breaking the ceasefire maintained that they were politically justified in doing so because of the government's assault on the Basque Statute of Autonomy through the introduction of the new LOAPA legislation. There were also arguments that violence was needed to maintain ETA-pm's strategy and to keep the organization relevant. On the opposite side, it was maintained that resuming hostilities would sever ETA-pm's relationship with the EE coalition, which would jeopardize their plan to unify the left and would put their very existence under threat. There were also arguments that the Basque people no longer wanted violence. This was supported by recent pacifist protests and strikes, in particular those against the killing of Ryan. In addition to this, some speakers also expressed concerns that ETA-pm had been so depleted by counterterrorism measures and inactivity that it no longer had the capacity to enact a successful armed campaign.

The chapter closed with a discussion of the significance of this debate. Terrorist and other violent protest groups are not formed with the intention of becoming perpetual organizations. Rather, they emerge in response to specific conditions. Once these conditions improve, the assumption is the group will change its tactics or dissolve. ETA-pm now found itself facing the prospect of its own dissolution. Some of the members who spoke at this debate acknowledged this fact. Others argued for a continuation of armed action, either to advance the cause or purely to sustain the organization. These transcripts evidence a clear divide within the organization. There were two distinct camps within ETA-pm, each of which advocated for an opposing and irreconcilable course of action. No resolutions were taken at this meeting. The cells were provided with the transcripts of the debate to continue the discussion and to prepare their positions for Assembly VIII of

1982. In the next chapter, I analyze ETA-pm's Assembly VIII. This was the final debate that the organization held as ETA-pm. I examine the records from the Assembly, the vote that ETA-pm held on the future of its organization, and the drivers that motivated members to adopt a position that was inconsonant with the social and political development of the Basque Country.

10

Assembly VIII of 1982

This chapter examines ETA-pm's Assembly VIII, which took place in February 1982. This was the final meeting that ETA-pm held as one united organization. The result of the Assembly was that the two main factions of the organization realized that they had irreconcilable differences in the way they viewed the future of ETA-pm. One side believed the only way to ensure the survival of the organization was to re-engage in armed action. The other believed that such a course would signify the end of ETA-pm. After Assembly VIII, ETA-pm split into two separate groups. In this chapter, I analyze the documents that were produced from Assembly VIII to provide an explanation for the split, as well as for the imminent dissolution of ETA-pm.

Two different proposals for the future of ETA-pm were presented at the Assembly. Proposal A called for an immediate end to the ceasefire and an escalated campaign of violence. It also argued that one of ETA-pm's main objectives should be "the accumulation of violence" and the creation of a military force capable of defending the Basque Country from any future right-wing coup. On the other end of the spectrum, Proposal B argued in favor of maintaining the ceasefire. Its authors warned that any initiation of hostilities would cause a definitive break in the relationship between ETA-pm and EE. This, they argued, would be the death knell for the organization. They also argued that ETA-pm did not have the capabilities to engage in armed practice at the level that would be required to pose any significant threat to the central government. Neither did they have the support of the people for such a course of action. Instead, they argued, the best way forward was to maintain the ceasefire and to negotiate with the central government.

In this chapter, I examine these two position papers and the comments that were recorded in the transcripts of the debate. The result of the debate was that Proposal A was approved by 70 per cent of the voting members. I argue that the reason the majority approved Proposal A was that it was the only alternative for those who wished to continue operating within ETA-pm.

Euskadi Ta Askatasuna. Nell Bennett, Oxford University Press. © University of Maryland National Consortium for the Study of Terrorism and Responses to Terrorism (START) (2025). DOI: 10.1093/9780197764268.003.0010

The organization was struggling from a lack of funds, resources, and personnel, and this situation was only exacerbated by the ceasefire. As several leaders argued, without action the organization would die "a slow death."[1] Accordingly, it is arguable that the majority of members accepted Proposal A not because it was the most practical, nor the most realistic. Rather, they voted for this proposal because the alternative would be organizational dissolution. This chapter is significant because it shows a terrorist organization adopting a radical strategy when faced with an existential threat. After years of moderating their position to expand their base and influence, the organization took a sharp strategic turn. It reverted to the ideological position it held back in 1974, before the separation of ETA into the political-military and the military branches. The reason for this shift is that the majority of the organization's members perceived this as the only way to continue as an armed organization.

Background to Assembly VIII

Much like the debate of 1981, Assembly VIII took place against a backdrop of heightened tension between ETA-pm and EE. EE wanted ETA-pm to maintain the ceasefire they had declared a year earlier. The moderate majority within EE, those who had approved the Aketegi proposal that renounced the use of armed or illegal tactics in the nationalist cause, wanted ETA-pm to pursue a negotiated settlement with the Spanish government. This would allow the organization to lay down its arms permanently in exchange for amnesty and additional political concessions.[2] The pressure from EE was amplified by increased opposition to political violence across the Basque Country. In April 1981, the PNV held a meeting to discuss measures that could be taken against ETA. The PNV, which was the majority party in the Basque government, condemned ETA's violence "once again, with all the moral force of that the institution provides," and said that terrorist attacks "debase their perpetrators" and "degrade the public image of our people."[3]

On November 14, 1981, the leadership of EIA gathered for a meeting to pass a resolution that would ask ETA-pm to maintain the ceasefire.

[1] ETA-pm, "Debate III," 3.

[2] Domínguez, "El fin de ETA político militar," 12; Soldevilla, *Historia de una Heterodoxia Abertzale*, 307–309.

[3] Etxarri, "Campaña del PNV para convencer."

Around one third of the attendees chose to abstain from voting in the belief that doing so would be akin to interfering in ETA-pm's internal management. It may be assumed that most of the abstainers belonged to EIA's hard-lined New Left faction. Most of the attendees voted in favor of the resolution. The final numbers were 43 in favor, two opposed, and 24 abstentions.[4]

The resolution was drafted as follows:

> The BT of EIA agrees to address the political-military organisation ETA... to express:
>
> 1 Although the concrete achievements achieved are not yet very significant, it positively values the truce in general terms due to the effects produced in Basque society...
> 2 The [leadership] considers that the maintenance of the truce on your part is absolutely necessary as an element that enables the advancement of the process of autonomy, the development of the participation of the masses in the political struggle and as an element that allows the development and consolidation of a left-wing and national alternative like Euskadiko Ezkerra.[5]

Despite this clear directive to maintain the ceasefire, on December 29, 1981, ETA-pm kidnapped Julio Iglesias Puga, the father of the famous singer. The kidnapping was enacted to raise funds for the organization.[6] ETA-pm operatives held Iglesias for three weeks, until he was rescued by a group of special operations police officers. Several officers were killed in the operation.[7] ETA-pm initially did not assume responsibility for the kidnapping, because they did not want to be seen to be breaking the ceasefire. However, after one of their operatives was arrested in connection with the event, they issued a public statement taking responsibility, with the caveat that "this does not at all mean the breaking of the ceasefire that we have been maintaining since February 27 of last year. The provision of financial means is a permanent necessity of the organisation, this does not signify any alteration to our decision to hold fire."[8] EE publicly condemned the kidnapping and ETA-pm's

[4] Domínguez, "El fin de ETA político militar," 12.
[5] Ibid.
[6] Varela, "El Dramático Secuestro."
[7] *El Español*, "Qué sucedió hoy, 17 de enero."
[8] *Punto y Hora*, "Lectura de una historia de novela," 10.

actions, saying that they were, "contrary to democratic normalisation and the most elementary criteria of coexistence."[9]

The kidnapping of Julio Iglesias Puga was also criticized by ETA-m, who said that it reflected badly on the nationalist left as a whole.[10] However, ETA-m and its affiliated political party Herri Batasuna were engaging in frequent demonstrations and clashes with police, which undermined ETA-pm's ceasefire. In February 1982, Herri Batasuna called for a day of struggle and mobilization in memory of an ETA-m operative, Joseba Arregui, who had died in police custody the year before. The call resulted in unauthorized protests around the Basque Country. In Gipuzkoa, groups of up to several hundred people set up flaming barricades across roads and threw Molotov cocktails at police.[11] To make matters worse for ETA-pm, on January 20 the police discovered the organization's weapons cache in a village named Erandio in the province of Bizkaia. The police seized 356 firearms and 50 kilograms of explosives.[12] The haul included 336 shotguns, 2,565 cartridges, 4 machine guns, 7 assault rifles, a bazooka, 5 grenades, 4 pistols, and 4 revolvers.[13] This loss significantly reduced ETA-pm's offensive capabilities.[14]

ETA-pm was accordingly facing a fraught political situation at the time at which they called Assembly VIII. They had felt the necessity to break the ceasefire to raise funds for the organization, and their actions were condemned by their political allies, ETA-m, and the broader Basque society. By 1982, there was little doubt that the organization had lost the support of the Basque people. Survey data from that year showed that only 6 percent of the Basque population completely supported the organization, while 42 percent completely rejected it.[15] ETA-pm was thus financially and militarily weakened. They had a diminished ability to recruit new members, waning popular support, and were facing opposition from both the nationalist and radical sides of Basque politics. In addition, the violent acts of ETA-m undermined the narrative they were trying to develop by adhering to the ceasefire. It was clear that the organization was in a dire situation and facing multiple threats to its continued existence.

[9] Ibid.; Soldevilla, "Agur a las armas," 86.
[10] *Punto y Hora*, "Lectura de una historia de novela," 10.
[11] de Azua, "Manifestaciones y violentos incidentes."
[12] Soldevilla, *Historia de una Heterodoxia Abertzale*, 315.
[13] ABC, "Con este Arsenal."
[14] Domínguez, "El fin de ETA político militar," 15.
[15] Llera Ramo, "Violencia y Opinion Publica," 92.

The Two Proposals

Assembly VIII was held at a time at which the organization was deeply divided. On one side were those who believed in maintaining the cease-fire. On the other were those who wanted to return to armed activity. These two factions each wrote a proposal for the future of ETA-pm. The proposals were simply titled Proposal A and Proposal B. Proposal A was written by the hard-line faction that supported a return to armed action. This proposal was referred to as "Orreaga." Proposal B supported a continuation of the Otsagabia Proposal, which had been approved in Assembly VII.[16] ETA-pm described the two proposals in their internal magazine, *Zutik*. The radical proposal was described as one that defended "the return to armed action and the promotion of a debate throughout the left for the strengthening of the political-military positions." The moderate proposal was characterized as one that argued "the impossibility and impracticability of the armed struggle and the unconditional relinquishment of 'political action.'"[17] ETA-pm also acknowledged in *Zutik* that the organization was going through a crisis due to the polarization caused by the debate.[18]

Proposal A or "Orreaga"

Proposal A presented an aggressive new strategy for ETA-pm. It was a clear break from the strategic direction that the organization had been pursuing since the Otsagabia Proposal in 1976. Proposal A was for a political-military strategy that would allow the left to "seize power from the ruling class" and "establish socialism and full national sovereignty through independence." It would do this by accumulating, organizing, and exercising "the necessary coercion" to support the struggle.[19] Proposal A was centered on the use of violence in furtherance of the nationalist cause. One of its key initiatives was the creation of a Basque pseudo-army that would be prepared for deployment in the event of a confrontation between the bourgeois power structures of the state and the Basque working class. Furthermore, the proposal argued that such a confrontation was inevitable. Therefore, an armed revolutionary vanguard was needed to protect the working class.[20]

[16] Casanova, *ETA, 1958–2008*, 279.
[17] ETA-pm, *Zutik*, 13.
[18] Ibid.
[19] ETA-pm, "Ponencia A," 20.
[20] Ibid., 26.

This proposal did not just contradict ETA-pm's existing strategic plan. It went as far as to blame the organization's internal and external problems on that plan. Its authors argued that the internal crisis that ETA-pm was experiencing had its roots in Assembly VII and the enactment of the Otsagabia Proposal. More specifically, they argued that the fault lay in a series of errors in the predictions on which the resolutions of that assembly were based.[21] It was due to the fact that events had largely invalidated the organization's predictions that "we find ourselves in this crisis situation: of indecision, vacillation and doubt."[22] Therefore, it argued, Assembly VII was out of date and needed to be replaced with a new and more militant plan.[23]

Proposal A acknowledged that under democracy, domination was achieved more from consensus than coercion. However, it argued that bourgeois power structures were underpinned by violence. Therefore, the Basque working classes also needed to have violence at their disposal. They argued that it was a priority for the left to "accumulate violence."[24] Although the meaning of this phrase was not elucidated in the document. In addition, the proposal recommended an escalation of *kale borroka,* or urban guerrilla tactics. The authors wrote that the Basque people "should learn to use violence from [ETA-pm's] exercises (attacks) or rather from the coercive power of the simple accumulation of violence (armed organization, military experience . . .)." This way coercion could be brought into specific conflicts.[25] In a fundamental break with the political-military strategy as it had been understood and practiced since 1976, Proposal A argued that violence would no longer be used as a measure of last resort. Violence was not to be reserved for a final and decisive confrontation with the bourgeois power structures. Instead, it was to be used in "all moments of the process."[26]

At a tactical level, the proposal identified three priorities. The first was to support the people's own struggle and negotiation processes. However, "the people" were only ever referred to in general terms. Which people and what they were negotiating was not clarified. In fact, there was little reference made to what the Basque people wanted. The first mention of the will or desires of the Basque people, aside from abstract discussions of supporting "the people's projects," was at page 38 of the proposal. There it said, ". . . we

[21] Ibid., 1.
[22] Ibid.
[23] Ibid., 26.
[24] Ibid., 32.
[25] Ibid., 30.
[26] Ibid., 32.

believe that the success or failure of our strategy will be in the degree to which the people accept our political practice." However, the assumption was that the Basque people *would* accept their practice. The authors went on to argue that as their practice was accepted by the people, so it would also become more accepted in the "sectors of the left that today remain in a vacillating position."[27] The inference here was that once the Basque people got behind the new ETA-pm, so too would the EE coalition and the rest of the Basque left.

The second priority was to develop a propaganda campaign with the objective of reinstating a political-military approach within EE. Here, they referred to the EE's rejection of violence and other illegal tactics, which was formalized by the Aketegi proposal. The hard-line faction, known as the "New Left," persisted within EE. The assumption of Proposal A was that propaganda, combined with a series of successful attacks, could be used to persuade the majority of EE to join the New Left in their support of violence.[28] The third tactical priority was the accumulation of coercive power to be used against attempts at reducing or annulling democratic freedoms or nationalist conquests.[29] The Proposal stated that it was time for ETA-pm to make a strategic about-face: "we should be capable of varying and abandoning the current state of political action. . . ."[30] Thus, the authors and supporters of Proposal A sought to call an immediate end to the ceasefire and initiate an escalated campaign of terrorist violence.[31]

Proposal B

Unlike the first proposal, Proposal B was for a continuation of the political-military strategy as it had been interpreted since Assembly VII in 1976. It stated at the outset that it was intended to complement Congress III of EIA, at which the Aketegi proposal was adopted. That was the conference at which EIA resolved to renounce and reject all armed action in favor of legal and democratic means of effecting political change.[32] Proposal B began by noting that violence was inherent in political power structures. Even in

[27] Ibid., 38.
[28] Ibid., 33–34.
[29] Ibid.
[30] Ibid., 35.
[31] Ibid.
[32] ETA-pm, "Ponencia B," 1.

a bourgeois democracy, the domination of the ruling class over the working class was underpinned by violence.[33] However, it warned against the "fetishization of violence," which they explained was "seeing violence as a thing to which miraculous virtues are attributed. . . . It is sometimes thought to have pedagogic virtues, in that it shows the people the repressive character of the state. . . ."[34]

Proposal B did not shy away from the difficulties ETA-pm was facing. It characterized the extant situation as one of "encirclement." They explained "encirclement" as being "the moment at which the deterrence of armed practice and the social consensus on which it is based lose their expansive character." That is to say, violence was no longer having the desired effect on either the political or the social front. The first consequence of this "encirclement" was that armed action began to lose its ability to influence politics. "The dissuasive capacity of an armed organisation is not principally in itself or in its practice, but in its capacity to catalyse more and more—that is to say, be expansive—a movement in response to an aggression."[35] They argued that the attacks perpetrated in 1978–1979 had much greater political repercussions than those of the current time and the "enemy" was aware of this. ETA-pm could no longer continue to expect to provoke political change because the bourgeois democratic powers knew that neither the people nor the moderate Basque political parties would accept armed action. Therefore, it was not possible to continue with the same strategy.[36] In support of this argument, the proposal referred to the recent actions of ETA-m, in particular the kidnapping and killing of José María Ryan. The authors stated that the killing of Ryan was one of the key events in the decline of armed struggle.[37]

The proposal observed that there were two other reasons why the Basque people no longer accepted violence. One was the new democratic freedoms that the region had been afforded. The second was social fatigue: "It is impossible to constantly maintain a society at the degree of agitation and mobilization like that which Euskadi has lived in the period 74–80."[38] This argument was a new addition to the debate. The proposal argued that the Basque people were tired of violence. Thus, ETA's attacks no longer had the

[33] Ibid., 6.
[34] Ibid., 4–5.
[35] Ibid., 20.
[36] Ibid., 21.
[37] Ibid., 30.
[38] Ibid., 31.

symbolic and communicative power they had had in earlier years: "Before, every armed action, whether it was ours or the milis', was analysed, studied, commented upon, created sympathy, etc. . . . today, however. . . it is hardly commented upon, except to criticise harshly when the attack goes too far. . . ."[39] While the authors of Proposal B took a degree of responsibility for the decline of armed struggle, they did place much of the blame on ETA-m. They argued that the quantity of violence that the milis had perpetrated had upset the relationship between the dissuasive capacity of violence and its popular acceptance. The result was that "today, for an action to be truly dissuasive . . . it has to be of such a magnitude or such brutality that it is difficult that it would achieve popular acceptance."[40] This had destroyed ETA-pm's ability to effect political change through violence.

Proposal B was in favor of maintaining the ceasefire. It said that it had been of great benefit to EE. It had allowed EE to escape from the political trap of being affiliated with a revolutionary organization and enabled it to "situate itself at an ideological and political level in the center of the left in our country."[41] This was in line with ETA-pm's overarching strategy of uniting the Basque left. The proposal argued that the ceasefire should only be broken if the social and political conditions permitted ETA-pm to break out of the "encirclement," that is, the opposition of both the Basque left and the Basque people to armed struggle. They argued that overcoming this "encirclement" would require "mobilization in favor of armed struggle that again creates an image of its necessity." However, they said that the reality was that in the existing atmosphere any error the organization might make was "fuel for the anti-armed struggle forces."[42] Thus, breaking the ceasefire would only damage their organization as well as EE.

Critiques of the Proposals

Critiques of the two proposals were also included with the materials that were distributed among the militants ahead of the debate. These were presumably penned by opponents to each proposal, as they highlighted what each faction perceived to be the shortcomings in the other's strategy.

[39] Ibid., 33.
[40] Ibid., 60.
[41] Ibid., 61–62.
[42] Ibid., 42.

The first paper presented a strong criticism of Proposal A. The first criticism leveled against Proposal A was that it failed to consider the damage to the image of armed struggle in the Basque Country and the resultant difficulties that produced. It observed that the proposal did not make even the minimum acknowledgment of the actual political situation. The discussions of political support and popular acceptance were at odds with the reality in the Basque Country. The paper also stated that Proposal A failed to engage in even the slightest degree of self-reflection on the reasons that had led ETA-pm to the situation in which it found itself, a situation that was by any measure, far from ideal.[43] The critique went on to point out that the expression "accumulation of violence" was not defined anywhere in the proposal. Not only was there no definition, but neither were there examples given by which the reader could deduce what was meant by the phrase. The authors of the critique argued that it was not possible to understand from the proposal whether its authors were referring to the accumulation of acts of violence or the accumulation of the capacity to commit violence.

If it was the former, the critics warned, this would be a grave mistake, as it would be nothing more than what ETA-m had been doing: "accumulate very considerable quantities of violence and without achieving practically any of their objectives, but rather the contrary: produce in society and the apparatus of the state a certain immunity to violence. . . ."[44] This is similar to the argument that the authors of Proposal B made when they stated that the Basque people were suffering from conflict fatigue, and this was impeding their willingness to mobilize.[45] If it was the latter, the authors were in agreement that ETA-pm should be enhancing its operational and logistical capacity. However, they observed that the dissuasive capability the authors of Proposal A discussed seemed to have little grounding in the reality of "organizational weakness" that ETA-pm was experiencing. This was not only in reference to their diminishing ability to recruit new members but also to the recent loss of their arsenal in the Erandio cache.[46] The critics argued that the organization would need an extraordinary increase in its logistical base to be able to move from a phase of "harassment" to one of "dissuasion."[47]

43 ETA-pm, "Enmienda a la Ponencia Orreaga," 7.
44 Ibid., 8.
45 Ibid., 31.
46 ABC, "Con este Arsenal se Podria Armar."
47 ETA-pm, "Enmienda a la Ponencia Orreaga," 10.

The main criticism of Proposal A was that it was out of touch with reality. The critics argued that the political situation appeared to be a dead end and that they could not see how armed action could have the "miraculous capacity to unblock the current situation and awaken the masses from their lethargy."[48] It criticized Proposal A's plan to use violence at all stages of the revolutionary process, saying that a coercive instrument is rarely if ever used in a democratic system.[49] Indeed, it went so far as to say that breaking the ceasefire would be "suicide for the organization" because it would leave them without the political cover of EE.[50] Instead, what was needed was "time and serenity to recover from the blows that we have suffered."[51] In short, the organization should continue with the ceasefire and maintain its relationship with EE.

On the other side of the argument were the critics of Proposal B. They distributed a document titled "A Group of Militants from the Base in Support of the Orreaga Proposal." The Orreaga Proposal was another name for Proposal A. The authors took aim at Proposal B's support for the ceasefire: "Armed struggle ALWAYS has to be presented as an answer to the repressions of the oligarchy and the State against popular conquests." They argued that the use of the truce as a negotiating tool was demonstrably inefficient, as they had made little if any progress on their main public goals, including securing amnesty for Basque political prisoners, the inclusion of Navarre in the Basque Country, blocking the proposed nuclear power plant at Lemoniz, decreasing unemployment, diminishing police brutality, and so forth. Indeed, they stated that new grievances had been added to the list, including the LOAPA, the common market, multinational corporations, and other social problems.[52] The rest of the critique consisted of a prolonged discussion of Marxist and Leninist theory. It concluded with the following remark: "Starting from the principle that 'Silence is a cowardice,' we believe that as we all have something to say . . . we have to participate as well as we can."[53] Overall, the critique provided minimal discussion of the political or social situations in the Basque Country and did not engage with the argument that breaking the ceasefire would signify the end of ETA-pm's relationship with EE.

[48] Ibid., 4.
[49] Ibid., 5.
[50] Ibid., 7.
[51] Ibid., 10.
[52] ETA-pm, "Critica a Ponencia B," 4–5.
[53] Ibid., 5–6.

Between the Organization and the Party

In addition to the debate on the two proposals, in February 1982 ETA-pm held a meeting to discuss the relationship between the organization and EE. The majority of ETA-pm members had realized by this time that the political party they had created to advance their agenda had turned away from armed action.[54] In fact, it had shifted so far from being the party that ETA-pm created in Assembly VII that they no longer knew what its strategic direction would be: "The party will maintain a line . . . political, strategic, ideological. . . . Undoubtedly, when I said before that it isn't clear what politics the party will develop, I think no one really knows."[55] One difficulty was that since ETA-pm created the party, new entrants to the party had diluted its original political-military membership. As one speaker at the debate explained, the result of this was that ETA-pm "can only exist on the basis that it does not act. . . ."[56]

This concern, that ETA-pm could only maintain its relationship with EE if it did nothing at all, was echoed by other members. One put it thus: "now the only way to get along with the organization is that [ETA-pm] does not act . . . what do you have to do? Well, be there and do nothing."[57] This speaker observed that unless ETA-pm was able to engage in armed action, it would not be able to develop its technical capabilities.[58] Neither would it be able to boost recruitment. As another speaker observed, over the period of the ceasefire ETA-pm had lost significant political influence and capacity for armed action. "It is evident that over six or seven years of ceasefire, without armed practice, that capacity will not increase . . "[59] However, to break with EE would mean that their only political ally would turn on them. This was especially clear because, as another leader observed, there were sectors within the party that would support the elimination of ETA-pm.[60] If they were to break the truce, they would be playing into the hands of the anti-political-military factions. Therefore, the organization was in a position in which it could either break with EE and lose its only political ally, or, as another leader put, die "a slow

[54] Ibid., 9.
[55] Ibid., 23.
[56] Ibid., 2–3.
[57] ETA-pm, "'Debate III,'" 2.
[58] Ibid.
[59] Ibid., 26.
[60] Ibid., 10.

death."[61] However, there were some within ETA-pm who held on to the fact that there was a small faction within EE, the New Left, that did support the political-military strategy. This was an argument that was used by the proponents of Proposal A, or the Orreaga Proposal.

The transcript of the debate ended without resolution on any issues. The closing remark summed up the conflict within ETA-pm: "There are some who support one proposal and others who support another, that is, some who support the one to promote the negotiated solution and the reorganisation of the organisation and others who say: violence always."[62] These were two irreconcilable positions, and there appeared to be little intention of bridging the gap between the two sides of the debate.

Criticism of the Debate

In addition to the critiques and discussions on the two proposals, one member submitted a paper that criticized the entire process of the debate. While the identity of the author is not known, it appears to have been written by a member of long standing. The author wrote that the debate had descended to such a level that the participants were not interested in discussing the ideas that were presented, only which ideological faction they belonged to. "They make lists of names, not ideas. Shameful." The author wrote that the debate had been cursory and superficial but that the positions adopted by the members were "disproportionately radical and wrapped in insults and epithets for the 'opposite side.'"[63]

The author blamed the organization's leadership for fostering this atmosphere by reducing the debate to two options, rather than analyzing the broader context. Rather than being an opportunity to discuss ideas, it had become a competition: "They only listen to attack quickly and forcefully the 'other position.'" The member also criticized the two proposals, saying they were "drawn up to justify previously established conclusions."[64] The intractable conflict the author observed within ETA-pm was reflected by the fact that the debates of 1982 failed to resolve the differences between the two factions.

61 Ibid., 3.
62 Ibid., 29.
63 "Criticas al Debate," 1–2.
64 Ibid.

The Decision

The outcome of the debate was that Proposal A/Orreaga was approved by approximately 70 percent of voting members. This caused a split in ETA-pm between the majority who supported Proposal A and the remaining 30 percent who wanted to maintain the ceasefire.[65] The two sides of the debate split into separate organizations. The majority became "ETA-pm Assembly VIII," adopting the name of the debate at which they had approved the Orreaga proposal and the return to active militancy. The remaining members became "ETA-pm Assembly VII," in recognition of the Otsagabia Proposal that had been approved at Assembly VII and which subordinated armed action to political action. The names were shortened to "Octavos," or "Eighths" for the majority Orreaga supporters and "Septimos" or "Sevenths" for the Otsagabia/Proposal B supporters.

ETA-pm Assembly VIII, or the Octavos, explained their decision to adopt Proposal A to the Basque people in a manifesto published in March 1982. The manifesto had a slogan written in Euskera across the cover, "Always fighting until the liberation of the Basque Country." It began by saying that the previous five years of armed struggle through the transition to democracy had been crystallized in Assembly VIII. They said that the assembly had opened up "a new way of considering the armed struggle as a **political instrument**," one more weapon that the Basque working class could use to bring about "social, economic and political change."[66] They wrote that there was a "current and permanent need for armed activity" to boost "the political-military project on the basis of an **accumulation of violence**."[67] [emphasis in original].

In explaining their reasoning for returning to violence, the Octavos adopted a Marxist interpretation of state power: "The existence of the State is a symptom of the existence of opposing classes in society and therefore implies, in the current circumstances, relations of exploitation and violence. . . ."[68] Referring specifically to the Basque situation, they argued that little progress had been made under the ceasefire that ETA-pm had been observing for the past year. In fact, they argued that they were in a worse situation than they had been twelve months previously. The Octavos even

[65] ETA-pm, *Zutik*, 13.
[66] ETA-pm. "VIII Asamblea, 'Manifiesto de la VIII Asamblea,'" 2.
[67] Ibid., 3
[68] Ibid., 4–5.

went so far as to discount the possibility of future ceasefires: "The Organisation can never make the Organisation itself or the continuity of the armed practice an element to negotiate. . . . Direct negotiation with the armed Organization will only be possible as a consequence of the very exercise of violence."[69] This constituted a radical departure from the Otsagabia Proposal and the political-military strategy as it had previously been practiced.

The Proponents of Proposal B

On September 30, 1982, ten leaders of ETA-pm Assembly VII gave a press conference in Biarritz in the French Basque Country at which they announced the dissolution of their organization. With their faces uncovered, they read from a preprepared statement in which they committed themselves to continuing the Basque struggle through nonviolent political means. These leaders, along with 20 percent of the former membership of ETA-pm, some 300 people, would renounce violence for good.[70] The declaration was made in exchange for a promise from the Spanish government that 110 ETA exiles and prisoners be granted amnesty and allowed to return to the Basque Country. However, it was also due to a recognition that armed action would no longer benefit the Basque people. As they stated, "We thought that armed violence was necessary at a certain time, but today we are convinced that it is the values and the democratic struggle that . . . can provide real solutions to the problems of Euskadi."[71] In their statement the former militants said that there was no longer the necessary popular support for armed struggle in the Basque Country. "On the contrary," they stated, "violent practice now constitutes a negative ingredient in the Basque Country's struggle for self-government."[72]

Consideration

The result of this debate is surprising, because it marks a sharp and sudden divergence from the strategy that ETA-pm had been developing since Assembly VII in 1976. In this debate, for the first time, there was a stark

69 Ibid., 12.
70 Eitb.eus, "30 años de la disolución."
71 Ibid.
72 Barbaria, "ETA Político-militar VII Asamblea."

division between the two factions of ETA-pm. In previous debates there had been a consensus on certain issues, such as the importance of the relationship with the party and the need for violence to serve concrete strategic objectives. In this debate, however, the proponents of Proposal A were prepared to sacrifice the relationship with EE to break the ceasefire and argued that violence was a necessary element of the nationalist struggle "at all moments of the process."[73] This position is a direct contradiction of the principles that had been developed in Assembly VII.

One notable aspect of Proposal A is that it resembled the strategy of ETA-m. Perhaps even more notable is the similarity between Proposal A and ETA's proposal for a Basque National Front, replete with army, to destroy the apparatus of the State. This was discussed back 1971, three years before the organization divided into ETA-pm and ETA-m. In a 1971 issue of *Kemen* the organization wrote: "The destruction of the State brings with it the destruction of the repressive apparatus . . . the people in power will demand the creation of a popular army."[74] These words could have been lifted directly out of Proposal A. The authors of Proposal B warned of the "fetishization of violence," which they said had been reflected in ETA-m's strategy. By this they meant the belief that violence in and of itself had a "miraculous" ability to unite the Basque people and solve political problems.[75] The social and political reality of the Basque Country demonstrated that this view was erroneous. One speaker in the debate had observed that ETA-m was suffering a slow death, because armed attacks that had enjoyed substantial popular support, even majority support, were no longer accepted.[76] In spite of this, Proposal A was approved with a 70 percent majority.

The question this raises is: why was a proposal that was completely at odds with ETA-pm's accepted wisdom, which was demonstrably out of touch with social and political realities, and which was logistically impractical, approved by the majority of the organization? At first glance, this result appears to be puzzling. However, one way to understand the decision is to examine the alternative course of action that was open to the organization. Proposal B argued for a continuation of the ceasefire to allow for negotiation with the government and to protect the organization's relationship with EE. This course presented several difficulties. Looking first at the

[73] ETA-pm, "Ponencia A," 32.
[74] ETA, *Kemen*, no. 6, 1971.
[75] ETA-pm, "Ponencia B," 4–5.
[76] ETA-pm, "Debate III," 3.

ETA-pm's relationship with EE, as several leaders observed in the debate, EE had been co-opted by more moderate political forces, the majority of whom were opposed to political violence. Some even supported the idea of eliminating ETA-pm altogether.[77] Therefore, the relationship could be maintained only if ETA-pm made a commitment to "doing nothing."[78] As one leader observed in the debate, an armed organization cannot maintain its capabilities and personnel if it does not engage in any armed activity.[79] It is easy to imagine that the prospect of continued political negotiation may have been concerning for the supporters of Proposal A. Proposal B stated that ETA-pm would continue to seek concessions from the Spanish government on important issues such as the release of hundreds of Basque prisoners, the dismantling of the nuclear power station at Lemoiz, and the incorporation of the province of Navarre into the Basque Country. However, if these negotiations were to continue under the ceasefire, ETA-pm's main bargaining chip would be the dismantling of their own organization.

There were at least two reasons why the members of ETA-pm would not want the organization dissolved. The first is that many members would want to continue operating within the organization. This could be because they genuinely believed that the organization was the best vehicle for advancing the nationalist cause. It could also be for a range of personal reasons, including the fact that ETA-pm provided members with a place to live, a stipend, camaraderie, and purpose. Another reason many members may have objected to the dismantling of ETA-pm could be that they did not trust the Spanish government. If ETA-pm were to dissolve in exchange for concessions, the Spanish government could always reinstate repressive policies. Indeed, this had happened back in 1979. The Spanish government had promised to move Basque prisoners to jails in the Basque Country in exchange for ETA-pm halting their bombing campaign. However, the government never fulfilled its end of the bargain.[80] Therefore, it is understandable that the militants would be reluctant to enter into a demobilization agreement with the government.

With these considerations in mind, it is understandable that 70 percent of ETA-pm members approved Proposal A. This proposal was the only alternative to the dissolution of the organization. Members who voted for Proposal

[77] Ibid., 10.
[78] Ibid., 2.
[79] Ibid., 2–3.
[80] Fernandez, "Between Francoism and Democracy," 30–31.

A may have been aware of the probable consequences of breaking the ceasefire, the inevitable loss of political cover, and even that most Basque people opposed their activities. But to vote for Proposal B would be to become a "liquidacionista."[81] A liquidationist was one who turned their back on the revolutionary vanguard.

Conclusion

This chapter has examined the documents ETA-pm created for Assembly VIII, along with the transcripts of that debate. This was the final meeting ETA-pm held as one united organization. Two proposals were presented for debate at the assembly. One was a strategic plan that involved breaking the ceasefire and engaging in "the accumulation of violence." Exactly what this accumulation would entail was never explained. The second proposal was to maintain the ceasefire and to seek a negotiated solution to the Basque situation. As the documents revealed, the division within the organization was so marked that the members were unable to overcome their differences. The result of Assembly VIII was that Proposal A was approved by 70 percent of the voting membership of the organization. The remaining 30 percent who had supported Proposal B split from the organization. ETA-pm divided into two new organizations: ETA-pm VIII Assembly and ETA-pm VII Assembly.

This chapter has also examined the significance of the Assembly and the arguments that were advanced. On its face, Proposal A appeared to be quite irrational. It proposed an escalated armed campaign, even though the Basque people had demonstrated through protest marches and strikes that a large proportion of the society opposed political violence. The proposal also argued that it would be possible to convert EE to supporting a political-military strategy through propaganda.[82] EE had not only shown its opposition to ETA-pm and ETA-m's actions through public and private criticism, it had also formalized its rejection of violence in the Aketegi proposal. Thus, the idea that the coalition could be persuaded into supporting a new campaign of violence was implausible.

Perhaps the key to understanding why this impractical proposal was approved lies in examining the alternative. Proposal B was to maintain the ceasefire. For an organization that was struggling financially and losing both

[81] Soldevilla, "Agur a las armas," 74.
[82] ETA-pm, "Ponencia A," 33–34.

capabilities and personnel, this could have been interpreted as being as good as "liquidationism." To support Proposal B could have been seen as a tacit acceptance of the argument that ETA-pm no longer had a role to play in Basque politics and that its dissolution was inevitable. For many members of ETA-pm, this may have been an unacceptable position to take. The only alternative to organizational dissolution was to pursue an aggressively militaristic strategy. The fact that this was not a viable means of advancing the goals that ETA had formed to pursue may not have weighed as heavily as the concern that the organization would be dispersed. In the next chapter, I conclude the case study with a discussion of the trajectory of ETA-pm VII Assembly and ETA-pm VIII Assembly and an analysis of what their histories reveal about the validity of both proposals and the majority decision to revert to radicalism.

11
The Aftermath

In this chapter I provide a brief overview of the trajectory of ETA-pm after Assembly VIII. I first discuss the minority ETA-pm VII Assembly group that dissolved in exchange for amnesty.[1] I then follow ETA-pm VIII Assembly, the majority group that supported Proposal A and called an end to the ceasefire. In this chapter I argue that the brief history of ETA-pm after Assembly VIII reveals several things. The first is that any militants who viewed Proposal B as "liquidationism" were in fact correct. The Septimos dissolved their organization the same year as the split. Many former Septimos joined EE, and others took advantage of the government's reintegration program to return to civilian life.

The other insight that can be drawn is that Proposal A was as impractical as it appeared on its face. EE took little time to denounce the organization, which indicated that the Octavos' plan to convince EE of the value of terrorism was at best wishful thinking. The loss of support from the political party left the Octavos isolated and vulnerable. The members who were not detained, defected. They joined either the reintegration program or ETA-m. I argue in this chapter that a legitimate desire to maintain the organization led most members to approve an impractical and ill-conceived proposal. There was a clear reason why the majority adopted an unworkable position. While it may have appeared irrational to continue fighting when the political and social trends in the Basque Country favored democracy, the alternative was to accept the dissolution of the organization. For most members, this was an acceptable option.

ETA-pm VII Assembly (the Septimos)

After their split from the majority Octavos, the Septimos held another meeting that they termed the second part of Assembly VII. At this gathering

[1] Domínguez, "El fin de ETA político militar," 13.

Euskadi Ta Askatasuna. Nell Bennett, Oxford University Press. © University of Maryland National Consortium for the Study of Terrorism and Responses to Terrorism (START) (2025). DOI: 10.1093/9780197764268.003.0011

they reconfirmed the Otsagabia proposal and their intention to maintain the ceasefire while they negotiated with the Spanish government. However, by September 1982 the Septimos officially announced the dissolution of their organization. Twelve leaders, who included most of the leadership of the former ETA-pm, held a press conference in Biarritz in the French Basque Country.[2] The representatives of the Septimos encouraged other militants to participate in the reintegration program. The spokesperson for the group was Miren Alkorta, who read the following statement:

> The draft resolution of amnesty measures presented by EE and the PNV in the Parliament of Euskadi (the legitimate representative of the Basque people) causes us to present our official dissolution at this time. We want our organisational decision and the fact that we have achieved an honourable solution to the issue of the prisoners and exiles to be taken into account by the rest of the armed organisations. The armed struggle of ETA has already fulfilled its role.[3]

After the press conference, the former members of the Septimos celebrated their decision to lay down their arms with a dinner party attended by several hundred people, including the leaders of EE. According to the newspaper *El Pais,* the dinner was followed by emotional speeches and hugs. Many former militants took the opportunity to request entry into EE. Halfway through the dinner, several hooded men caused a commotion by storming into the room carrying a banner that read "We do not regret." They then turned the banner to reveal the message ". . . being in EE." This provoked laughter and applause from those gathered.[4]

Miren Alkorta participated in several interviews after the dissolution of the organization. Speaking with *El Pais* she gave her view on the utility of armed struggle:

> . . . the polymilis [ETA-pm] already said in our seventh assembly . . . that armed struggle is not a lucky charm, but something that can also be co-opted and used by the oligarchy. And this is the case now. Armed struggle

[2] Barberia, "El precio de la Libertad"; Barberia, "El mosaico de las organizaciones"; Soldevilla, "Agur a las armas," 87.
[3] Giacopucci, *ETA-pm: El otro camino*, 244.
[4] Ridruejo, "Vamos a integrarnos."

> today plays mainly in favour of coups and destabilisation and its effects in this new stage are, in my opinion, much more negative than positive.[5]

Alkorta, a leader who had participated in numerous ETA-pm debates, restated the view that in the existing climate, political violence could be exploited by the right and used as a justification for repression. For this reason, she and her husband, another ETA leader, voted for Proposal B. They both took advantage of the reintegration program to return to civilian life.[6]

Around 300 militants participated in the government's reintegration initiative. EE helped them to find housing and employment. The Septimos did not collaborate with police, apologize for their past actions, or make amends in any other way. The Spanish government did not require any demonstrations of remorse from the demobilized militants. They adopted this permissive approach to ensure that the maximum number of militants accepted the reintegration program. The government also opened the program to any members of ETA, either ETA-pm or ETA-m, who were willing to participate.[7] Speaking of the program, EE leader Bandres said:

> The term repentant terrorists . . . has not caught on in the Basque Country in relation to the Septimos. On the contrary, the latter have been welcomed with respect even in highly radicalised environments. According to many observers, this illustrates a significant evolution of the Basque political situation.[8]

Soldevilla argued that the reintegration program was so successful that the Octavos and ETA-m were concerned that their members would also choose to lay down their arms. In response, the Octavos made death threats against demobilized militants and their lawyers. They tried to socially ostracize former members after they returned to their villages by organizing physical assaults and inflammatory graffiti and by setting fire to their cars. ETA-m even went as far as to kill two of its former members who joined the program: Miguel Francisco Solaun Angulo in February 1984 and María Dolores González Catarain (also known as "Yoyes") in September 1986.[9]

[5] Barberia, "Miren Alkorta."
[6] Ibid.
[7] Soldevilla, "Agur a las armas," 90.
[8] Iñesta, "'Los que Volvieron a Casa,'" 39.
[9] Soldevilla, "Agur a las armas," 89.

ETA-pm VIII Assembly (the Octavos)

After Assembly VIII and the division of ETA-pm, the majority of the organization's members sided with the Octavos. This also included most of the incarcerated ETA-pm members.[10] The Octavos signaled their decision to break the ceasefire by placing a bomb on the Bilbao electrical grid. However, aside from this they did not engage in any further terrorism for several months.[11] In the summer of 1982, the Octavos committed a series of kidnappings to raise funds for the organization. Josu Ugarte Gastaminza estimated that the organization was able to raise somewhere between 6 and 6.5 million euros, in the currency of 2016.[12]

Despite the fact that EE had renounced armed action, the Octavos had continued to support them in the hope that the radical faction within the party, the New Left, would eventually be able to revive the political military strategy.[13] As part of this continued support, they issued a communication to EE in which they offered what they termed their constructive criticism of EE's attitude and its failure to accommodate the views of the New Left faction in its decision-making processes. The communication argued that the behavior of EE was resulting in "its progressive distancing from the political spectrum of the nationalist left," as well as deepening "the internal unrest in the party."[14] The Octavos also encouraged the New Left to split from EE. However, the New Left spokesperson put an end to that plan by declaring that they would not become the Octavos' political wing and that they were against armed action.[15] This left the Octavos with no political affiliation. Their response was to make threats against EE leaders Bandrés and Onaindia, whom they labeled as traitors.[16]

The loss of political support left the Octavos vulnerable to government repression. In the words of one of the leaders of the Octavos, Josu Abrisketa Korta, also known as "Txutxo", "the repression hit us hard, the political allies were depressed and despite all this, we launched a strong offensive almost desperately in 1983; fundamental objective was in our sights: to discredit,

[10] Barberia, "El mosaico de las organizaciones."
[11] Giacopucci, *ETA-pm: el otro camino*, 234; Gastaminza, *La bolsa y la vida*.
[12] Gastaminza, *La bolsa y la vida*.
[13] Soldevilla, "Agur a las armas," 90.
[14] ETA-pm, "Comunicado de la organizacion," 125.
[15] Soldevilla, "Agur a las armas," 91.
[16] Iñesta, "'Los que Volvieron a Casa,'" 37.

dismantle, put an end to the disastrous policy of repentance."[17] However, by early 1983 there was a further division within the ranks of the Octavos. A subset of about twenty of their members defected and formed a new group called the ETA-pm KAS line or the "milikis." This group was in favor of joining ETA-m.[18]

ETA-m would only allow the milikis to join their organization on two conditions. The first was that they had to demonstrate that could carry out attacks without the infrastructure of the Octavos. The second condition was that they apply as individuals, not as a group. The milikis agreed to these conditions and committed seven attacks. They then dissolved their organization, and in February 1984 they individually sought entry into ETA-m.[19] One of those miliki members, Arnaldo Otegi, went on to become the spokesperson for ETA-m's political party, Herri Batasuna.[20] At the time of writing, Otegi was the General Secretary of the Basque nationalist party EH Bildu, which was a leading left-wing nationalist party in the Basque Country.[21]

Throughout 1983, a steady stream of Octavo members defected and joined the reintegration program.[22] The remaining Octavos were plagued with internal tensions and divisions. One of their responses to this was to kidnap their own members who they suspected of defection.[23] On September 27, several members detained five members of the organization who wanted to take up the government's reintegration offer. They were held for ten days and made to sign, at gunpoint, a document in which they agreed not to carry out any activity for a year.[24] In 1984 the majority of the remaining members of the Octavos decided to dissolve their organization. In the official declaration of their dissolution, the Octavos placed the blame for their failure on EE. They argued that the EE took advantage of the "prestige of armed struggle" and its financial reward to advance their political project, while all the time they were preparing for the dissolution of the armed organization.[25] The Octavos described the history of ETA-pm as "a dark and dirty history on the part of the EE, a betrayal of the Basque

[17] Soldevilla, "Agur a las armas," 91.
[18] Barberia, "El mosaico de las organizaciones."
[19] Soldevilla, "Agur a las armas," 92.
[20] Martínez and Pagola, "Arnaldo Otegi."
[21] EH Bildu, "Nor Gara?"
[22] Barberia, 'Miembros de grupos activos."
[23] Iñesta, "'Los que Volvieron a Casa,'" 37.
[24] Efe, "Miembros de ETApm secuestraron."
[25] ETA-pm, "ETApm-ren autodisolbatzea."

Workers and a struggle for personal interests.... Meanwhile, in the bureaucracy of the party, vicious competition was taking place to seize positions of responsibility in the apparatus. . . ."[26]

The main leaders of the Octavos, including Txutxo Abrisketa, went into voluntary exile over the following years. Most ended up living in Cuba. The remaining members suffered continuous arrests until the last remaining commando was detained in March 1985. A few members continued in a nonmilitant capacity and issued occasional statements. They were absorbed into ETA-m in 1992.[27]

Conclusion

This chapter has provided a brief overview of the aftermath of Assembly VIII. It has shown that the Septimos voluntarily dissolved their organization in September of the same year. This may explain why around 70 percent of the voting members of ETA-pm had rejected their strategy. The Octavos, however, did not fare much better. Their organization subsisted until 1984. It could be argued that it persisted, albeit in a purely nominal form, until 1992. However, the group was politically ostracized and the target of state repression. Most of its members were either arrested or defected. Many joined ETA-m and were able to continue to operate as militants until 2011.

The conclusions that can be drawn from this brief history is that most ETA-pm members adopted an ill-conceived course of action because they perceived it as the best, or perhaps the only, way to maintain the integrity of their organization. After years of developing a pragmatic political-military philosophy, the majority of members made the apparently irrational move of approving a strategy that was patently impractical. Yet, if one considers the choices they faced at the time, it is easy to see that many could have considered this to be the only possible alternative to dissolution.

[26] Ibid.
[27] Efe, "Miembros de ETApm secuestraron."

12
Conclusion

This book began with a puzzle: why is it that so many terrorists choose to continue using violence beyond the point at which they can reasonably expect to achieve a meaningful victory? To provide an answer, I combined organizational theory with rational choice explanations of terrorism to create the organizational survival approach to terrorism. According to this approach, terrorist groups will prioritize organizational maintenance over their espoused political objectives. This causes them to persist with losing causes for longer than conventional rational choice analyses would predict.

I argue that although terrorist organizations form with the objective of advancing the political goals of their base, over time this objective is supplanted by internal goals that are related to organizational expansion and maintenance. The publicly professed goals can be pursued in tandem with the internal organizational goals until these goals conflict. When this occurs, organizational survival will prevail over the terrorist's professed political goals. This point of conflict is foreseeable, as terrorist groups usually form to bring about social change that would render their own existence redundant.[1] I argue, therefore, that terrorist groups that have had sufficient success to be able to exact political concessions from the government may find themselves in a situation in which they will have to choose between their political objectives and maintaining their organization.

In support of this argument, I have examined one branch of the Basque separatist group ETA, called ETA-politico-militar, or ETA-pm. Internal documents produced by ETA-pm enabled me to examine the internal decision-making processes of this organization for a period of six years, between 1976 and 1982. While these documents covered a wide range of topics and issues, I have focused on the organization's decision-making regarding their use of violence. A remarkable feature of ETA-pm is that they kept detailed records of their debates. These were highly confidential but were distributed among the militants so that all active members of the organization were abreast of

[1] Beckett, "Future of Insurgency," 265.

Euskadi Ta Askatasuna. Nell Bennett, Oxford University Press. © University of Maryland National Consortium for the Study of Terrorism and Responses to Terrorism (START) (2025). DOI: 10.1093/9780197764268.003.0012

developments in the organization's strategic and philosophical orientation. Of relevance to this study are the transcripts from the debates on the utility of armed action, in which the members gave their frank opinions on the strategic options that were available to the organization.

The results of this analysis are striking. In 1976, ETA-pm took a pragmatic approach to armed struggle by establishing a legitimate political party that would work to bring about political change within the new Spanish democracy. In Assembly VII, the organization resolved to subordinate their armed action to the political party's strategic direction. This continued to be ETA-pm's strategy until 1982. In that year, the organization found itself in a situation in which is it was condemned by its own political party and opposed by most Basque people.[2] At a crucial decision point, the members were asked to choose between a course of action that would result in the ultimate dissolution of the organization or to adopt a radical militant stance. The majority, approximately 70 percent of the members, adopted the latter position.

This radical about-face contradicts the orthodox rational choice prediction that militants will lay down their arms when the cost of continuing is outweighed by the benefits of disarming.[3] In this case, the militants who persisted relinquished the opportunity to participate in the generous demobilization agreement and to take up positions in Basque politics. They also chose to continue fighting in the knowledge that they had lost popular support and that the Spanish government would not accede to their demands. While this may appear to be irrational on its face, I argue that it is not so. The decision to continue fighting is readily explained by rational choice models if the terrorists' utility function is expanded to include the desirability of maintaining their organization. Once this is integrated into existing understandings of terrorist incentive structures, it is easy to understand why so many conflicts drag on beyond the point at which militants can reasonably expect to achieve a meaningful victory.

In this chapter, I provide a summary of the theoretical model employed in this book, the organizational survival approach. I then present a summary of the findings of the empirical section. I argue that this case study provides evidence of the applicability of goal displacement to a terrorist

[2] *El Pais*, "El terrorismo va a condenar."

[3] Abrahms, "What Terrorists Really Want"; Shapiro, "Terrorist Decision-Making," 6; Crenshaw, "The Causes of Terrorism," 380; Stohl, "Counterterrorism and Repression," 62; Muller and Weede, "Cross-National Variation," 625.

organization. This is followed by a discussion of the theoretical implications of this research. I argue that the accuracy of rational choice models of conflict duration and resolution can be enhanced by incorporating an expanded understanding of terrorist utility that encompasses the desirability of maintaining their organization and/or the benefits that accrue to them from their positions within that organization. I also discuss the implications for the literature on outbidding and spoiling. An interesting aspect of this research is that after the division of ETA into two rival armed organizations in 1974, the two groups did not engage in outbidding. Instead, ETA-pm became more moderate. This suggests that more attention should be paid to the phenomenon of "underbidding."[4]

This research also has implications for counterterrorism and DDR practitioners. I argue that parties concerned with conflict resolution and peace negotiations should understand that the terrorists have an interest in maintaining their organization. Therefore, the survival of the organization should be factored in as a benefit of continued conflict and should also be considered an additional cost of demobilization. Research on status quo bias and loss aversion has demonstrated that when faced with a choice, individuals disproportionately opt to maintain the status quo.[5] Accordingly, an attractive peace offering should be one that minimizes the terrorists' perception of disruption and loss through the dissolution of their organization.

This chapter concludes with a discussion of the limitations of this study and directions for future research. As this book uses one case study, it is not possible to make generalizable claims about the applicability of the organizational survival approach to terrorist and/or separatist organizations. I therefore encourage researchers to examine additional cases to assess the extent to which goals related to organizational maintenance displaced the group's original political objectives. I also discuss the limitations in building arguments based on documentary evidence. While this evidence gives the reader rare insights into the internal workings of a terrorist organization, there may be additional factors that influenced the organization's trajectory that were not recorded in the documents. Therefore, future researchers could combine documentary research with interviews with former terrorists to construct more accurate representations of the inner workings of terrorist organizations.

[4] Kydd and Walter, "Outbidding and Overproduction," 4.

[5] Samuelson and Zeckhauser, "Status Quo Bias"; Fernandez and Rodrik, "Resistance to Reform"; Kahneman and Tversky, "Prospect Theory"; Levy, "Prospect Theory," 89; Hancock, Weiss, and Duerr, "Prospect Theory and Framing," 185.

Summary of Findings

The history of ETA-pm is a clear example of the operation of goal displacement within a terrorist organization. ETA was originally formed in the late 1950s with the objective of protecting Basque culture and advancing the nationalist cause.[6] By the late 1970s, the organization needed to develop a new strategy to maintain its relevance and efficacy within the new democracy.[7] The political-military strategy was a means of tempering ETA's militant character.[8] It also enabled ETA-pm to continue to operate as it always had, as a clandestine armed organization, while reaping the benefits of participating in electoral politics.

Since the division of ETA into two separate groups in 1974, ETA-pm positioned itself as the more moderate and pragmatic organization. While ETA-pm was an illegal militant organization, the leadership took a restrictive view of violence. Armed action was only to be used in support of political objectives.[9] This was in contrast with ETA-m, which ETA-pm perceived as being overly militant and acting to the detriment of the movement. In the internal documents, ETA-pm's leaders emphasized the fact that their organization only used violence to advance and support the political objectives of Basque nationalism and to defend the political victories that had been achieved by the Basque people.[10]

In 1976, ETA-pm conducted an internal debate, known as Assembly VII, in which the members discussed the future of the organization. At the close of the debate, most ETA-pm members approved a plan to create a political party that would participate in the new democratic system. This was over the objections of the organization's internal militant faction, the Komando Bereziak. The Bereziak ultimately defected in protest over the decision.[11] However, despite this internal dissent, the majority of ETA-pm supported the political-military strategy.

By the early 1980s, the social and political climate had changed in the Basque Country. The nation had transitioned from a right-wing, centralist

[6] Muro, "ETA: Basque Nationalist and Separatist Organization"; Barros, "Intervention Analysis of Terrorism," 402.
[7] ETA-pm, "El Partido de los Trabajadores," 1.
[8] Calvo, "Izquierda abertzale," 383–384.
[9] Iñesta, "'Los Que Volvieron A Casa,'" 31.
[10] ETA-pm, "El Partido de los Trabajadores."
[11] Komando Bereziak, "Comunicado Denuncia de ETA."

dictatorship to a democracy that recognized limited regional autonomy.[12] The Basque Country had been granted a degree of self-determination, and its representatives were seated in the national parliament in Madrid.[13] Basque people were allowed to freely express their culture and language and organize in labor unions.[14] In consequence, most Basque people opposed terrorist violence. They made their opposition known by participating in anti-ETA protests and strikes. This sentiment was echoed by prominent Basque intellectuals and sections of the liberal Basque press.[15] In addition, the peace movement was gaining strength in Basque politics.[16]

The crucial implication of these developments was that political violence would no longer bring about the desired political change. Members of ETA-pm explicitly stated in the debates that they were aware that in the existing climate, attacks would not bring about the desired results. This was because the Spanish government would be able to join the Basque government and even ETA-pm's affiliated party, EIA, in condemning any use of terrorist tactics. Using violence in the early 1980s in the Basque Country would do little more than position ETA-pm as the enemy of the Basque people. The result of this was that by 1981 ETA-pm found itself at a crossroads. The fundamental premise of its strategic direction was that it would use violence only to advance political objectives, yet its own political party was publicly denouncing all forms of armed action. The organization could either continue with the ceasefire, with a view to dissolving the organization under favorable terms, or break with its political party and re-establish itself as a militant group.

The members of ETA-pm gathered for three debates over 1981–1982 to discuss these possibilities and decide on the future of the organization. The results of the final debate show that 70 percent of the membership of ETA-pm chose to continue within the armed organization.[17] Not only that, the majority approved a position paper that advocated for a more radical stance than that which the organization had held in 1974. The approved proposal

[12] Meisler, "Spain's New Democracy"; Sánchez-Navarro and Vale, "Political Transition of the Francoist Cortes," 8.

[13] Atienza, "Autonomy of the Basque Country," 5–6.

[14] Lasagabaster, "Language Use," 66.

[15] El Correo Español, El Pueblo Vasco, "Intellectuales Vascos," 11.

[16] Bibiloni, "Movilizaciones pacifistas," 229–230.

[17] ETA-pm, *Zutik*, 13.

included plans to create an army and to "accumulate violence" in a manner reminiscent of the declarations that ETA had made before the organization divided into ETA-pm and ETA-m.[18]

Proposal A, which most of the organization approved, was disconnected from the political and social reality of the Basque Country in 1982. It was a return to the radical stance the organization had held under the dictatorship, which had been motivated and justified by the repressive policies of the central government. The majority position did not reflect the changes that had occurred in the Basque Country over the preceding six years.[19] The decision to adopt this proposal could therefore be considered irrational. However, it is only irrational if the majority of ETA-pm held their political goals to be their organizational priority.

Viewed in the context of organizational survival, the terrorists made a rational choice. This was to preserve the integrity of their organization. Proposal B took full account of the public opposition to armed action and the opportunities that were available in the new liberal democracy. In that regard it was the more pragmatic proposal. However, it advocated maintaining the ceasefire even though the organization was suffering.[20] Without recourse to violence, ETA-pm was unable to generate revenue or attract recruits. In the meantime, its existing members were vulnerable to arrest. Therefore, the ultimate outcome of Proposal B would be the dissolution of ETA-pm.

Proposal A advocated for a course of action that was at once ambitious and radical. A key aspect of this proposal was that it stated that under this strategy there would be no further ceasefires and no concessions made to the Spanish government.[21] The plan was to create a perpetual organization that would operate as the Basque national army.[22] In that regard, it was the very antithesis of Proposal B. It also provided an assurance to the members that their positions within the organization would continue and that their power and responsibilities would increase. I argue, therefore, that the reason 70 percent of the members of ETA-pm selected Proposal A was that their priority was organizational survival and that this was more important than advancing the Basque nationalist cause.

[18] ETA-pm, "Ponencia A," 20; ETA, *Kemen*.
[19] ETA-pm, "Enmienda a la Ponencia Orreaga," 7.
[20] ETA-pm, "Ponencia B," 61–62.
[21] ETA-pm, "Ponencia A," 33.
[22] Ibid., 26.

Implications for Rational Choice Theory

The results of this book have implication for rational choice analyses of conflict resolution. I argue that the rational choice calculations often employed in terrorism studies do not provide an accurate prediction for conflict resolution. However, this is not because rational choice theory itself is at fault. I argue that a key part of the terrorist organization's utility has been neglected, that is, the desirability of maintaining their organization. Once this is included in the terrorists' utility function, analysts should be able to make more accurate predictions about conflict resolution.[23] Conventional rational choice understandings of terrorism hold that terrorists should lay down their arms when the cost of continuing outweighs the benefits that could be obtained from persisting. Some scholars have argued that terrorists will not continue if they can see that victory is unattainable and there is a preferable alternative to conflict.[24] I argue that this understanding of incentive structures is incomplete. This is because they overlook the changes that occur in collections of individuals when they form organizations.

According to organizational theory, the benefits that group membership bestows on individuals causes them to form an attachment to their position within the organization.[25] This notion was discussed by Mancur Olson, who used the term "selective incentives" to describe the special benefits that are afforded to group members.[26] Terry M. Moe elaborated on Olson's theory and found selective incentives to be superior to general group goals as member inducements.[27] These incentives can be material but may also include intangible benefits, such as a sense of purpose and dedication to a cause.[28] The desire to preserve these benefits needs to be included in the incentive structures of terrorist organizations and of individual militants.

This research is also significant for studies of terrorist tactics. An interesting aspect of the empirical material is that it shows that ETA-pm took a rational and instrumental view of violence. Violence was just a tool that the

[23] For a discussion of expanding the utility function in rational choice theory, see Lindenburg and Fey, "Alternatives, Frames and Relative Prices," 191–205.

[24] Chai, "'An Organizational Economics Theory,'' 99–110.

[25] Tolbert and Hiatt, "On Organizations and Oligarchies."

[26] Olson, *Logic of Collective Action*.

[27] Moe, *Organization of Interests*, 35.

[28] Wood, "Emotional Benefits of Insurgency"; Morrow and Meadowcroft, "Rise and Fall of the English Defence League," 547–548; Gauja, "Construction of Party Membership," 238–239; Malešević and Ó Dochartaigh, "Why Combatants Fight."

organization could use, in the same way that strikes, civil disobedience, and ceasefires were tools.[29] This supports the research that argues that political violence is just one of a number of alternatives that terrorists have at their disposal.[30]

However, violence also served organizational purposes. By 1981, ETA-pm was organizationally weakened by the ceasefire. So long as it did not engage in violence it could not raise funds or attract new recruits. One of the arguments made by the proponents of Proposal A was that if the ceasefire were to continue, the organization would lose its capacity to engage in armed action.[31] Thus, violence was necessary for organizational maintenance. This contradicts the research that argues that terrorists will refrain from using violence if it consistently fails to achieve the group's political goals or if legitimate means of enacting change become available.[32] In this case, the ability to maintain operations was prioritized over political objectives, and violence was used in pursuit of that goal.

Implications for Research on Outbidding

The results of the empirical study are also relevant for the literature on outbidding. In 1976, ETA-pm was in a weakened condition and facing external competition. However, the organization chose to become more moderate, rather than radicalizing. After the split with ETA-m and after ETA-pm had been infiltrated by a mole, the organization was left with barely one active commando unit.[33] And yet, most of the members approved the Otsagabia Proposal and decided to subordinate its armed activities to the strategic direction that would be set by the new political party. What makes this even more significant is that it took place during a period of regime shift in which the future political direction of Spain was uncertain.

According to the literature on outbidding, these three factors—organizational weaknesses, competition, and uncertainty—should have caused

[29] ETA-pm, "Debate I," 38.
[30] Abrahms, "What Terrorists Really Want," 81.
[31] ETA-pm, "Debate III," 2.
[32] For example, Matthew Valasik and Matthew Phillips argue that ISIS shifts from instrumental violence to symbolic violence when instrumental violence fails to deliver the desired results: Valasik and Phillips, "Understanding Modern Terror," 197.
[33] Soldevilla, *Historia de una Heterodoxia Abertzale*, 111.

ETA-pm to become more radical.[34] A weakened organization could be expected to use violence to demonstrate strength and resolve in order to attract recruits and resources.[35] Competition should instigate more brutal attacks to establish the organization as the most credible challenger.[36] And during a transitional period, terrorists may be expected to use violence as a means of securing a position of influence in the new political order.[37]

However, between the years 1976 and 1981, ETA-pm progressively moderated their strategy. One argument for this could be that ETA-pm was engaging in "underbidding" to gain a greater share of popular support than their more militant rival, ETA-m. Andrew Kydd and Barbara F. Walter observed back in 2009 that the outbidding literature frequently overlooks the fact that there could also be process of underbidding. This would occur when terrorist groups are in competition, but the public is known to want peace. In such scenarios, the rival organizations would try to become more moderate to win popular support.[38] However, underbidding has not received the same scholarly attention as outbidding.[39]

This case, however, does not fit neatly within the underbidding theory either. This is because while ETA-pm and their political party EE became more moderate, ETA-m maintained its radical militant strategy, as did the Komando Bereziak. Another possible explanation is that the theory of outbidding is not applicable to this case. Michael G. Findley and Joseph K. Young have suggested that outbidding may not be as generally applicable as Kydd and Walter and Mia M. Bloom suggest.[40] While not discounting the outbidding theory altogether, they cautioned against generalizing from specific case studies, writing: "[f]uture research could explore case-specific characteristics more systematically, but our results clearly suggest that the outbidding argument may not be generalizable to a wide variety of countries and conflicts."[41] This adds further weight to the argument for more detailed

[34] Shapiro, "Terrorist Decision-Making," 8; Kydd and Walter, "Strategies of Terrorism"; Bloom, "Palestinian Suicide Bombing"; Findley and Young, "More Combatant Groups, More Terror?," 707.

[35] Del Pino, "Family, Culture, and 'Revolution,'" 168

[36] Chenoweth, "Democratic Competition."

[37] Fein, "More Murder in the Middle," 173–174.

[38] Kydd and Walter, "Outbidding and Overproduction," 4.

[39] The underbidding phenomenon was referred to in a recent paper from Vogt, Gleditsch, and Cederman, "From Claims to Violence," in which they say that "one promising avenue for future research . . . would be a systematic analysis of the causes and consequences of de-escalation in terms of movement demands. . . .".

[40] Kydd and Walter, "Outbidding and Overproduction," 4.

[41] Findley and Young, "More Combatant Groups, More Terror?," 719.

case study analyses of different conflicts. Fine-grained examinations of terrorist organizations from a range of geographic and historical contexts are needed to ascertain which phenomena are truly generalizable.

Levels of Analysis

Another implication of this research is that it demonstrates that organizations are more than just the sum of their members. I argue that it is the organizational structure and the individual's position within that structure that alters their incentives. Thus, while individual terrorists may have joined the movement for a variety of motives, from idealism to anger to boredom to greed, once they are assigned a role within the organization, they begin to develop an interest in maintaining and advancing that position.[42]

Laia Balcells and Patricia Justino observed that there is an emphasis on macro-level research in civil war and insurgency studies, that is, research that takes place at the level of the sovereign state. This has been tempered with an increase in micro-level studies that have focused on individuals and households. Recent applications of organizational approaches have also expanded the meso-level research.[43] Research at this level of analysis "connects individuals and households with larger communities and broader processes."[44] Anthony Vinci argues that analyses conducted at the group level may be able to provide valuable explanations for conflict persistence that cannot be found at other levels of analysis.[45] Vinci found that organizations' need to survive and accrue power was one such explanation.[46] Balcells and Justino note that one difficulty in bridging levels of analysis is "the identification and isolation of the precise mechanisms, whereby macro-level processes (e.g., peace negotiations, the employment of different warring technologies, and recruitment patterns) may affect actors, institutions, and processes at the micro level."[47] This book has demonstrated that micro and meso-level processes can also affect macro-level processes. The history of

[42] Michels, *Political Parties*, 353.

[43] Examples of meso-level studies of insurgency include: Shapiro, *The Terrorist's Dilemma*; Shapiro and Siegel, "Moral Hazard, Discipline, and Management"; Gates, "Recruitment and Allegiance"; Staniland, *Networks of Rebellion*; Staniland, "Organizing Insurgency"; Bueno de Mesquita, "Terrorist Factions"; Pearlman, "Spoiling Inside and Out."

[44] Balcells and Justino, "Bridging Micro and Macro Approaches," 1344.

[45] Vinci, "Greed-Grievance Reconsidered," 27.

[46] Vinci, *Armed Groups and the Balance of Power*, 37–38.

[47] Balcells and Justino, "Bridging Micro and Macro Approaches," 1345–1346.

ETA-pm has shown that decision processes that took place at individual and group levels caused most of the organization to refuse to participate in the demobilization agreement and to continue to engage in political violence. It is therefore possible that studies that seek to test micro-level theories with macro data overlook processes that occur at the meso level. Thus, key processes in decision-making may be overlooked.

Valuable insights could also be gained from conducting civil war research from the levels of analysis employed in organizational ecology. In that field, the lowest level of analysis is that of the organization, the meso level is that of the population of organizations, meaning the different organizations operating in a particular area.[48] In terrorism studies, this could refer to all the rival terrorist organizations in one particular conflict. Meso-level organizational studies would examine the density of these organizations, their relationships with one another, and the growth and decline of the population as a whole. Macro-level studies, or macro-evolutionary approaches, concern the emergence and the disappearance of particular organizational forms.[49] Studies at the macro-level could allow researchers to take a broader view of the kinds of organizations that engage in terrorism in specific historical periods with a view to identifying their unique drivers.

Implications for Counterterrorism

Contemporary counterterrorism practice is premised on the assumption that terrorists want what they claim to want.[50] Accordingly, if their demands are met, they will lay down their arms.[51] On the other hand, if they can be shown that they have no prospect of achieving their objectives, they should also disband. This assumption explains much of contemporary counterterrorism strategy.[52] Deterrence, target-hardening, punitive sanctions, and incentives for defection and demobilization are examples of approaches that

[48] Carroll, "Organizational Ecology," 72.

[49] Ibid. Examples of the macroevolutionary approach include Skocpol, "Review: Wallerstein's World Capitalist System."

[50] Hazelton, "The 'Hearts and Minds' Fallacy"; Lichbach, "Deterrence or Escalation?"; Fortna, "Do Terrorists Win?"; Kydd and Walter, "Strategies of Terrorism," 52; Kilcullen, "Countering Global Insurgency."

[51] Mason, "Insurgency, Counterinsurgency"; Brym and Andersen, "Rational Choice and Political Bases," 483; Fitzsimmons, "Hard Hearts and Open Minds?"

[52] Gawthorpe, "All Counterinsurgency Is Local," 848; Cramer, "Homo Economicus Goes to War," 1845.

are premised on conventional rational choice calculations of individual and group utility.[53]

The assumption that terrorists should lay down their arms when the cost of engaging in violence outweighs the benefits developed out of rational choice criminology. The argument was that crime could be reduced by increasing the perceived effort and risk of the crime while reducing rewards and justifications.[54] This notion, referred to as deterrence, is prevalent in social policy and criminal law, as well as in military strategy and nuclear doctrine.[55] Yet research on the efficacy of repression and deterrence is mixed.[56] Some have even argued that it does not work. Laura Dugan and Erica Chenoweth have observed that "empirically, unwanted behaviors continue—and indeed often increase—despite the threat of punishment."[57]

One reason why counterterrorists may find deterrence and repression to yield suboptimal results is that they are based on an incomplete understanding of the terrorists' incentive structures. If the terrorists' primary goal is the maintenance of their organization, repression would encourage the terrorists to shore up their organizational resources and use the government's repressive policies in propaganda to encourage recruitment. Indeed, literature on terrorist mobilization has shown that repression can have the undesired effect of increasing popular sympathy and function as a mobilizing tool.[58] This is because external threat is one of the most powerful motivating and unifying factors for an identity group.[59]

The organizational survival approach can explain why many terrorist groups actively seek to provoke incumbent forces into disproportionate reactions.[60] So-called propaganda of the deed has been a popular tactic since it was brought into prominence by anarchist terrorists in the late nineteenth century.[61] It may appear to be irrational for terrorists to encourage the opposition to inflict indiscriminate and brutal attacks on the people that they

[53] Schultz, "Breaking the Will of the Enemy"; Friedman, "End of Counterinsurgency"; Galula, *Counterinsurgency Warfare*, 4; Dixon, "Hearts and Minds?"; Hack, "Everyone Lived in Fear."

[54] Becker, "Crime and Punishment"; Felson and Clarke, "Opportunity Makes the Thief," vi.

[55] Dugan and Chenoweth, "Moving Beyond Deterrence," 597.

[56] Opp and Roehl, "Repression, Micromobilization," 523.

[57] Dugan and Chenoweth, "Moving Beyond Deterrence," 597–598.

[58] Miller, "Confronting Terrorisms," 332.

[59] Condit, *Case Study in Guerrilla War*, 267–268; Sanchez-Cuenca and de la Calle, "Domestic Terrorism," 42; Molnar, *Human Factors Considerations*, 169.

[60] Sanchez-Cuenca and de la Calle, "Domestic Terrorism," 41.

[61] Molnar, *Human Factors Considerations*, 169.

claim to be defending. Yet, such attacks may benefit the organization by providing popular support, resources, personnel, and legitimacy.[62] Thus, if the maintenance and expansion of the organization is the terrorists' primary goal, it is entirely rational for them to provoke the government into indiscriminate violence.

Implications for Conflict Resolution

One factor that peace brokers should bear in mind when constructing demobilization agreements is that dismantling a terrorist organization involves a loss to the members. Once the organization is dissolved, the members will be deprived of a range of tangible and intangible benefits. These losses may be more pronounced among the leadership, who would also be the key decision makers in a peace negotiation process.[63] According to Daniel Kahneman and Amos Tversky, individuals weigh losses more heavily than gains.[64] This is even more pronounced in decisions taken under risk.[65] In such circumstances, individuals would be expected to be hesitant to accept even-chance gambles, unless the potential payoffs are very generous. Kahneman and Tversky found that in many cases people will only accept an even-chances gamble if the payoff is at least double the loss.[66] Loss aversion is particularly salient when the reference point against which the potential loss is measured is the status quo. Any disadvantages to alternatives to the status quo have been found to also be weighted more heavily than advantages. This causes the phenomenon known as status quo bias, which is highly significant for conflict resolution.[67]

As Robert Jervis states, loss aversion can explain why people "persevere in losing ventures much longer than standard rationality would lead one to expect."[68] Jervis argues that this theory is particularly relevant for conflict and international bargaining.[69] Kahneman and Tversky applied the concepts of loss aversion and status quo bias to conflict resolution and

[62] Lichbach, "Deterrence or Escalation?"
[63] Morrison, "Some Notes Toward Theory."
[64] Weyland, "Latin American Economic Restructuring"; Kahneman et al. "The Endowment Effect."
[65] Kahneman and Tversky, "Prospect Theory."
[66] Kahneman and Tversky, "Conflict Resolution," 738.
[67] Masatlioglu and Ok, "Rational choice"; Samuelson and Zeckhauser, "Status Quo Bias in Decision Making"; Fernandez and Rodrik, "Resistance to Reform."
[68] Jervis, "Political Implications of Loss Aversion," 190.
[69] Ibid., 192.

developed the term "concession aversion." They observed that in peace negotiations, the most effective concessions a party can make are ones that reduce the opponent's losses.[70] However, to effectively implement this, negotiators need to understand exactly what it is that the opponent values and what they stand to lose. If key terrorist decision makers will lose positions of power and influence by agreeing to demobilize, an effective concession could be to grant them positions of greater power and influence within legitimate political parties or similar activist organizations. Negotiators also need to be mindful of the losses that will be suffered by the rank and file. A common occurrence in peace agreements is that the leadership and a large proportion of the membership may agree to accept the terms, but a section of the militancy continues with armed action.[71] Therefore, the benefits must be tailored to the wider membership. Such generous concessions may be politically unpopular but could result in more durable peace.

It is important to note that loss is not limited to material factors. Intangible and psychological processes also play a key role in individuals' decisions to lay down their arms or continue fighting. Militants may lose an aspect of their identity by demobilizing. In a study of FARC militants, Rachel Schmidt found that the "fighter identity" was highly significant for ex-combatants. Thus, government policies that attempted to eliminate this identity were counterproductive. Schmidt argued that in order to understand the efficacy of dembolization and reintegration programs, "it is not enough to study why combatants abandon armed groups—we must also understand why other combatants stay and how they make sense of those choices."[72]

The dissolution of an organization will also result in a loss of collective identity. A significant intangible benefit that group members receive is camaraderie and companionship. This is amplified in a terrorist or militant organization. Discussing the Colombian group ELN, Barbara Gruber and Jan Pospisil observed, "The members are divided into small units in which they work, live and fight. This creates lasting ties and group cohesion. Combat, of course, also has an unequivocal impact on the unity of the organization." Within a terrorist organization, group identity is created in

[70] Kahneman and Tversky, "Conflict Resolution," 739–740.

[71] For example, see Dnes and Brownlow, "Formation of Terrorist Groups," and Okado-Gough, "Coiste na n-Iarchimí," 149–150.

[72] Schmidt, "Contesting the Fighter Identity," 52.

opposition to the government, which is perceived as the enemy. This makes it even more difficult for members to accept demobilization offers, even if such offers seem generous to impartial observers.[73]

Limitations and Future Research

The research I have presented in this book is not without its limitations. Perhaps the most significant of these is that it only uses one case study. There are inherent dangers in making claims based on a single case.[74] The case may be an outlier or there could be contextual factors that set it apart from other similar cases. An analysis of one case cannot provide confirmation of a theory, and indeed, I did not set out to make any definitive claims. Instead, I present proof of concept. It is an analysis of one terrorist organization that demonstrates that goal displacement can be applied to terrorism. I also use this case to argue that this theory could have significant implications for counterterrorism and conflict resolution theory and practice.

Another limitation of this study is that it only analyzes ETA-pm's decision processes as they can be understood from the internal documents. Most of these documents, such as the minutes and transcripts, were made contemporaneously with the decision points that they describe. They are remarkably candid documents, and they even record criticisms of the leadership. Yet, it is impossible to obtain the full story from documents alone. Factors including the personalities of members, internal loyalties, and alliances may also have had significant impacts on the decisions reached. Indeed, this was suggested by the author of the anonymous letter that criticized the process of the final debates. As the author stated: "Private cliques and clubs are created" and "[t]hey only listen to attack quickly and forcefully the 'other position.'"[75] This indicates that there may have been additional factors that affected the conduct of the final debates that are not apparent in the documents.

These limitations aside, I would encourage more researchers to analyze the ETA documents. In this project, I have examined more than 2,000 documents produced by ETA and its affiliated organizations. However, this is

[73] Gruber and Pospisil, "Ser Eleno," 238.
[74] For a discussion of the benefits and dangers of theory generation from a single case study see Armato and Caren, "Mobilizing the Single-Case Study."
[75] "Criticas al Debate y Algunas Propuestas," 1.

just a small portion of the material that is available for analysis. In addition, I have approached these documents with a narrow focus. My objective has only been to analyze ETA-pm's strategic decision-making processes regarding their use of violence. In these papers, the members discuss a broad range of organizational, social, and political issues that would provide valuable insights for the study of terrorism and political violence. They discuss target selection, their relationships with rival organizations, popular support, propaganda, and branding. Comparisons can also be made between the paths taken by ETA-pm and ETA-m. There is important knowledge that can be gained from this material that is beyond the scope of this book.

Another advantage of analyzing the ETA documents, or the archives of other militant groups, is that they provide the researcher with fine-grained data. Archival research and analysis of documentary records "gets the researcher behind the closed doors that are so hard to penetrate as a participant observer" and gives them "insight into processes that are largely unseen by participant observers . . . the researcher is able to draw back the curtain on multiple and long-term decision processes to understand and appreciate the complexity of individual behaviors."[76] As noted above, there are limitations to basing a research project on documents alone. Researchers could complement their analyses of the ETA documents with interviews with former members who were present at the debates. This could provide additional insights into ETA's internal politics and dynamics.

Researchers could also investigate the validity of the organizational survival model in other organizations. Such studies could take the form of single case studies, comparative cases, or studies that examine a larger selection of conflicts.[77] One possible approach would be to compare persistent conflicts with conflicts of shorter duration. Robert Jervis has noted that actors who chose to cut their losses early in a conflict may be of less historical significance and could therefore have fallen into obscurity. Long, drawn-out conflicts may be more salient, which could bias the population.[78] Therefore, a comparison between both long and short conflicts could generate important findings. Nevertheless, persistent conflicts have been a feature

[76] Frisch and Kelly, "Political Science and Archival Research," p. 42.
[77] Christopher Paul, Colin P. Clarke, Beth Grill, and Terrance Savitsky discuss the benefits of "medium-*n*" analyses of insurgencies in: Paul et al., "Between Large-*N* and Small-*N* Analyses."
[78] Jervis, "Political Implications of Loss Aversion," 190.

of modern warfare.[79] In this book, I have proffered an explanation for this phenomenon that reconciles the apparently irrational behavior of terrorist organizations. Further applications of organizational theory to the study of conflict will enable researchers to understand the conditions under which conflicts can be resolved and the requirements for constructing a lasting peace.

[79] Beckett, "Future of Insurgency," 261–262.

APPENDIX

A Guide to the ETA Documents

In this appendix I provide an overview of the documents that are used in this book, along with their location and access options.[1] These documents are available at various locations and are a valuable resource for researchers. The documents can be found in archives in the Basque Country, and certain documents can be found online and in a series of published volumes entitled *Documentos Y*. The resources described here are only the ones that are used in this book. There is a wealth of primary and secondary sources created by and related to ETA, which I encourage researchers to explore. At the end of this appendix, I have included references to additional archives in the Basque Country that hold collections related to ETA.

I have included this discussion of the ETA documents because it is my hope that this book inspires others to use them to further develop our collective understanding of terrorism, political violence, and conflict resolution. I encourage researchers to explore these sources and to build on the work presented in this book. The ETA documents provide a rare and unique insight into the operations of a terrorist organization. A wealth of knowledge can be gained from these documents. I also take this opportunity to acknowledge and to thank the archivists, librarians, and researchers who compile and safeguard these sources and make them available to scholars. Without their diligent work, many of these resources would have been lost.

A note on language—most of the ETA documents are written in Castilian Spanish. This includes the meeting minutes and position papers. More formal documents, including manifestos and communiques, were often written in both Spanish and Euskera. It is useful to remember that under the dictatorship, the use of Euskera was not permitted. Thus, many of the ETA members did not speak Euskera. The language subsisted in rural areas, and the formal linguistic unification process did not begin until 1968.[2] Therefore, researchers with a good understanding of Spanish should not be deterred from consulting the ETA documents.

Internal Documents

The analyses presented in this book rely in large part on the internal documents produced by ETA-pm. Much like legal organizations, ETA kept detailed records of its internal processes. ETA held regular "assemblies" or meetings, beginning in 1962. In the lead-up to these meetings, questions were often put to the militancy. The leaders requested submissions from cells and members and in some years from rival groups and associated legal organizations such as political parties and labor unions. These papers were

[1] The best and most thorough discussion of primary sources related to ETA is Soldevilla, Barandiaran, and Casanellas, "La documentación de (y sobre) ETA." I am indebted to the authors for their detailed explanation of the different categories of documents created by the various branches of ETA.

[2] Gaseni and Manuel, "Basque Language."

collected, distributed, and debated at the meetings. Agendas were set and minutes were taken. Resolutions were written up with justifications and were distributed among the militancy.

The result of these bureaucratic processes is that detailed records exist for many of ETA's internal debates. Much of this material is kept in the Lazkaoko Beneditarren Fundazioa, or the Lazkao Benedictine Foundation. This archive houses the ETA Collection, which comprises materials compiled by Aita Juan José Agirre. Some of these documents were donated to the Foundation by former ETA members. In such cases, these donations were anonymous and were made with the desire of preserving internal records from ETA that were never intended to see the light of day. The Lazkao Foundation holds a vast collection of ETA documents, much more than I was able to analyze for this book. The materials range primarily from the mid-1960s to the mid-1980s. The archive also holds a large collection of communiques, bulletins, newsletters, and manifestos, as well as media reports from the period.[3]

Newsletters and Bulletins

ETA used internal newsletters and bulletins to distribute material to the militancy. These publications often presented compilations of debate questions, position papers, records of the debates, and the decisions that were taken. The publication that I relied on most frequently was *Kemen*. *Kemen* was an internal bulletin produced by ETA between 1966 and 1973, and by ETA-pm between 1974 and 1982.[4] The *Kemen* collection provides an accessible means for researchers to conduct targeted or chronological investigations. These publications are written in a combination of Spanish and Euskera. Some issues contain translations in French.

Another important internal newsletter is *Zutik*. ETA began publishing *Zutik* in 1960. When the organization split into ETA-pm and ETA-m in 1974, ETA-m continued to publish *Zutik*. This was replaced in 1978 by *Zutabe*, then by *Zuzen*, and finally, *Barne Buletina* (Internal Bulletin).[5] These newsletters are an excellent source of information on ETA-m and would be valuable tools for any researchers seeking to conduct a comparative analysis of ETA-pm and ETA-m.

Documentos Y

An excellent resource for researchers and for anyone interested in the history of ETA is the eighteen-volume series *Documentos Y*, produced by Editorial Lur, Hordago. This series compiles primary sources from ETA's genesis up until 1977. It contains a collection of internal documents, media reports, ephemera, and editorial commentary. It also includes excerpts from internal bulletins including *Kemen* and *Zutik*. Unfortunately, this collection is difficult to find. Complete sets can be found in the Lazkao Foundation and in the Spanish National Library in Madrid.

[3] Soldevilla, Barandiaran, and Casanellas, "La documentación de (y sobre) ETA," 35–36.
[4] Ibid., 39.
[5] Other groups and factions also used the name *Zutik* for certain publications. For a more detailed discussion, see Soldevilla, Barandiaran, and Casanellas, "La documentación de (y sobre) ETA," 34.

Online Sources

In addition to the archival holdings, some of the ETA documents can also be found online. The website Abertzale Komunista has a Marxist Library that contains a collection of ETA's internal documents and publications. including issues of *Kemen* and *Zutik*. At the time of writing, these useful resources could be found at: https://www.abertzalekomunista.net/es/relato-historico/historia-del-mlnv.

The Abertzale Komunista website enables readers to consult a selection of original documents, without having to travel to the Basque Country. This website also contains a back catalog of the Basque publication *Punto y Hora,* which sometimes featured ETA communiques and interviews: https://www.abertzalekomunista.net/es/relato-historico/historia-del-mlnv/publicaciones/punto-y-hora.

In addition to this, several of the Spanish newspapers have excellent online archives. At the time of writing this book, *El Pais* had a particularly user-friendly website that made it easy to access original newspaper reports related to ETA, https://elpais.com. Online newspaper archives assisted me in interpreting some of the internal documents. As the ETA documents were records that were only intended to be read by the membership, they often included obscure references to events of the time, sometimes with little more than a date or the name of a town as an identifier. By cross-checking these references in the digital news archives, I was able to better understand the recorded discussions.

Other Historical Centers

In this book, I focused primarily on the trajectory of ETA-pm from 1976 to 1982. Thus, most of the material that I used came from the Lazkao Foundation. However, this is not the only archive for researchers who are interested in the history of ETA. The Eusko Ikaskuntza (Society for Basque Studies) in Donostia has an archive of documents relating to Basque history. Researchers may also find valuable material in the Archivo de la Memoria Histórica de Euskadi (Archive of the Historical Memory of Euskadi). This is part of the Mario Onaindia Foundation, located in Zarautz, Gipuzkoa. Several provinces of the Basque Country, including Bizkaia, Gipuzkoa, and Alava, also have their own historical archives. This is by no means an exclusive list of archives with material relating to ETA but a suggestion of places where researchers can begin their investigations.

The ETA documents are highly valuable and underutilized resources for the study of terrorism and political violence. This may be due to the remote location of the materials or the common misconception that the documents are written primarily in Euskera. I have provided this brief guide to the ETA materials in the hope that it will encourage more scholars to investigate this organization. The research presented in this book examines just one aspect of ETA's trajectory. I hope that this work will encourage others to use the archives, libraries, and online sources to further develop our understanding of conflict onset, conflict persistence, and conflict resolution.

References

Abasolo, Jose Antonio. "ETApm reivindica la muerte del dirigente de UCD de Alava." *El Pais*, September 30, 1980. https://elpais.com/diario/1980/10/01/espana/339202812_850215.html.

ABC. "Con este Arsenal se Podria Armar a un Batallon." January 21, 1982. https://www.abc.es/archivo/periodicos/abc-madrid-19820121.html.

ABC. "La ETA-V Asamblea expulsa a dos de sus más carecterizados elementos." December 12, 1974. https://linz.march.es/Documento.asp?Reg=r-67437.

Abrahms, Max. "What Terrorists Really Want: Terrorist Motives and Counterterrorism Strategy." *International Security* 32, no. 4 (2008): 78–105.

Acosta, Benjamin. "Live to Win Another Day: Why Many Militant Organizations Survive Yet Few Succeed." *Studies in Conflict & Terrorism* 37, no. 2 (2014): 135–161.

Addison, Tony, and Mansoob S. Murshed. "Credibility and Reputation in Peacemaking." WIDER Discussion Paper, No. 2001/45. Helsinki: United Nations University World Institute for Development Economics Research (UNU-WIDER), 2001, 1–14.

Aizpeolea, Luis R. "¿Qué fue de Pertur?" *El Pais*, July 24, 2016. https://elpais.com/politica/2016/07/22/actualidad/1469210135_812147.html.

Aizpeolea, Luis R. "El primer retiro masivo de etarras." *El Pais*, September 30, 2012. https://elpais.com/politica/2012/09/28/actualidad/1348859835_831476.html.

Aldrich, Howard, and Ellen R. Auster. "Even Dwarfs Started Small: Liabilities of Age and Size and Their Strategic Implications." *Research in Organizational Behavior* 8 (1986): 165–198.

Aljazeera. "Colombia Accuses FARC Dissidents of Car Bomb that Injured Dozens." March 27, 2021. https://www.aljazeera.com/news/2021/3/27/colombia-accuses-farc-dissidents-of-car-bomb-that-injured-dozens.

Almond, Gabriel A., and Stephen J. Genco. "Clouds, Clocks, and the Study of Politics." *World Politics* 29, no. 4 (1977): 489–522.

Alonso, Rogelio. "Spain." In *Routledge Handbook of Terrorism and Counterterrorism*, edited by Andrew Silke, 593–603. London: Routledge, 2018.

Alonso, Rogelio. "The Modernization in Irish Republican Thinking Toward the Utility of Violence." *Studies in Conflict & Terrorism* 24, no. 2 (2001): 131–144.

Alonso, Rogelio. "Why Do Terrorists Stop? Analyzing Why ETA Members Abandon or Continue with Terrorism. *Studies in Conflict & Terrorism* 34, no. 9, 2011: 696–716.

Alonso, Rogelio. *The IRA and Armed Struggle*. Abingdon: Routledge, 2007.

Anderson, James. "Separatism and Devolution: The Basques in Spain." In *Shared Space: Divided Space: Essays on Conflict and Territorial Organization*, edited by Michael Chisholm and David M. Smith, 135–156. Abingdon: Routledge, 1990.

Anderson, Noel. "Why Victories in Battle Have Not Yet Finished the War Against al-Shabaab." *Survival: Global Politics and Strategy* 58, no. 4 (2016): 51–62.

Anderson, Paul A. "Decision Making by Objection and the Cuban Missile Crisis." *Administrative Science Quarterly* 28, no. 2 (1983): 201–222.

Anderton, Charles H., and John R. Carter. "On Rational Choice Theory and the Study of Terrorism." *Defence and Peace Economics* 16, no. 4 (2006): 275–282.

Ansar, Atif. "The Fate of Ideals in the Real World: A Long View on Philip Selznick's Classic on the Tennessee Valley Authority (TVA)." *International Journal of Project Management* 36, no. 2 (2018): 385–395.

Ansell, Chris, Arjen Boin, and Moshe Farjoun. "Dynamic Conservatism: How Institutions Change to Remain the Same." In *Institutions and Ideals: Philip Selznick's Legacy for Organizational Studies*, edited by Matthew S. Kraatz, 89–119. Emerald: Bingley, 2015.

Aquino, Marco. "Peru's Shining Path Rebels Kill at Least 16 Ahead of Vote Military." Reuters, May 25, 2021. https://www.reuters.com/world/americas/perus-shining-path-rebels-kill-least-14-ahead-vote-military-2021-05-24/.

Arce, Daniel G., and Todd Sandler. "Terrorist Signalling and the Value of Intelligence." *British Journal of Political Science* 37, no. 4 (2007): 573–586.

Arjona, Ana, and Stathis N. Kalyvas. "Rebelling Against Rebellion: Insurgent and Counterinsurgent Recruitment." Paper presented at the International Studies Association Annual Conference, Chicago, 2007. https://stathiskalyvas.files.wordpress.com/2016/01/arjonaandkalyvasrecruitment2008.pdf.

Armato, Michael, and Neal Caren. "'Mobilizing the Single-Case Study: Doug McAdam's Political Process and the Development of Black Insurgency, 1930–1970." *Qualitative Sociology* 25, no. 1 (2002): 93–103.

Arnold, Thurman W. *The Folklore of Capitalism*. New Haven, CT: Yale University Press, 1937.

Arreguín-Toft, Ivan. "How the Weak Win Wars: A Theory of Asymmetric Conflict." *International Security* 26, no, 1 (2001): 93–128.

Asal, Victor, and R. Karl Rethemeyer. "The Nature of the Beast: Organizational Structures and the Lethality of Terrorist Attacks." *Journal of Politics* 70, no. 2 (2008): 437–449.

Asal, Victor, Mitchell Brown, and Angela Dalton. "Why Split? Organizational Splits among Ethnopolitical Organizations in the Middle East." *Journal of Conflict Resolution* 56, no. 1 (2012): 94–117.

Atienza, Javier Corcuera. "The Autonomy of the Basque Country." *Fundacion para la Libertad* (2008): 5–6. https://paralalibertad.org/wp-content/uploads/InformeCompleto_Ingles.pdf.

Atkins, Stephen E. *Encyclopaedia of Modern Worldwide Extremists and Extremist Groups*. Westport, CT: Greenwood Press, 2004.

Atran, Scott. *Talking to the Enemy*. London: Penguin, 2010.

Auñamendi Eusko Entziklopedia. "MUGICA ARREGUI, Iñaki." Fund Bernardo Estornes Lasa. http://aunamendi.eusko-ikaskuntza.eus/en/mugica-arregui-inaki/ar-82614/.

Aviles, Juan. "'Experiencing Terrorism in Spain: The Case of ETA." In *Fighting Terrorism in the Liberal State*, edited by S. Peleg and W. Kempf, 40–47. Amsterdam: IOS Press, 2006.

Azkarraga, Josemari Velez de Mendizabal. "Juan Jose Agirre. Creador del Archivo de Lazkao: El instinto me hizo ver que el esfuerzo de emprender el trabajo del archivo iba a merecer la pena." *Zenbakia* https://www.euskonews.eus/zbk/552/juan-jose-agirre-creador-del-archivo-de-lazkao-el-instinto-me-hizo-ver-que-el-esfuerzo-de-emprender-el-trabajo-del/ar-0552002001C/#.

Bader, Araj. "Harsh State Repression as a Cause of Suicide Bombing: The Case of the Palestinian–Israeli Conflict." *Studies in Conflict & Terrorism* 31, no. 4 (2008): 284–303.

Bahney, Benjamin W., Radha K. Iyengar, Patrick B. Johnston, Danielle F. Jung, Jacob N. Shapiro, and Howard J. Shatz. "Insurgent Compensation: Evidence from Iraq." *American Economic Review* 103, no. 3 (2013): 518–522.

Bahney, Benjamin, Howard J. Shatz, Carroll Ganier, Renny McPherson, and Barbara Sude. *An Economic Analysis of the Financial Records of al-Qa'ida in Iraq*. Santa Monica, CA: RAND Corporation, 2010.

Bakke, Kristin M., Kathleen Gallagher Cunningham, and Lee J. M. Seymour. "A Plague of Initials: Fragmentation, Cohesion, and Infighting in Civil Wars." *Perspectives on Politics* 10, no. 2 (2012): 265–283.

Balcells, Laia, and Patricia Justino. "Bridging Micro and Macro Approaches on Civil Wars and Political Violence: Issues, Challenges, and the Way Forward." *Journal of Conflict Resolution* 58, no. 8 (2014): 1343–1359.

Balcells, Laia, and Stathis N. Kalyvas. "Does Warfare Matter? Severity, Duration, and Outcomes of Civil Wars." *ICIP Working Papers: 2012/5* (2012): 1–41.

Banholzer, Lilli. "When Do Disarmament, Demobilisation and Reintegration Programmes Succeed?" Discussion Paper No. 8/2014, Bonn: Deutsches Institut für Entwicklungspolitik (DIE), 2014.

Barber, William E., and John N. Taylor. "The Importance of Goals, Objectives, and Values in the Fisheries Management Process and Organization: A Review." *North American Journal of Fisheries Management* 10, no. 4 (1990): 365–373.

Barberia, Jose Luis. "El mosaico de las organizaciones terroristas vascas." *El Pais*, October 15, 1983. https://elpais.com/diario/1983/10/15/espana/435020405_850215.html.

Barberia, Jose Luis. "El precio de la Libertad." *El Pais*, January 27, 1985. https://elpais.com/diario/1985/01/27/espana/475628413_850215.html.

Barberia, Jose Luis. "ETA Político-militar VII Asamblea anuncia su disolución." *El Pais*, October 1, 1982. https://elpais.com/diario/1982/10/01/espana/402274806_850215.html.

Barberia, Jose Luis. "Miembros de grupos activos de ETA Político-militar abandonan el terrorismo y se acogen a la vía de la negociación." *El Pais*, October 14, 1983. https://elpais.com/diario/1983/10/14/espana/434934005_850215.html.

Barberia, Jose Luis. "Miren Alkorta: la vuelta a la normalidad de una 'liberada' de ETA." *El Pais*, October 10, 1982. https://elpais.com/diario/1982/10/11/espana/403138822_850215.html.

Barkey, Henri J., and Graham E. Fuller. *Turkey's Kurdish Question*. Lantham: Rowman and Littlefield, 1998.

Barragán, Carlos, and Roberto R. Ballesteros. "13 víctimas, dos parejas rotas . . . Las cloacas del atentado que ETA nunca quiso asumir." *El Confidencial*, November 11, 2018. https://www.elconfidencial.com/espana/2018-11-11/eta-atentado-rolando-calle-correo-1974_1642741/.

Barros, Carlos Pestana. "An Intervention Analysis of Terrorism: The Spanish ETA Case." *Defence and Peace Economics* 14, no. 6 (2003): 401–412.

BBC News. "Small Basque Bomb Explodes Despite ETA Ceasefire." September 16, 2010. https://www.bbc.com/news/world-europe-11325067.

BBC News. "Peru's Shining Path Defeated, Rebel Leader Admits." December 7, 2011. https://www.bbc.com/news/world-latin-america-16066029.

Becker, Gary S. "Crime and Punishment: An Economic Approach." In *Essays in the Economics of Crime and Punishment*, edited by Gary S. Becker and William M. Landes, 1–54. Cambridge, MA: National Bureau of Economic Research, 1974.

Beckett, Ian. "The Future of Insurgency." *Australian Army Journal* 5, no. 2 (2008): 261–278.

Bedeian, Arthur G. *Organizations: Theory and Analysis: Text and Cases*. 2nd ed. New York: Drysden Press, 1984.

Beetham, David. *Max Weber and the Theory of Modern Politics*. Cambridge: Polity Press, 1985.

Bekker, Martin. "Protest as an Act of Love." *International Journal of Zizek Studies* 15, no. 1 (2021): 1–33.

Bendor, Jonathan, and Terry M. Moe. "An Adaptive Model of Bureaucratic Politics." *American Political Science Review* 79, no. 3 (1985): 755–774.

Bentley, Arthur F. *The Process of Government: A Study of Social Pressures*. Chicago: University of Chicago Press, 1908.

Berdal, Mats, and David H. Ucko. "Introduction to the DDR Forum: Rethinking the Reintegration of Former Combatants." *International Peacekeeping* 20, no. 3 (2013): 316–320.

Berkowitz, Leonard. "Whatever Happened to the Frustration-Aggression Hypothesis?" *American Behavioral Scientist* 21, no. 5 (1978): 691–708.

Berman, Eli, Jacob N. Shapiro, and Joseph H. Felter. "Can Hearts and Minds Be Bought? The Economics of Counterinsurgency in Iraq." *Journal of Political Economy* 119, no. 4 (2011): 766–819.

Biberman, Yelena, and Farhan Zahid. "Why Terrorists Target Children: Outbidding, Desperation, and Extremism in the Peshawar and Beslan School Massacres." *Terrorism and Political Violence* 31, no. 2 (2016): 169–184.

Bibiloni, Irene Moreno. "Movilizaciones pacifistas en el País Vasco: Los inicios de Gesto por la Paz." *Revista de Paz y Conflictos* 8, no. 2 (2015): 227–242.

Bischof, Daniel, and Simon Fink. "Repression as a Double-Edged Sword: Resilient Monarchs, Repression and Revolution in the Arab World." *Swiss Political Science Review* 21, no. 3 (2015): 377–395.

Bloom, Mia M. "Palestinian Suicide Bombing: Public Support, Market Share, and Outbidding." *Political Science Quarterly* 119, no. 1 (2004): 61–88.
Boeker, Warren. "The Development and Institutionalization of Subunit Power in Organizations." *Administrative Science Quarterly* 34, no. 3 (1989): 388–410.
Bolleyer, Nicole. "The Irish Green Party: From Protest to Mainstream Party?" *Irish Political Studies* 25, no. 4 (2010): 603–623.
Bosi, Lorenzo, and Donatella Della Porta. "Micro-mobilization into Armed Groups: Ideological, Instrumental and Solidaristic Paths." *Qualitative Sociology* 35 (2012): 361–383.
Bosi, Lorenzo, and Donatella Della Porta. "Processes of Disengagement from political Violence: A Multilevel Relational Approach." In *Researching Terrorism, Peace and Conflict Studies*, edited by Ioannia Tellidis and Harmonie Toros, 81–100. Abingdon: Routledge, 2015.
Boucek, Françoise. "Rethinking Factionalism: Typologies, Intra-Party Dynamics and Three Faces of Factionalism." *Party Politics* 15, no. 4 (2009): 455–485.
Boudreau, Vincent. "State Repression and Democracy Protest in Three Southeast Asian Countries." In *Social Movements: Identity, Culture and the State*, edited by David S. Meyer, Nancy Whittier, and Belinda Robnett, 28–46. New York: Oxford University Press, 2002.
Boukhars, Anouar. "The Logic of Violence in Africa's Extremist Insurgencies." *Perspectives on Terrorism* 14, no. 5 (2020): 117–129.
Bourne, Angela K. "Political Parties and Terrorism: Why Ban Batasuna?" Paper presented at Elections, Public Opinion and Parties Annual Conference, University of Exeter, September 9–11, 2010. http://www.exeter.ac.uk/media/universityofexeter/research/microsites/epop/papers/Bourne_-_Political_Parties_and_Terrorism.pdf.
Braithwaite, John, and Bina D'Costa. *Cascades of Violence: War, Crime and Peacebuilding across South Asia*. Acton: Australian National University Press, 2018.
Bray, Zoe. "Basque Militant Youths in France: New Experiences of Ethnonational Identity in the European Context." In *Political Transformation and National Identity Change*, edited by Jennifer Todd, Lorenzo Cañás Bottos, and Nathalie Rougier, 219–239. London: Routledge, 2008.
Brenner, David. "Recognition and Rebel Authority: Elite-Grassroots Relations in Myanmar's Ethnic Insurgencies." *Contemporary Politics* 23, no. 4 (2017): 408–426.
Brym, Robert J., and Robert Andersen. "Rational Choice and the Political Bases of Changing Israeli Counterinsurgency Strategy." *British Journal of Sociology* 62, no. 3 (2011): 482–503.
Bueno de Mesquita, Ethan. "Terrorist Factions." *Quarterly Journal of Political Science* 3 (2008): 399–418.
Buharg, Halvard. "Dude, Where's My Conflict?: LSG, Relative Strength, and the Location of Civil War." *Conflict Management and Peace Science* 27, no. 2 (2012): 107–128.
Buhaug, Halvard, and Kristian Skrede Gleditsch. "Contagion or Confusion? Why Conflicts Cluster in Space." *International Studies Quarterly* 52, no. 2 (2008): 215–233.
Bulut, Ercan. "A Checkmate, Not a Stalemate: Turkey versus the PKK." Master's thesis, Naval Postgraduate School, Monterey, CA, 2014.

Burch, Michael. "Natural Resources and Recurrent Conflict: The Case of Peru and Sendero Luminoso." Washington, DC: United States Institute of Peace, 2013.

Burns, Tom. "Massive Basque Protests Reject ETA Terrorism.", *Washington Post*, February 11, 1981. https://www.washingtonpost.com/archive/politics/1981/02/11/massive-basque-protests-reject-eta-terrorism/a6a7fe8e-6ada-4a97-be3a-9663cd4a91e1/.

Byman, Daniel, Peter Chalk, Bruce Hoffman, William Rosenau, and David Brannan. *Trends in Outside Support for Insurgent Movements*. Santa Monica, CA: RAND Corporation, 2001.

Caballero, José Antonio Rubio. "Los Nacionalistas Vascos y Catalanes Ante La Loapa: Ajustes y Desajustes En Los Inicios Del Estado De Las Autonomías." *Historia Actual Online*, no. 5 (2004): 65–80.

Cála, Andres. "Is the End Near for Basque Separatist Group ETA?" *Time*, September 25, 2010. https://content.time.com/time/world/article/0,8599,2021333,00.html.

Calvo, Rafael Leonisio. "Izquierda abertzale: De la heterogeneidad al monolitismo." *Historia de Nuestro Tiempo* (2012): 377–388.

Cameron, Kim S. "Effectiveness As Paradox: Consensus and Conflict in Conceptions of Organizational Effectiveness." *Management Science* 32, no. 5 (1986) 539–553.

Cameron, Kim. "Critical Questions in Assessing Organizational Effectiveness." *Organizational Dynamics* (1980): 66–80.

Caplan, Bryan. "Terrorism: The Relevance of the Rational Choice Model." *Public Choice* 128 (2006): 91–107.

Carroll, Glenn R. "Organizational Ecology." *Annual Review of Sociology* 10 (1984): 71–93.

Carty, R. K. "Parties as Franchise Systems: The Stratarchical Organizational Imperative." *Party Politics* 10, no. 1 (2004): 5–24.

Casanova, Iker. *ETA, 1958–2008: Medio siglo de historia*. Tafalla: Txalaparta, 2007.

Ceberio, Jesús. "Fusión de ETA-militar y los comandos especiales." *El Pais*, September 30, 1977. https://elpais.com/diario/1977/09/30/espana/244422022_850215.html.

Cederman, Lars-Erik, Nils B. Weidmann, and Kristian Skrede Gleditsch. "Horizontal Inequalities and Ethnonationalist Civil War: A Global Comparison." *American Political Science Review* 105, no. 3 (2011): 478–496.

Chai, Sun-Ki. "An Organizational Economics Theory of Antigovernment Violence." *Comparative Politics* (1993): 99–110.

Chang, Wen-Lung. "A Study of Political Coercion in Urban Taiwan." PhD diss., Northwestern University, 1972.

Chenoweth, Erica, and Jay Ulfelder. "Can Structural Conditions Explain the Onset of Nonviolent Uprisings?" *Journal of Conflict Resolution* (2015):1–27.

Chenoweth, Erica. "Democratic Competition and Terrorist Activity." *Journal of Politics* 72, no. 1 (2010):16–30.

Chun, Young Han, and Hal G. Rainey. "Goal Ambiguity and Organizational Performance in U.S. Federal Agencies." *Journal of Public Administration Research and Theory* 15, no. 4 (2005): 529–557.

Cicourel, Aaron V. "The Front and Back of Organizational Leadership: A Case Study." *Pacific Sociological Review* 1, no. 2 (1958): 54–58.

Clark, Burton R. "Organizational Adaptation and Precarious Values: A Case Study." *American Sociological Review* 21, no. 3 (1956): 327–336.

Clark, Robert P. *The Basques, the Franco Years and Beyond.* Reno: University of Nevada Press, 1979.

Clayton, Govinda. "Relative Rebel Strength and the Onset and Outcome of Civil War Mediation." *Journal of Peace Research* 50, no. 5 (2013): 609–622.

Cohen, Michael D., James G. March, and Johan P. Olsen. "A Garbage Can Model of Organizational Thought." *Administrative Science Quarterly* 17, no. 1 (1972): 1–25.

Collard-Wexler, Simon. "Understanding Resistance to Foreign Occupation." PhD diss., Columbia University, 2013.

Collier, David, and James Mahoney. "Insights and Pitfalls: Selection Bias in Qualitative Research." *World Politics* 49 (1996): 56–91.

Collier, Paul, and Nicholas Sambanis, eds. *Understanding Civil War, Volume 1: Africa.* Herndon, VA: World Bank Publications, 2005.

Collier, Paul, Anke Hoeffler, and Nicholas Sambanis. "The Collier-Hoeffler Model of Civil War Onset and the Case Study Project Research Design." In *Understanding Civil War, Volume 1: Africa*, edited by Paul Collier and Nicholas Sambanis, 1–34. Herndon, VA: The World Bank, 2005.

Condit, D. M. *Case Study in Guerrilla War: Greece during World War II.* Washington, DC: Special Operations, 1961.

Connable, Ben, and Martin C. Libicki. *How Insurgencies End.* Santa Monica, CA: RAND Corporation, 2010. https://apps.dtic.mil/sti/pdfs/ADA519917.pdf.

Conrad, Justin, and Kevin Greene. "Competition, Differentiation, and the Severity of Terrorist Attacks." *Journal of Politics* 77, no. 5 (2015): 546–561.

Cordes, Bonnie, Bruce Hoffman, Brian M. Jenkins, Konrad Kellen, Sun Moran, and William Sater. *Trends in International Terrorism 1982 and 1983.* Santa Monica, CA: RAND Corporation, 1984. https://www.rand.org/content/dam/rand/pubs/reports/2005/R3183.pdf.

Council on Foreign Relations. "Understanding Intrastate Conflict," May 16, 2023. https://world101.cfr.org/understanding-international-system/conflict/understanding-intrastate-conflict.

Cramer, C. "Homo Economicus Goes to War: Methodological Individualism, Rational Choice and the Political Economy of War." *World Development* 30, no. 11 (2002): 1845–1864.

Crenshaw, Martha. "Terrorism Research: The Record." *International Interactions* 40, no. 4 (July 2014): 556–567. https://doi.org/10.1080/03050629.2014.902817.

Crenshaw, Martha. "The Causes of Terrorism." *Comparative Politics* 13, no. 4 (1981): 379–399.

Crenshaw, Martha. "Theories of Terrorism: Instrumental and Organizational Approaches." *Journal of Strategic Studies* 10, no. 4 (1987): 13–31.

Crenshaw, Martha." "How Terrorism Declines." *Terrorism and Political Violence* 3, no. 1 (1991) 69–87.

"Criticas al Debate y Algunas Propuestas," 1982." Euskadi ta Askatasuna (ETA) Bilduma (1960–2018) ETA_B, 01.02. Debate interno (1960–1982). Lazkaoko Beneditarren Fundazioa Dokumentazio Gunea, Lazkao, Gipuzkoa.

Crocker, Chester A. *Taming Intractable Conflicts.* Washington, DC: United States Peace Press, 2004.

Cronin, Audrey Kurth. "How Al-Qaida Ends: The Decline and Demise of Terrorist Groups." *International Security* 31, no. 1 (2006): 7–48.

Crosby, Faye. "A Model of Egoistical Relative Deprivation." *Psychological Review* 83, no. 2 (1976): 85–113.

Cunningham, David E. "Veto Players and Civil War Duration." *American Journal of Political Science* 50, no. 4 (2006): 875–892.

Cunningham, David E. *Barriers to Peace in Civil Wars.* New York: Cambridge University Press, 2011.

Cunningham, David E., Kristian Skrede Gleditsch, and Idean Salehyan. "It Takes Two: A Dyadic Analysis of Civil War Duration and Outcome." *Journal of Conflict Resolution* 53, no. 4 (2009): 570–597.

Cunningham, Kathleen Gallagher, Kristin M. Bakke, and Lee J. M. Seymour. "Shirts Today, Skins Tomorrow: Dual Contests and the Effects of Fragmentation in Self-Determination Disputes." *Journal of Conflict Resolution* 56, no. 1 (2012): 67–93.

Cunningham, Kathleen Gallagher. "Actor Fragmentation and Civil War Bargaining: How Internal Divisions Generate Civil Conflict." *American Journal of Political Science* 57, no. 3 (2013): 659–672.

Daly, Sarah Zukerman. "The Dark Side of Power-Sharing: Middle Managers and Civil War Recurrence." *Comparative Politics* 46, no. 3 (April 2014), 333–353.

Davis, David R., and Michael D. Ward. "They Dance Alone: Deaths and the Disappeared in Contemporary Chile." *Journal of Conflict Resolution* 34, no. 3 (1990): 449–475.

Daxecker, Ursula E., and Michael Hess. "Repression Hurts: Coercive Government Responses and the Demise of Terrorist Campaigns." *British Journal of Political Science* 43, no. 3 (July 2013): 559–577. https://doi.org/10.1017/S0007123412000452.

de Azua, Victorino Ruiz. "Manifestaciones y violentos incidentes en numerosas localidades del País Vasco." *El Pais*, February 14, 1982. https://elpais.com/diario/1982/02/14/espana/382489214_850215.html.

de la Calle, Luis. "Compliance vs. Constraints: A Theory of Rebel Targeting in Civil War." *Journal of Peace Research* 54, no. 3 (2017): 427–441.

Del Pino, H. Ponciano. "Family, Culture, and 'Revolution': Everyday Life with Sendero Luminoso." In *Shining and Other Paths: War and Society in Peru, 1980–1995*, edited by Steve J. Stern, 158–192. Durham, NC: Duke University Press, 1998.

Della Porta, Donatella. *Social Movements: Political Violence, and the State: A Comparative Analysis.* New York: Cambridge University Press, 1995.

DeNardo, James. *Power in Numbers: The Political Strategy of Protest and Rebellion.* Princeton, NJ; Princeton University Press, 1985.

DiMaggio, Paul J., and Walter W. Powell. "The Iron Cage Revisited: Institutional Isomorphism and Collective Rationality in Organizational Fields." *American Sociological Review* 48, no. 2 (1983): 147–160.

Divins, Thomas J. "Four Days that Transformed Spain 11-M Impact on Memory Recovery Examined through the Lens of Duality." Master's thesis, West Virginia University, 2016. https://core.ac.uk/download/pdf/230481446.pdf.

Dixon, Paul. "'Hearts and Minds'? British Counter-Insurgency from Malaya to Iraq." *Journal of Strategic Studies.* 32, no. 3 (2009): 353–381.

Dnes, Antony W., and Graham Brownlow." "The Formation of Terrorist Groups: An Analysis of Irish Republican Organizations." *Journal of Institutional Economics* (2017): 1–25.

Do, Quy-Toan, and Lakshmi Iyer. "Geography, Poverty and Conflict in Nepal." *Journal of Peace Research* 47, no. 6 (2020): 735–748.

Documentos Y, vol. 16. Donostia: Hordago, 1979.

Documentos Y, vol. 17., Donostia: Hordago, 1979.

Documentos Y, vol. 18., Donostia: Hordago, 1979.

Domínguez, Florencio. "El fin de ETA político militar." Fundacion Manuel Gimenez Abad, 2010, 1–15.

Doyle, Michael, and Nicholas Sambanis. "International Peacebuilding: A Theoretical and Quantitative Analysis." *American Political Science Review* 94, no. 4 (2000): 779–801.

Drago, William A. "Predicting Organisational Objectives: Role of Stakeholder Influence and Volatility of Environmental Sectors." *Management Research News* 21, no. 9 (1998): 16–28.

Drucker, Peter F. *Managing in Turbulent Times.* New York: Harper & Row, 1980.

Druckman, Daniel, and Cecilia Albin. "Distributive Justice and the Durability of Peace Agreements." *Review of International Studies* 37 (2011): 1137–1168.

Dudouet, Véronique. "Dynamics and Factors of Transition from Armed Struggle to Nonviolent Resistance." *Journal of Peace Research* 50, no. 3 (2013): 401–413.

Dugan, Laura, and Erica Chenoweth. "Moving Beyond Deterrence: The Effectiveness of Raising the Expected Utility of Abstaining from Terrorism in Israel." *American Sociological Review* 77, no. 4 (2012): 597–624.

Duhart, Philippe. "Directing Disengagement." *European Journal of Sociology* 57, no. 1 (2016): 31–63.

Dutton, Jane E. "Understanding Strategic Agenda Building and Its Implications for Managing Change." *Scandanavian Journal of Management Studies* 3, no. 1 (1986): 3–24.

Dutton, Jane E., and Janet M. Dukerich. "Keeping an Eye on the Mirror: Image and Identity in Organizational Adaptation." *Academy of Management Journal* 34, no. 3 (1991): 517–554.

Duva, Jesus. "La primera victima de ETA." *El Pais*, January 31, 2010. http://extranet.fundacionfernandobuesa.com/download/docs/pelpais_d0000938.pdf.

Eastin, Joshua, and Stephen T. Zech. "Joining the Counterinsurgency: Explaining Pro-Government Militia Participation in the Philippines." *Studies in Conflict and Terrorism* (2019): 1–25.

Edles, Laura Desfor. *Symbol and Ritual in the New Spain: The Transition to Democracy After Franco.* Cambridge: Cambridge University Press, 1998.

Efe. "Miembros de ETApm secuestraron a cinco de sus militantes que querían dejar las armas." *El Pais*, October 20, 1984. https://elpais.com/diario/1984/10/20/espana/467074813_850215.html.

Egido, José Antonio. *Viaje a la nada: principio y fin de Euskadiko Ezkerra*. Tafalla: Txalaparta, 1993.

EH Bildu. "Nor Gara?" https://ehbildu.eus/#norgara.

Eisenhardt, Kathleen M., and L. J. Bourgeois III. "Politics of Strategic Decision Making in High-velocity Environments: Towards a Midrange Theory." *Academy of Management Journal* 31, no. 4 (1988): 737–770.

Eisenhardt, Kathleen M., and Mark J. Zbaracki. "Strategic Decision Making." *Strategic Management Journal* 13 (1992): 17–37.

Eitb.eus. "30 años de la disolución de ETA pm." September 30, 2012. https://www.eitb.eus/es/noticias/politica/detalle/960982/30-anos-disolucion-eta-pm—30-aniversario-disolucion-eta-pm.

El Correo Español, El Pueblo Vasco. "Impresionante Manifestacion Contra la Violencia." October 29, 1978. http://www.gesto.org/archivos/201312/1.-19781029-prensa-manifa-pnv.pdf?0.

El Correo Español, El Pueblo Vasco. "Intellectuales Vascos Contra la Violence." May 17, 1980. http://www.gesto.org/archivos/201312/2.-19800527-prensa-llamamiento-intectuales.pdf?0.

El Diario Vasco. "El portero del 'Mondra' que patentó el 'aurrera bolie." February 26, 2017. https://www.diariovasco.com/politica/201702/26/portero-mondra-patento-aurrera-20170226011452-v.html.

El Español. "Qué sucedió hoy, 17 de enero: ETA libera a Julio Iglesias Puga y otras efemérides." January 17, 2019. https://www.elespanol.com/sociedad/efemerides/20190117/sucedio-eta-libera-julio-iglesias-puga-efemerides/368964176_0.html.

El Mundo. "Pedro I. Pérez Beotegui, dirigente de ETA." Obituarios. https://www.elmundo.es/elmundo/2008/03/11/obituarios/1205238407.html.

El Pais. "El Gobierno de Euskadi, dispuesto a asumir el mando y las funciones de policía en el País Vasco." April 16, 1981. https://elpais.com/diario/1981/04/16/espana/356220004_850215.html.

El Pais. "El terrorismo va a condenar a Euskadi al fascismo, dice Mario Onaindía." March 22, 1981. https://elpais.com/diario/1981/03/22/espana/354063610_850215.html.

El Pais. "ETA (p-m) reivindica el triple atentado de Madrid y anuncia de nuevas acciones. July 31, 1979. https://elpais.com/diario/1979/07/31/portada/302220004_850215.html.

El Pais. "ETA asume el asesinato de 13 personas en la calle del Correo de Madrid tras negarlo durante 44 años." November 7, 2018. https://elpais.com/politica/2018/11/06/actualidad/1541508078_589338.html.

El Pais. "ETA fracasa en su objetivo de buscar apoyo popular para su causa, según la CIA." June 25, 1981. https://elpais.com/diario/1981/06/25/espana/362268012_850215.html.

El Pais. "Huelga general y grandes manifestaciones populares contra el terrorismo de ETA en el País Vasco." February 10, 1981. https://elpais.com/diario/1981/02/10/espana/350607609_850215.html.

El Pais. "J. M. Bandrés: 'Mi sorpresa inicial se tornó en profunda consternación.'" July 31, 1979. https://elpais.com/diario/1979/07/31/espana/302220013_850215.html.

El Pais. "Puestos en libertad los monjes benedictinos detenidos por su relación con ETA." February 11, 2005. https://elpais.com/elpais/2005/02/11/actualidad/1108113423_850215.html.
Elbadawi, Ibrahim A., and Nicholas Sambanis. "External Interventions and the Duration of Civil Wars." *Policy Research Working Paper 2433*. New York: The World Bank, 2000, 1–20.
Emerson, Stephen A. "Desert Insurgency: Lessons from the Third Tuareg Rebellion." *Small Wars & Insurgencies* 22, no. 4 (2011): 669–687.
ETA. *Kemen*, no. 6 (1971). Abertzale Komunista. https://www.abertzalekomunista.net/es/relato-historico/historia-del-mlnv/publicaciones/kemen/2535-kemen-6-zk-1971.
ETA-m. "A Todo el Pueblo Vasco," 1975. *Documentos Y* 16 (1979), 300.
ETA-m. "Declaracion del Biltzar Tripia de ETA." *Punto y Hora*, June 28, 1977.
ETA-m. "Dos aportaciones de ETAm a la VII Asamblea1976." Abertzale Komunista. https://www.abertzalekomunista.net/es/relato-historico-2/historia-del-mlnv/vii-asamblea/documentos-vii-asamblea/657-dos-aportaciones-de-etam-a-la-vii-asamblea-1976.
ETA-m. "La Lucha Continua." *Punto y Hora*, no. 216 March 5–12, 1981, 26–29.
ETA-pm. "'ETApm-ren autodisolbatzea,'" February 1984. https://www.abertzalekomunista.net/es/relato-historico/historia-del-mlnv/viii-asamblea/documentos-viii-asamblea/659-etapm-ren-autodisolbatzea.
ETA-pm. "Adios as las Armas." *Punto y Hora*, no. 216 March 5–12, 1981. 21–26.
ETA-pm. "Carta a la militancia—interno," 1977. In *Documentos Y* 18 (1979): 504–505.
ETA-pm. "Comunicado de ETA. A la clase trabajadora y a todo el Pueblo Vasco," 1977. In *Documentos Y* 18 (1979): 524.
ETA-pm. "Comunicado de la organizacion sobre la actitud de EE," May 27, 1982. *Zutik*, no. 65, (1982). https://www.abertzalekomunista.net/images/Liburu_PDF/MLNV/VIII_BATZARRA/ZUTIK_65_zk.pdf.
ETA-pm. "Convocatorio a toda la militancia para la celebracion de una conferencia de cuadros," 1977. In *Documentos Y* 18 (1979): 483.
ETA-pm. "Critica a Ponencia B," 1982. Euskadi ta Askatasuna (ETA) Bilduma (1960–2018) ETA_B, 01.02. Debate interno (1960–1982). Lazkaoko Beneditarren Fundazioa, Lazkao, Gipuzkoa, Spain.
ETA-pm. "Debate desde la Base," 1981. Euskadi ta Askatasuna (ETA) Bilduma (1960–2018) ETA_B, 01.02. Debate interno (1960–1982). Lazkaoko Beneditarren Fundazioa, Lazkao, Gipuzkoa, Spain.
ETA-pm. "Debate I," 1981. Euskadi ta Askatasuna (ETA) Bilduma (1960–2018)ETA_B, 01.02. Debate interno (1960–1982). Lazkaoko Beneditarren Fundazioa, Lazkao, Gipuzkoa, Spain.
ETA-pm. "Debate II," 1981. Euskadi ta Askatasuna (ETA) Bilduma (1960–2018) ETA_B, 01.02. Debate interno (1960–1982). Lazkaoko Beneditarren Fundazioa, Lazkao, Gipuzkoa, Spain.
ETA-pm. "Debate III," 1982. Euskadi ta Askatasuna (ETA) Bilduma (1960–2018) ETA_B, 01.02. Debate interno (1960–1982). Lazkaoko Beneditarren Fundazioa, Lazkao, Gipuzkoa, Spain.

ETA-pm. "El Partido de los Trabajadores Vascos: Una necesidad urgente en la coyuntura actual." Apuntes de un debate sobre el Partido, 1976. Euskadi ta Askatasuna (ETA) Bilduma (1960–2018) ETA_B, 01.01.04. VII Asamblea (1976) (pm). Lazkaoko Beneditarren Fundazioa Dokumentazio Gunea, Lazkao, Gipuzkoa.

ETA-pm. "Enmienda a la Ponencia Orreaga," February 1982. Euskadi ta Askatasuna (ETA) Bilduma (1960–2018) ETA_B, 01.02. Debate interno (1960–1982). Lazkaoko Beneditarren Fundazioa, Lazkao, Gipuzkoa, Spain.

ETA-pm. "Euskal Herriari: ETA-ren Seigarren Biltzar Nagusiko bigarren zatiaren agyria," 1975. *Documentos Y* 16 (1979): 302.

ETA-pm. "Informe de una Reunion de Herrialdeburus," *Kemen* no. 15, 1977, Lazkaoko Beneditarren Fundazioa, Lazkao, Gipuzkoa, Spain.

ETA-pm. "Informe sobre la Conferencia de Cuandros, Mayo del 77 (Resumen de Actas), *Kemen*, no. 15 (1977): 3, Lazkaoko Beneditarren Fundazioa, Lazkao, Gipuzkoa, Spain.

ETA-pm. "Ponencia A," January 20, 1982. Euskadi ta Askatasuna (ETA) Bilduma (1960–2018) ETA_B, 01.02. Debate interno (1960–1982). Lazkaoko Beneditarren Fundazioa, Lazkao, Gipuzkoa, Spain.

ETA-pm. "Ponencia B," January 1982. Euskadi ta Askatasuna (ETA) Bilduma (1960–2018) ETA_B, 01.02. Debate interno (1960–1982). Lazkaoko Beneditarren Fundazioa, Lazkao, Gipuzkoa, Spain.

ETA-pm. "VIII Asamblea, Manifiesto de la VIII Asamblea de ETA al Pueblo Vasco,'" 1982. Euskadi ta Askatasuna (ETA) Bilduma (1960–2018) ETA_B. Lazkaoko Beneditarren Fundazioa Dokumentazio, Gunea Lazkao, Gipuzkoa.

ETA-pm. "VIII Asamblea." *Kemen*, no. 65 (1982). Abertzale Komunista. http://www.abertzalekomunista.net/images/Liburu_PDF/MLNV/VIII_BATZARRA/ZUTIK_65_zk.pdf.

ETA-pm. Boletin Interno, November 1980. Euskadi ta Askatasuna (ETA) Bilduma (1960–2018)ETA_B, 01.02. Debate interno (1960–1982). Lazkaoko Beneditarren Fundazioa Dokumentazio Gunea, Lazkao, Gipuzkoa.

ETA-pm. Boletin Interno, September 1980. Euskadi ta Askatasuna (ETA) Bilduma (1960–2018) ETA_B, 01.02. Debate interno (1960–1982). Lazkaoko Beneditarren Fundazioa Dokumentazio Gunea, Lazkao, Gipuzkoa.

ETA-pm. ETAren Agiria. Abertzale Komunista. http://www.abertzalekomunista.net/es/relato-historico-2/historia-del-mlnv/vii-asamblea/documentos-vii-asamblea/658-etaren-agiria-1974.

ETA-pm. ETAren VII Batzarra, 1976. Abertzale Komunista. http://www.abertzalekomunista.net/es/relato-historico-2/historia-del-mlnv/vii-asamblea/documentos-vii-asamblea/655-etaren-vii-batzarra-resena.

ETA-pm. *Hautsi* February 15, 1976. Lazkaoko Beneditarren Fundazioa Dokumentazio Gunea, Lazkao, Gipuzkoa.

ETA-pm. *Kemen*, no. 10 (1977). Lazkaoko Beneditarren Fundazioa Dokumentazio Gunea, Lazkao, Gipuzkoa.

ETA-pm. *Kemen*, no. 11 (1977). Lazkaoko Beneditarren Fundazioa Dokumentazio Gunea, Lazkao, Gipuzkoa.

ETA-pm. *Kemen*, no. 12 (1977). Lazkaoko Beneditarren Fundazioa Dokumentazio Gunea, Lazkao, Gipuzkoa.

ETA-pm. *Kemen*, no. 13 (1977). Lazkaoko Beneditarren Fundazioa Dokumentazio Gunea, Lazkao, Gipuzkoa.

ETA-pm. *Kemen*, no. 14 (1977). Lazkaoko Beneditarren Fundazioa Dokumentazio Gunea, Lazkao, Gipuzkoa.

ETA-pm. *Kemen*, no. 15 (1977). Lazkaoko Beneditarren Fundazioa Dokumentazio Gunea, Lazkao, Gipuzkoa.

ETA-pm. *Zutik*, no. 65 (1982). Abertzale Komunista. https://www.abertzalekomunista.net/images/Liburu_PDF/MLNV/VIII_BATZARRA/ZUTIK_65_zk.pdf.

Etxarri, Tonia. "Campaña del PNV para convencer al pueblo vasco de la inutilidad de la violencia." *El Pais*, April 14, 1981. https://elpais.com/diario/1981/04/14/espana/356047217_850215.html.

Etzioni, Amitai. "Mixed-Scanning: A "Third" Approach to Decision-Making." *Public Administration Review* 27, no. 5 (1967): 385–392.

Etzioni, Amitai. "Two Approaches to Organisational Analysis: A Critique and Suggestions." *Administrative Science Quarterly* 5, no. 2 (1960): 257–278.

Eustat. "1.7. Population by Place of Birth and Sex. Basque Country1970." Eustat: Population and Housing Census 1970. https://en.eustat.eus/elementos/ele0006000/17-population-by-place-of-birth-and-sex-basque-country/tbl0006047_i.html.

Fabbe, Kristin Elisabeth. "Disciples of the State: Secularization and State Building in the Former Ottoman World." PhD diss., Massachusetts Institute of Technology, 2012.

Fair, C. Christine. "Diaspora Involvement in Insurgencies: Insights from the Khalistan and Tamil Eelam Movements." *Nationalism and Ethnic Politics* 11, no. 1 (2005): 125–156.

Fearon, James D. "Rationalist Explanations for War." *International Organization* 49, no. 3 (1995): 379–414.

Fearon, James D., and David D. Laitin. "Ethnicity, Insurgency and Civil War." *American Political Science Review* 97, no. 1 (2003): 75–90

Fearon, James D., and David D. Laitin. "Weak States, Rough Terrain, and Large-Scale Ethnic Violence Since 1945." Paper presented at the 1999 Annual Meetings of the American Political Science Association, Atlanta, GA, September 1999.

Fein, Helen. "More Murder in the Middle: Life-Integrity Violations and Democracy in the World 1987." *Human Rights Quarterly* 17, no. 1 (1995): 170–191.

Felson, Marcus, and Ronald V. Clarke. "Opportunity Makes the Thief: Practical Theory for Crime Prevention." Police Research Series Paper 98, 1998. https://popcenter.asu.edu/sites/default/files/opportunity_makes_the_thief.pdf.

Fernandez, Gaizka. "The Origins of ETA: Between Francoism and Democracy, 1958–1981." In *ETA's Terrorist Campaign: From Violence to Politics, 1968–2015*, edited by Rafael Leonisio, Fernando Molina, and Diego Muro, 19–34. Abingdon: Routledge, 2017.

Fernandez, Raquel, and Dani Rodrik. "Resistance to Reform: Status Quo Bias in the Presence of Individual-Specific Uncertainty." *American Economic Review* 81, no. 5 (1991): 1146–1155.

Findley Michael G., and Joseph K. Young. "More Combatant Groups, More Terror?: Empirical Tests of an Outbidding Logic." *Terrorism and Political Violence* 25, no. 5 (2012): 706–721.

Fitzsimmons, Michael. "Hard Hearts and Open Minds? Governance, Identity and the Intellectual Foundations of Counterinsurgency Strategy." *Journal of Strategic Studies* 31, no. 3 (2008): 337–365.

Fleming, Stephen M., Charlotte L. Thomas, and Raymond J. Dolan." "Overcoming Status Quo Bias in the Human Brain." *Proceedings of the National Academy of Sciences* 107, no. 13 (2010): 6005–6009.

Fortna, Virginia Page. "Do Terrorists Win? Rebels' Use of Terrorism and Civil War Outcomes." *International Organization* 69, no. 3 (2015): 519–556.

Fortna, Virginia Page. "Does Peacekeeping Keep Peace? International Intervention and the Duration of Peace After Civil War." *International Studies Quarterly* 48 (2004): 269–292.

Fortna, Virginia Page. *Does Peacekeeping Work? Shaping Belligerents' Choices After Civil War*. Princeton, NJ: Princeton University Press, 2008.

Friedman, George. "The End of Counterinsurgency." *Real Clear World*, June 5, 2012. https://www.realclearworld.com/articles/2012/06/05/the_end_of_counterinsurgency_100074.html.

Friend, Julius W. *Stateless Nations: Western European Regional Nationalisms and the Old Nations*. New York: Palgrave Macmillan, 2015.

Frisch, Scott A., and Sean Q Kelly. "Political Science and Archival Research." In *Doing Archival Research in Political Science*, edited by Scott A. Frisch, Douglas B. Harris, Sean Q Kelly, and David C. W. Parker, 35–58. Amherst, NY: Cambria Press, 2012.

Gaertner, Gregory H., and S. Ramnarayan. "Organizational Effectiveness: An Alternative Perspective." *Academy of Management Review* 8, no. 1 (1983): 97–107.

Gaibulloev, Khusrav, James A. Piazza, and Todd Sandler. "Regime Types and Terrorism." *International Organization* 71, no. 3 (2017): 491–522.

Gallimore, Timothy. "Unresolved Trauma: Fuel for the Cycle of Violence and Terrorism." In *Psychology of Terrorism: Coping with the Continuing Threat*, edited by C. E. Stout, 67–93. Westport, CT: Praeger Publishers/Greenwood Publishing Group, 2004.

Galula, David. *Counterinsurgency Warfare*. Westport, CT: Praeger Security International, 2006.

Garcia, Jose Manuel Valdes. "La 'Kale Borroka' como Instrumento Politico Violento." *Revista Cientifica DOCRIM*, no. 2, 2019. https://dialnet.unirioja.es/servlet/articulo?codigo=7344467.

Gaseni, López, and José Manuel. "Basque Language—A History of Translation." *Encyclopaedia of Translation and Interpreting, AIETI*. https://www.aieti.eu/enti/basque_ENG/.

Gastaminza, Genoveva. "Duelo en Guipúzcoa por muerte de dos militantes de ETA." *El Pais*, March 10, 1977. https://elpais.com/diario/1977/03/10/espana/226796418_850215.html.

Gastaminza, Josu Ugarte. *La bolsa y la vida: La extorsión y la violencia de ETA contra el mundo empresarial.* Madrid: La Esfera de Libros, 2018.

Gates, Scott. "Recruitment and Allegiance: The Microfoundations of Rebellion." *Journal of Conflict Resolution* 46, no. 1(2002): 111–130.

Gauja, Anika. "The Construction of Party Membership." *European Journal of Political Research* 54 (2015): 232–248.

Gaus, John M. "A Theory of Organization in Public Administration." In *The Frontiers of Public Administration*, edited by John M. Gaus, Leonard D. White, and Marshall E. Dimock, 66–91. Chicago: University of Chicago Press, 1936.

Gawthorpe, Andrew J. "All Counterinsurgency Is Local: Counterinsurgency and Rebel Legitimacy." *Small Wars & Insurgencies* 28, no. 4–5 (2017): 839–852.

George, Alexander L., and Andrew Bennett. *Case Studies and Theory Development in the Social Sciences.* Cambridge, MA: MIT Press, 2004.

Georgiou, Petro. "The Goal Paradigm and Notes Towards a Counter Paradigm." *Administrative Science Quarterly* 18, no. 3 (1973): 291–310.

Gerring, John. 'What Is a Case Study and What Is It Good for?" *American Political Science Review* 98, no. 2 (2004): 341–354.

Gerth, H. J., and C. W. Mills. eds. *From Max Weber: Essays in Sociology.* New York: Oxford University Press, 1946.

Giacopucci, Giovanni." *ETA pm: El otro camino*, Tafalla: Txalaparta, 1997.

Giezendanner, Eliane, and Bert Ingelaere. "How to Understand Ex-Combatants' Political Participation Against the Background of Rebel-to-Party Transformations?" Discussion Paper/2021.02. Instituut voor Ontwikkelingsbeleid en-Beheer.

Gilpin, Robert. "Economic Evolution of National Systems." *International Studies Quarterly* 40, no. 3 (1996): 411–431.

Gimeno, Javier, and Carolyn Y. Woo. "'Hypercompetition in a Multimarket Environment: The Role of Strategic Similarity and Multimarket Contact in Competitive De-escalation." *Organization Science* 7, no. 3 (1996): 322–341.

Glassmyer, Katherine, and Nicholas Sambanis. "Rebel: Military Integration and Civil War Termination." *Journal of Peace Research* 45, no. 3 (2008): 365–384.

Glynn, Mary Ann. "When Cymbals Become Symbols: Conflict over Organizational Identity within a Symphony Orchestra." *Organization Science* 11 (2000): 285–298.

Gobierno de España. Consulta de Resultado Electorales. http://www.infoelectoral.mir.es/min/home.html.

Goffman, Erving. *The Presentation of Self in Everyday Life.* Edinburgh: University of Edinburgh Press, 1956.

Goñi, Fermin. "'Cinco miembros de ETA (p-m) roban mil kilos de "goma-2" en las afueras de Pamplona." *El Pais*, March 7, 1979. https://elpais.com/diario/1979/03/07/espana/289609207_850215.html.

Goñi, Fermin. "Multa de dos millones de pesetas al dueño de la armería asaltada por ETA (pm)." *El Pais*, March 8, 1979. https://elpais.com/diario/1979/03/08/espana/289695625_850215.html.

Gonzalez, Antonio. "Treinta y tres personalidades vascas vinculadas a la cultura, contra la violencia de ETA." *El Pais*, May 28, 1980. https://elpais.com/diario/1980/05/28/espana/328312806_850215.html.

Gorospe, Pedro. "ETA asume el asesinato de 13 personas en la calle del Correo de Madrid tras negarlo durante 44 años." *El Pais*, November 7, 2018. https://elpais.com/politica/2018/11/06/actualidad/1541508078_589338.html.

Grandy, Gina. "Instrumental Case Study." In *Encyclopedia of Case Study Research*, edited by Albert J. Mills, Gabrielle Durepos, and Elden Wiebe, 473–475. Los Angeles: SAGE Publications, 2012.

Green, Donald, and Ian Shapiro. *Pathologies of Rational Choice Theory: A Critique of Applications in Political Science*. New Haven, CT: Yale University Press, 1994.

Greenhill, Kelly M., and Paul Staniland. "Ten Ways to Lose at Counterinsurgency." *Civil Wars* 9, no. 4 (2007): 402–419.

Greenhill, Kelly M., and Solomon Major. "The Perils of Profiling: Civil War Spoilers and the Collapse of Intrastate Peace Accords." *International Security* 31, no. 3 (2006–2007): 7–40.

Gruber, Barbara, and Jan Pospisil. "'Ser Eleno': Insurgent Identity Formation in the ELN." *Small Wars & Insurgencies* 26, no. 2 (2015): 226–247.

Guevara, Ernesto Che. *Guerrilla Warfare*. Lanham, MD: SR Books, 2004.

Gunther, Richard, José Ramón Montero, and Joan Botella. *Democracy in Modern Spain*. New Haven, CT: Yale University Press, 2004.

Gurney, Joan Neff, and Kathleen J. Tierney. "Relative Deprivation and Social Movements: A Critical Look at Twenty Years of Theory and Research." *Sociological Quarterly* 23, no. 1 (1982): 33–47.

Gurr, Ted R. "Some Observations on Resistance and Revolution in Contemporary Africa." *Journal of Asian and African Studies* 47, no. 3 (2012): 279–290.

Hack, Karl. "Everyone Lived in Fear: Malaya and the British Way of Counter-insurgency." *Small Wars & Insurgencies* 23, no. 4–5 (2012): 671–699.

Hamilton, Carrie. *Women and ETA: The Gender Politics of Radical Basque Nationalism*. Manchester: Manchester University Press, 2007.

Hancock, Landon E., Joshua N. Weiss, and Glen M. E. Duerr. "Prospect Theory and the Framing of the Good Friday Agreement." *Conflict Resolution Quarterly* 28, no. 2 (2010) 183–203.

Hands, Gordon. "Roberto Michels and the Study of Political Parties." *British Journal of Political Science* 1, no. 2 (1971): 155–172.

Haney, Patrick J. *Organizing for Foreign Policy Crises: Presidents, Advisers, and the Management of Decision Making*. Ann Arbor: University of Michigan Press, 2002.

Hannan, Michael T., and John Freeman. "Obstacles to Comparative Studies." In *New Perspectives on Organizational Effectiveness*, edited by Paul S. Goodman, Johannes M. Pennings, and Associates, 106–131. San Francisco: Jossey-Bass, 1977.

Hannan, Michael T., and John Freeman. "Structural Inertia and Organizational Change." *American Sociological Review* 49 (1984): 149–164.

Hannan, Michael T., and John Freeman. *Organizational Ecology.* Cambridge, MA: Harvard University Press, 1989.
Harris, Douglas B. "Behavioral Reality and Institutional Change: Historical Methods for Political Science's Historical-Institutional Turn." In *Social Research: Philosophy, Politics and Practice*, edited by Martyn Hammersley, 61–100. London: Sage Publications, 2004.
Hart, Peter. *The I.R.A. at War: 1916–1923.* Oxford: Oxford University Press, 2003.
Hartzell, Caroline, Matthew Hoddie, and Donald Rothchild. "Stabilizing the Peace after Civil War: An Investigation of Some Key Variables." *International Organization* 55, no. 1 (2001): 183–208.
Hayes, Brigadier Vere. "Establishing the Credibility of a Regional Peacekeeping Capability." *ACCORD Occasional Paper* 2000, no. 1 (2000): 2–12.
Heath, Julia A., T. David Mason, William T. Smith, and Joseph P. Weingarten. "The Calculus of Fear: Revolution, Repression, and the Rational Peasant." *Social Science Quarterly* 81, no. 2 (2000): 622–633.
Hechter, Michael, and Satoshi Kanazawa. "Sociological Rational Choice Theory." *Annual Review of Sociology* 23 (1997): 191–214.
Henderson, Elisa. "Negotiating for Survival." *British Accounting Review* 50, no. 2 (2018): 185–198.
Henderson, Rebecca M., and Kim B. Clark. "Architectural Innovation: The Reconfiguration of Existing Product Technologies and the Failure of Established Firms." *Administrative Science Quarterly* 35, no. 1 (1990): 9–30.
Hironaka, Ann. *Neverending Wars: The International Community, Weak States, and the Perpetuation of Civil Wars.* Cambridge, MA: Harvard University Press, 2005.
Hirose, Kentaro, Kosuke Imai, and Jason Lyall. "Can Civilian Attitudes Predict Insurgent Violence? Ideology and Insurgent Tactical Choice in Civil War." *Journal of Peace Research* 54, no. 1 (2017): 47–63.
Hirsch, Eric L. "Sacrifice for the Cause: Group Processes, Recruitment, and Commitment in a Student Social Movement." *American Sociological Review* 55, no. 2 (1990): 243–254.
Hirschman, Alberto O. *Exit, Voice and Loyalty: Responses to Decline in Firms, Organizations and States.* Cambridge, MA: Harvard University Press, 1970.
Hoddie, Matthew, and Caroline Hartzell. "Civil War Settlements and the Implementation of Military Power-Sharing Arrangements." *Journal of Peace Research* 40, no. 3 (2003): 303–320.
Högbladh, Stina. "Peace Agreements 1975–2011—Updating the UCDP Peace Agreement Dataset." In *States in Armed Conflict 2011*, edited by Therése Pettersson and Lotta Themnér, 39–56. Department of Peace and Conflict Research Report 99, Uppsala University, 2012.
Hogg, Michael A., and Dominic Abrams. "Towards a Single-Process Uncertainty-Reduction Model of Social Motivation in Groups." In *Group Motivation: Social Psychological Perspectives*, edited by Michael Hogg and Dominic Abrams, 173–190. London: Harvester Wheatsheaf, 1993.

Hogg, Michael A., and Janice Adelman. "Uncertainty–Identity Theory: Extreme Groups, Radical Behavior, and Authoritarian Leadership." *Journal of Social Issues* 69, no. 3 (2013): 436–454.

Holland, Paul. "Statistics and Causal Inference." *Journal of the American Statistical Association* 81, no. 396 (1986): 945–960.

Horchem, Hans Josef. "The Decline of the Red Army Faction." *Terrorism and Political Violence* 3, no. 2 (1991): 61–74.

Howard, Lise Morjé, and Alexandra Stark. "How Civil Wars End: The International System, Norms, and the Role of External Actors." *International Security* 42, no. 3 (2017/18): 127–171.

Huff, Connor Dezzani. "Why Rebels Reject Peace." PhD diss., Harvard University, 2019.

Hug, Simon. "Further Twenty Years of Pathologies? Is Rational Choice Better Than It Used to Be?" *Swiss Political Science Review* 20, no. 3(2014): 486–497.

Huizinga, Kees, and Martin de Bree. "Exploring the Risk of Goal Displacement in Regulatory Enforcement Agencies: A Goal-Ambiguity Approach." *Public Performance and Management Review* 44, no. 4 (2021): 868–898.

Hultman, Lisa. "Battle Losses and Rebel Violence: Raising the Costs for Fighting.", *Terrorism and Political Violence* 19, no. 2 (2007): 205–222.

Hultquist, Philip. "Power Parity and Peace? The Role of Relative Power in Civil War Settlement." *Journal of Peace Research* 50, no. 5 (2015): 623–634.

Humphreys, Macartan, and Jeremy M. Weinstein. "Handling and Manhandling Civilians in Civil War." *American Political Science Review* 100, no. 3 (2006): 429–447.

Humphreys, Macartan, and Jeremy M. Weinstein. "Who Fights? The Determinants of Participation in Civil War." *American Journal of Political Science* 52, no. 2 (2008): 436–455.

Iglesias, Leyre. "El pueblo que alimentó a ETA." *El Mundo*, October 12, 2014. https://www.elmundo.es/pais-vasco/2014/10/12/543a491f22601daa1c8b456e.html.

Iñesta, Eduardo Parra. "'Los Que Volvieron A Casa': El Fin De ETA Político Militar y La Reinserción De Sus Miembros (1974–1985)." *Historia Actual Online* 32 (2013): 31–41.

Ishiyama, John, and Anna Batta. "Swords into Plowshares: The Organizational Transformation of Rebel Groups into Political Parties." *Communist and Post-Communist Studies* 44, no. 4 (2011): 369–379.

Islam, Gazi. "Social Identity Theory." In *Encyclopedia of Critical Psychology*, edited by Thomas Teo, 1781–1783. New York: Springer, 2014.

Jacques, Karen, and Paul J. Taylor. "Male and Female Suicide Bombers: Different Sexes, Different Reasons?" *Studies in Conflict & Terrorism* 31, no. 4 (2008): 304–326.

Jennings, Kathleen M. "The Struggle to Satisfy: DDR Through the Eyes of Ex-combatants in Liberia." *International Peacekeeping* 14, no. 2 (2007): 204–218.

Jerolmack, Colin, and Shamus Khan. "Talk Is Cheap: Ethnography and the Attitudinal Fallacy." *Sociological Methods & Research* 43, no. 2 (2014): 178–209.

Jervis, Robert. "Political Implications of Loss Aversion." *Political Psychology* 13, no. 2 (1992): 187–204.

Joly, Lionel. "La cause basque et l'euskera." *Mots: Les langues du politique* 74 (2004): 73–90.

Jones, Seth G. *Counterinsurgency in Afghanistan*. RAND Counterinsurgency Study, Vol. 4. Santa Monica, CA: RAND Corporation, 2008.

Jones, Seth G. *Waging Insurgent Warfare: Lessons from the Vietcong to the Islamic State*. Oxford: Oxford University Press, 2017.

Jordan, Jenna. "Attacking the Leader, Missing the Mark: Why Terrorist Groups Survive Decapitation Strikes." *International Security* 38, no. 4 (2014): 7–38.

Joyce, Renanah Miles, and Virginia Page Fortna. "Extremism and Terrorism: Rebel Goals and Tactics in Civil Wars." *Perspectives on Politics* (May 2024): 1–21.

Kahneman, Daniel, and Amos Tversky. "Conflict Resolution: A Cognitive Perspective." In *Preference, Belief, and Similarity: Selected Writings of Amos Tversky*, edited by Eldar Sharif, 729–746. Cambridge, MA: MIT Press, 2004.

Kahneman, Daniel, and Amos Tversky. "Prospect Theory: An Analysis of Decision under Risk." *Econometrica* 47, no. 2 (1979): 263–292.

Kahneman, Daniel, Jack L. Knetsch, and Richard H. Thaler. "The Endowment Effect, Loss Aversion, and Status Quo Bias." *Journal of Economic Perspectives* 5, no. 1 (1991): 193–206.

Kalyvas, Stathis N. "'New' and 'Old' Civil Wars: A Valid Distinction?" *World Politics* 54, no. 1 (2001): 99–118.

Kalyvas, Stathis N. "Promises and Pitfalls of an Emerging Research Program: The Micro-dynamics of Civil War." In *Order Conflict and Violence*, edited by Stathis N. Kalyvas, Ian Shapiro, and Tarek Masoud, 397–421. New York: Cambridge University Press, 2010.

Kalyvas, Stathis N. "The Paradox of Terrorism in Civil Wars." *Journal of Ethics* 8 (2008): 97–138.

Kalyvas, Stathis N. *The Logic of Violence in Civil War*. New York: Cambridge University Press, 2006.

Kalyvas, Stathis N., and Matthew Adam Kocher. "The Dynamics of Violence in Vietnam: An Analysis of the Hamlet Evaluation System (HES)." *Journal of Peace Research* 46, no. 3 (2009): 335–355.

Kathman, Jacob D. "Civil War Contagion and Neighboring Interventions." *International Studies Quarterly* 54, no. 4 (2010): 989–1012.

Kaufmann, Chaim. "Intervention in Ethnic and Ideological Civil Wars: Why One Can Be Done and the Other Can't." *Security Studies* 6, no. 1 (1996): 62–101.

Kaylvas, Stathis N. "The Urban Bias in Research on Civil Wars." *Security Studies* 13, no. 3 (2004): 160–190.

Keeney, Gregory L., and Detlof von Winterfeldt. "Identifying and Structuring the Objectives of Terrorists." *Risk Analysis* 30, no. 12 (2010): 1803–1816.

Kenny, Paul D. "Structural Integrity and Cohesion in Insurgent Organizations: Evidence from Protracted Conflicts in Ireland and Burma." *International Studies Review* 12 (2010):533–555.

Khieng, Sothy, and Heidi Dahles. "Resource Dependence and Effects of Funding Diversification Strategies Among NGOs in Cambodia." *Voluntas* (2014).

Kilcullen, David J. "Countering Global Insurgency." *Journal of Strategic Studies* 28, no. 4 (2005): 597–617.

King, Gary, Robert O. Keohane, and Sidney Verba. *Designing Social Inquiry: Scientific Inference in Qualitative Research*. Princeton, NJ: Princeton University Press, 1994.

Kingma, Kara, Bryan Cramer, and Erica Chenoweth. "Regime Type and Terrorist Attacks." In *Emerging Trends in the Social and Behavioral Sciences*, edited by Robert A. Scott, Stephen M. Kosslyn, and Marlis C. Buchmann, 1–15. New York: John Wiley, 2015.

Knight, Mark. "Expanding the DDR Model: Politics and Organisations." Cranfield Centre for Security Sector Management 6, no. 1 (2008): 1–16.

Koelble, Thomas A. "Party Structures and Democracy: Michels, McKenzie, and Duverger Revisited via the Examples of the West German Green Party and the British Social Democratic Party." *Comparative Political Studies* 22, no. 2 (1989): 199–216.

Komando Bereziak. "Comunicado Denuncia de ETA a la clase trabajadora y al Pueblo de Euskadi," 1977. In *Documentos Y* 18 (1979): 487.

Komando Bereziak. "Ponencia retirada, en el VII B. N, Septiembre de 1976," 1979, 200.

Korobkin, Russell. "Status Quo Bias and Contract Default Rules." *Cornell Law Review* 83, no. 3 (1998): 608–687.

Krakowski, Shmuel. *The War of the Doomed: Jewish Armed Resistance in Poland, 1942–1944*. New York: Holmes and Meier, 1984.

Krause, Peter. "The Political Effectiveness of Non-State Violence: A Two-Level Framework to Transform a Deceptive Debate." *Security Studies* 22, no. 2 (2013): 259–294.

Kreutz, Joakim. "Civil War Outcomes and a Durable Peace: Setting the Record Straight." Briefing Paper 17/2015, German Development Institute. https://uu.diva-portal.org/smash/get/diva2:870480/FULLTEXT01.pdf.

Kreutz, Joakim. "How and When Armed Conflicts End." *Journal of Peace Research* 47, no. 2 (2010): 243–250.

Kreutz, Joakim. *How Civil Wars End (and Recur)*. Abingdon: Routledge, 2014.

Kruglanski, Arie W., and Edward Orehek. "The Role of the Quest for Personal Significance in Motivating Terrorism." In *The Psychology of Social Conflict and Aggression*, edited by J. P. Forgas, Arie W. Kruglanski, and K. D. Williams, 153–164. London: Psychology Press, 2011.

Kydd, Andrew H., and Barbara F. Walter. "The Strategies of Terrorism." *International Security* 31, no. 1 (2006): 49–80.

Kydd, Andrew, and Barbara F. Walter. "Outbidding and the Overproduction of Terrorism." Unpublished manuscript, 2009. http://citeseerx.ist.psu.edu/viewdoc/download?doi=10.1.1.520.7525&rep=rep1&type=pdf.

Kydd, Andrew, and Barbara F. Walter. "Sabotaging the Peace: The Politics of Extremist Violence." *International Organization* 56, no. 2 (2002): 263–296.

La Vanguardia. "Carta del obispo de Malaga a los terroristas." June 29, 1980. http://hemeroteca.lavanguardia.com/preview/1980/07/01/pagina-6/32905810/pdf.html?search=eta-pm.

La Verdad. "'Antxon' culpa de la desaparición de 'Pertur' a los servicios de inteligencia españoles." November 4, 2008. https://www.laverdad.es/murcia/20081104/espana/eta-juicio-desaparicion-pertur-antxon-culpa-servicios-inteligencia-200811041439.html.

Markham, James M. "4 Killed by Bombs at Madrid Airport and Rail Terminals." *New York Times*, July 30, 1979. https://www.nytimes.com/1979/07/30/archives/4-killed-by-bombs-at-madrid-airport-and-rail-terminals-113-hurt-as.html.

Lacina, Bethany. "Explaining the Severity of Civil Wars." *Journal of Conflict Resolution* 50, no. 2 (2006): 276–289.

Laitin, David D. "National Revivals and Violence." *European Journal of Sociology* 36, no. 1 (1995): 3–43.

Lamb, Christina. "Chronicle of a Defeat Foretold: Why America Failed in Afghanistan." *Foreign Affairs* (July/August 2021). https://www.foreignaffairs.com/reviews/review-essay/2021-06-22/chronicle-defeat-foretold.

Langley, Ann, Henry Mintzberg, Patricia Pitcher, Elizabeth Posada, and Jan Saint-Macary. "Opening Up Decision Making: The View from the Black Stool." *Organization Science* 6, no. 3 (1995): 260–279.

Larrea, Iñaki Vázquez. "Los Orígenes del Nacionalismo Vasco." *Socio Tam* 16, no. 1 (2006): 141–161.

Lasagabaster, David. "Language Use and Language Attitudes in the Basque Country." In *Multilingualism in European Bilingual Contexts*, edited by David Lasagabaster and Ángel Huguet Canalís, 65–89. Bristol: Blue Ridge Summit, 2006.

Leach, Darcy K. "The Iron Law of What Again? Conceptualizing Oligarchy Across Organizational Forms." *Sociological Theory* 23, no. 3 (2005): 312–337.

Lebovic, James H. "How Organizations Learn: U.S. Government Estimates of Foreign Military Spending." *American Journal of Political Science* 39, no. 4 (1995): 835–863.

Lehtinen, Aki. and Jaakko Kuorikoski. "Unrealistic Assumptions in Rational Choice Theory." *Philosophy of the Social Sciences* 37, no. 2, 2007: 115–138.

León, Ángel Dámaso Luis. "Un Árbol En Tierra Yerma: Génesis y Formación De Euskadiko Ezkerra." *Ab. Initio*, no. 4 (2011): 111–139.

Letamendia, Francisco. "Sobre la necessidad del Partido independentista de los trabajadores vascos, 1976." *Documentos Y* 18 (1979): 191.

Levy, Jack S. "Prospect Theory, Rational Choice, and International Relations." *International Studies Quarterly* 41, no. 1 (1997): 87–112.

Lichbach, Mark Irving. "Deterrence or Escalation?: The Puzzle of Aggregate Studies of Repression and Dissent." *Journal of Conflict Resolution* 31, no. 2 (1987): 266–297.

Lichbach, Mark Irving. "Will Rational People Rebel against Inequality? Samson's Choice." *American Journal of Political Science* 34, no. 4 (1990): 1049–1076.

Lichbach, Mark Irving. *The Rebel's Dilemma*. Ann Arbor: University of Michigan Press, 1995.

Licklider, Roy, ed. *Stopping the Killing: How Civil Wars End*. New York: New York University Press, 1993.

Lidow, Nicholai Hart. *Violent Order: Understanding Rebel Governance through Liberia's Civil War*. New York: Cambridge University Press, 2016.

Lieberman, Sima. *Growth and Crisis in the Spanish Economy: 1940–1993*. Abingdon: Routledge, 2005.

Lieberson, Stanley. "Small N's and Big Conclusions: An Examination of the Reasoning in Comparative Studies Based on a Small Number of Cases." *Social Forces* 70, no. 2 (1991): 307–320.

Lindblom, Charles E. "The Science of 'Muddling Through.'" *Public Administration Review* 19, no. 2 (1959): 79–88.

Lindenburg, Siegwart, and Bruno S. Fey. "Alternatives, Frames and Relative Prices: A Broader View of Rational Choice Theory," *Acta Sociologica* 36 (1993): 191–205.

Lingelbach, William E. "The Defiant Basques." *Current History* 41, no. 1 (1934): 111.

Lipsky, Michael *Street-Level Bureaucracy, 30th Anniversary Edition: Dilemmas of the Individual in Public Services.* New York: Russell Sage Foundation, 2010.

Llera Ramo, Francisco J. "Violencia y Opinion Publica en el Pais Vasco, 1978–1992." *Revista Internacional de Sociología*, Tercera Epoca, no. 3, 84–111.

Llera, Francisco J. "ETA, Ejercito Secreto y Movimento Social." *Revista de Estudios Politicos* 78 (1992): 161–193.

Llera, Francisco J., José M. Mata, and Cynthia L. Irvin. "ETA: From Secret Army to Social Movement: The Post-Franco Schism of the Basque Nationalist Movement." *Terrorism and Political Violence* 5, no. 3 (1993): 106–134.

Lockyer, Adam. "Foreign Intervention and Warfare in Civil Wars: The Effect of Exogenous Resources on the Course and Nature of the Angolan and Afghan Conflicts." PhD diss., University of Sydney, 2008.

Lockyer, Adam. *Foreign Intervention, Warfare and Civil Wars: External Assistance and Belligerents' Choice of Strategy.* London: Routledge, 2018.

Lu, Lingyu, and Cameron G. Thies. "Economic Grievance and the Severity of Civil War." *Civil Wars* 13, no. 3 (2011): 215–231.

Lustick, Ian S. "History, Historiography, and Political Science: Multiple Historical Records and the Problem of Selection Bias." *American Political Science Review* 90, no. 3 (1996): 605–618.

Lutz, James M., and Brenda J. Lutz. "How Successful Is Terrorism?" *Forum on Public Policy: A Journal of the Oxford Round Table*, 2009.

Lyall, Jason, and Isaiah Wilson III. "Rage Against the Machines: Explaining Outcomes in Counterinsurgency Wars." *International Organization*, no. 63 (2009): 67–106.

Lyall, Jason. "Does Indiscriminate Violence Incite Insurgent Attacks? Evidence from Chechnya." *Journal of Conflict Resolution* 53, no. 3 (2009): 331–362.

Mack, Andrew. "The Utility of Terrorism." *Australian and New Zealand Journal of Criminology* 14, no. 4 (1981): 197–224.

Mack, Andrew. "Why Big Nations Lose Small Wars." *World Politics* 27, no. 2 (1975): 175–200.

Mahoney, Charles W. "End of the Cycle: Assessing ETA's Strategies of Terrorism." *Small Wars & Insurgencies* 29, no. 5–6 (2018): 916–940.

Mahoney, Charles W. "More Data, New Problems: Audiences, Ahistoricity, and Selection Bias in Terrorism and Insurgency Research." *International Studies Review* (2017): 1–26.

Malešević, Siniša, and Niall Ó Dochartaigh. "Why Combatants Fight: The Irish Republican Army and the Bosnian Serb Army Compared." *Theory and Society* 47 (2018): 293–326.

March, James G. *Explorations in Organizations*. Stanford, CA: Stanford University Press, 2008.

Markham, James M. "Kidnapping of Basque Industrialist Heightens Tension." *New York Times*, May 21, 1977. https://www.nytimes.com/1977/05/21/archives/kidnaping-of-basque-industrialist-heightens-tension.html.

Martin, Susanne, and Arie Perliger. "Turning to and from Terror: Deciphering the Conditions under Which Political Groups Choose Violent and Nonviolent Tactics." *Perspectives on Terrorism* 6, no. 4–5 (2012): 21–45.

Martínez, D., and J. Pagola. "Arnaldo Otegi, 'la voz de su amo.'" ABC, April 9, 2002. https://www.abc.es/espana/abci-arnaldo-otegi-200204090300-90611_noticia.html.

Martinez, Isabel C. "Treinta años del febrero más convulse." *El Pais*, February 20, 2011. https://elpais.com/diario/2011/02/20/paisvasco/1298234399_850215.html.

Masatlioglu, Yusufcan, and Efe A. Ok. "Rational Choice with Status Quo Bias." *Journal of Economic Theory* 121, no. 1 (2005): 1–29.

Mason, T. David, "Insurgency, Counterinsurgency, and the Rational Peasant." *Public Choice* 86 (1996): 63–83.

Mason, T. David, and Jason Quinn. "Sustaining the Peace: Determinants of Civil War Recurrence." Paper presented at Annual Meeting of the APSA, Chicago, 2004.

Mason, T. David, and Patrick J. Fett. "How Civil Wars End: A Rational Choice Approach." *Journal of Conflict Resolution* 40, no. 4 (1996): 546–568.

Masters, David. "Support and Nonsupport for Nationalist Rebellion: A Prospect Theory Approach." *Political Psychology* 25, no. 5 (2004): 703–726.

McCormick, Gordon H. "Terrorist Decision Making." *Annual Review of Political Science* 6, no. 1 (2003): 473–507.

McCreanor, Kyle. "ETA and the Public, 1959–1987." *The Ascendant Historian* 3, no. 2 (2015–2016): 71–92.

McLaren, Lauren M. *Constructing Democracy in Southern Europe: A Comparative Analysis of Italy, Spain and Turkey*. Abingdon: Routledge, 2008.

McLauchlin, Theodore, and Wendy Pearlman. "Out-group Conflict, In-group Unity? Exploring the Effect of Repression on Movement Fragmentation." Paper presented at the Annual Meeting of the American Political Science Association, Toronto, September 3–6, 2009.

Medrano, Juan Díez. *Divided Nations: Class Conflict, Politics, and Nationalism in the Basque Country and Catalonia*. Ithaca, NY: Cornell University Press, 1995.

Meier, Kenneth J. "Bureaucracy and Democracy: The Case for More Bureaucracy and Less Democracy." *Public Administration Review* 57, no. 3 (1997): 193–199.

Meisler, Stanley. "Spain's New Democracy." *Foreign Affairs* (1977). https://www.foreignaffairs.com/articles/spain/1977-10-01/spains-new-democracy.

Merari, Ariel. "Terrorism as a Strategy of Insurgency." *Terrorism and Political Violence* 5, no. 4 (1993): 213–251.

Merton, Robert K. *Social Theory and Social Structure*. Glencoe, IL: The Free Press, 1968.

Metelits, Claire M. "Bourdieu's Capital and Insurgent Group Resilience: A Field-Theoretic Approach to the Polisario Front." *Small Wars & Insurgencies* 29, no. 4 (2018): 680–704.

Meyer, John W., and Brian Rowan. "Institutionalized Organizations: Formal Structure as Myth and Ceremony." In *The New Institutionalism in Organizational Analysis*, edited by Walter W. Powell and Paul J. DiMaggio, 4–62. Chicago: University of Chicago Press, 1991.

Meyer, John W., W. Richard Scott, David Strang, and Andrew L Creighton. "Bureaucratization without Centralization: Changes in the Organizational System of American Public Education 1940–1980." In *Institutional Patterns and Organisations: Culture and Environment*, edited by Lynne G. Zucker, 139–160. Cambridge: Ballinger, 1988.

Michels, Robert. *Political Parties.*, Glencoe, IL: The Free Press, 1949.

Miller, Gregory D. "Confronting Terrorisms: Group Motivation and Successful State Policies." *Terrorism and Political Violence* 19, no. 3 (2007): 331–350.

Miller, N. E. "The Frustration-Aggression Hypothesis." *Psychological Review* 48, no. 4 (1941): 337–342.

Minkoff, Debra C. "From Service Provision to Institutional Advocacy: The Shifting Legitimacy of Organizational Forms." *Social Forces* 72, no. 4 (1994): 943–970.

Mira, Irene. "El 11-M de la Transición: 40 años del triple atentado de ETA en Madrid." *ABC Historia*, July 30, 2019. https://www.abc.es/historia/abci-olvidado-11-m-transicion-40-anos-atentado-estremecio-adolfo-suarez-201907290948_noticia.html.

Moe, Espen. "Mancur Olson and Structural Economic Change: Vested Interests and the Industrial Rise and Fall of the Great Powers." *Review of International Political Economy* 16, no. 2 (2009): 202–230.

Moe, Espen. "Vested Interests, Energy Efficiency and Renewables in Japan." *Energy Policy* (2011): 1–14.

Moe, Espen. *Governance, Growth and Global Leadership: The Role of the State in Technological Progress, 1750–2000.* Abingdon: Routledge, 2016.

Moe, Terry M. *The Organization of Interests: Incentives and the Internal Dynamics of Political Interest Groups.* Chicago: University of Chicago Press, 1988.

Molnar, Andrew R. *Human Factors Considerations of Undergrounds in Insurgencies.* Washington, DC: Special Operations, 1965.

Moore, Will H. "Tilting at a Windmill? The Conceptual Problem in Contemporary Peace Science." *Conflict Management and Peace Science* 32, no. 3 (2015): 1–15.

Moro, Mikel Saratxo. "Gerra iraultzaileetik nazionalismo iraultzailera. Nazio-arazoaren eta biolentziaren inguruko hausnarketaren garapena ETAn (1958–1970)." *Uztaro*, no. 87 (2013): 93–110.

Morrow, Elizabeth A., and John Meadowcroft. "The Rise and Fall of the English Defence League: Self-Governance, Marginal Members and the Far Right." *Political Studies* 67, no. 3 (2019): 539–556.

Morrow, James D. "Signalling Difficulties with Linkage in Crisis Bargaining." *International Studies Quarterly* 36, no. 2 (1992): 153–172.

Moskovich, Yaffa. "Goal Displacement in the New Israeli Labor Unions: Lessons Learned." *Current Politics and Economics of the Middle East* 10, no. 4 (2019): 411–439.

Muggah, Robert. "Innovations in Disarmament, Demobilization and Reintegration Policy and Research: Reflections on the Last Decade." NUPI Working Paper 774, Norwegian Institute of International Affairs, 2010.

Muller, Edward N., and Erich Weede. "Cross-National Variation in Political Violence: A Rational Action Approach." *Journal of Conflict Resolution* 34, no. 4 (1990): 624–651.

Mullins, Sam. *Twenty-Five Years of Terrorism and Insurgency in Southeast Asia, Hindsight, Insight, Foresight: Thinking about Security in the Indo-Pacific.* Asia Pacific Centre for Security Studies, 2020. https://apcss.org/dkiapcss25book/.

Muro, Diego. "ETA during Democracy, 1975–2011." In *ETA's Terrorist Campaign: From Violence to Politics, 1968–2015*, edited by Rafael Leonisio, Fernando Molina, and Diego Muro, 35–53. Abingdon: Routledge, 2017.

Muro, Diego. "ETA: Basque Nationalist and Separatist Organization." In *The Wiley-Blackwell Encyclopedia of Social and Political Movements*, edited by David A. Snow, Donatella della Porta, Bert Klandermans, and Doug McAdam, 1–3. Oxford: Blackwell Publishing, 2013.

Muro, Diego. "The Politics of War Memory in Radical Basque Nationalism." In *Nationalism and National Identities*, edited by Martin Bulmer and John Solomos, 73–91. London: Routledge, 2014.

Muro, Diego. *Ethnicity and Violence: The Case of Radical Basque Nationalism.* New York: Routledge, 2008.

Murua, Imanol. "The End of ETA (2007–2011): Narratives from the Media and from the Actors." PhD diss., University of Nevada, Reno, 2014.

Musa, Eşref, and Mohamad Misto. "2 Civilians Killed by YPG/PKK Terrorist Fire during Protest." *Andalou Agency*, May 18, 2021. https://www.aa.com.tr/en/middle-east/2-civilians-killed-by-ypg-pkk-terrorist-fire-during-protest/2246300.

National Foreign Assessment Center. "Western Europe Review,"' March 14, 1979. https://www.cia.gov/readingroom/docs/CIA-RDP79T00912A001700010011-9.pdf.

Nemeth, Stephen. "The Effect of Competition on Terrorist Group Operations." *Journal of Conflict Resolution* (2013): 1–27.

Newman, Edward, and Oliver Richmond, eds. *Challenges to Peacebuilding: Managing Spoilers During Conflict Resolution.* Tokyo: UNU Press, 2006.

NewsX, "NewsX Video: Interview with Col. Karuna Amman Part-4," News X, 12 May 2009, https://www.youtube.com/watch?v=uZTtX1fy1TE.

Ngaruko, Floribert, and Janvier D. Nkurunziza. "Civil War and Its Duration in Burundi." In *Understanding Civil War, Volume 1: Africa*, edited by Nicholas Sambanis and Paul Collier, 35–54. Herndon, VA: World Bank Publications, 2005.

Nilsson, Desirée. "Partial Peace: Rebel Groups Inside and Outside Civil War Settlements." Policy Research Working Paper 4572, The World Bank, 2008.

Nyden, Philip W. "Democratizing Organizations: A Case Study of a Union Reform Movement." *American Journal of Sociology* 90, no. 6 (1985): 1179–1203.

Okado-Gough, Damien. "Coiste na n-Iarchimí (the Irish Republican Army ex-prisoners network) and the Limitations of Hybrid Peacebuilding in Ireland." *Journal of Global Studies* 11 (2020): 145–168.

Olmeda, José A. "ETA Before and After the Carrero Assassination." *Strategic Insights* 10, no. 2 (2011): 3–16.

Olson, Mancur. *The Logic of Collective Action.* Cambridge, MA: Harvard University Press, 2002.

Olson, Mancur. *The Rise and Decline of Nations: Economic Growth, Stagflation, and Social Rigidities.* New Haven, CT: Yale University Press, 1982.

Oots, Kent L. "Bargaining with Terrorists: Organizational Considerations." *Studies in Conflict & Terrorism* 13, no. 2 (1990): 145–158.

Opp, Karl-Dieter, and Wolfgang Roehl. "Repression, Micromobilization, and Political Protest." *Social Forces* 69, no. 2 (1990): 521–547.

Orsini, Alessandro. "Interview with a Terrorist by Vocation: A Day Among the Diehard Terrorists, Part II." *Studies in Conflict & Terrorism* 36, no. 8 (2013): 672–684.

Ortuñez, José Ángel Etxaniz. "La Revitalización del Partido Comunista de Euskadi (1970–1975): El ingreso de militantes de ETA-VI Asamblea (Minos) en el EPK." *Historia del PCE: I Congreso, 1920–1977* 2 (2007): 313–334.

Osterman, Paul. "Overcoming Oligarchy: Culture and Agency in Social Movement Organizations." *Administrative Science Quarterly* 51 (2006): 622–649.

Ovalle, Carlos Alberto Ospina." "Was FARC Militarily Defeated?' *Small Wars & Insurgencies* 28, no. 3 (2017): 524–545.

Pape, Robert. *Dying to Win: The Strategic Logic of Suicide Terrorism*. New York: Random House, 2005.

Parra, Vega Rodíguez-Flores. "Nación Española y Estado Autonómico en el Partido Socialista Obrero Español (1974–1982)." PhD diss., Universitat de Valencia, 2017.

Parra, Vega Rodíguez-Flores. "PSOE y PSC-PSOE ante la LOAPA. ¿Derecho a la Diferencia O Igualdad En Derechos?" *Historia Actual Online* 51, no. 5 (2020): 79–92.

Patterson, Henry. *Ireland since 1939*. London: Penguin 2007.

See also Hart, Peter. *The I.R.A. at War: 1916–1923*. Oxford: Oxford University Press, 2003.

Paul, Christopher, Colin P. Clarke, Beth Grill, and Molly Dunigan. "Paths to Victory: Lessons from Modern Insurgencies." Santa Monica, CA: RAND Corporation, 2013. https://apps.dtic.mil/sti/pdfs/ADA586471.pdf.

Paul, Christopher, Colin P. Clarke, Beth Grill, and Terrance Savitsky. "Between Large-*N* and Small-*N* Analyses: Historical Comparison of Thirty Insurgency Case Studies.", *Historical Methods* 46, no. 4 (2013): 220–239.

Pearlman, Wendy, and Kathleen Gallagher Cunningham. "Nonstate Actors, Fragmentation, and Conflict Processes." *Journal of Conflict Resolution* 56, (2012): 3–15.

Pearlman, Wendy. "Spoiling Inside and Out: Internal Political Contestation and the Middle East Peace Process." *International Security* 33, no. 3 (2008/2009): 79–109.

Peña, Mario Aguilera. "Las FARC: auge y quiebre de su modelo de Guerra." *Análisis Político* 26, no. 77 (2013). http://www.scielo.org.co/scielo.php?script=sci_arttext&pid=S0121-47052013000100004.

Petersen, Roger D. *Resistance and Rebellion: Lessons from Eastern Europe*. Cambridge: Cambridge University Press, 2001.

Pettigrew, Andrew M. *The Politics of Organisational Decision-Making*. Abingdon: Taylor and Francis, 2014.

Pettigrew, Thomas F. "Samuel Stouffer and Relative Deprivation." *Social Psychology Quarterly* 78, no. 1 (2015): 7–24.

Phelan, Alexandra. "Engaging Insurgency: The Impact of the 2016 Colombian Peace Agreement on FARC's Political Participation." *Studies in Conflict & Terrorism* 42, no. 9 (2019): 836–852.

Phillips, Brian J. "Enemies with Benefits? Violent Rivalry and Terrorist Group Longevity." *Journal of Peace Research* 52, no. 1 (2015): 62–75.
Phillips, Brian J. "How Terrorist Organizations Survive: Cooperation and Competition in Terrorist Groups Networks." PhD diss., University of Pittsburgh, 2012.
Piazza, James A., and James Igoe Walsh. "Physical Integrity Rights and Terrorism." *PS: Political Science and Politics* 43, no. 3 (2010): 411–414.
Polletta, Francesca. *Freedom Is an Endless Meeting: Democracy in American Social Movements.* Chicago: University of Chicago Press, 2004.
Polo, Sara M. T., and Belén González. "The Power to Resist: Mobilization and the Logic of Terrorist Attacks in Civil War." *Comparative Political Studies* 53, no. 13 (2020): 2029–2060.
Porter, Michael E. *Competitive Strategy: Techniques for Analyzing Industries and Competitors.* New York: Free Press, 1998.
Powell, Charles. "The 1981 Coup d'État and Trial in Spain: Possible Lessons for Turkey." Working Paper 7/2019, Elcano Royal Institute.
Preston, Paul. *The Triumph of Democracy in Spain.* London: Taylor and Francis, 2005.
Pruitt, Dean G. "Readiness Theory and the Northern Ireland Conflict." *American Behavioral Scientist* 50, no. 11 (2007): 1520–1541.
Punto y Hora. "Lectura de una historia de novela." No. 250. January 22–29, 1982.
Punto y Hora. "No estoy implicado en el secuestro de Iparra." June 16–22, 1977.
Ramesh, Randeep. "Tamil Tigers Finished, Claims Former Leader." *Irish Times*, May 21, 2009. https://www.irishtimes.com/news/tamil-tigers-finished-claims-former-leader-1.727266.
Real Academia de la Historia. "Eduardo Moreno Bergaretxe." http://dbe.rah.es/biografias/134919/eduardo-moreno-bergaretxe.
Real Academia de la Historia. "José Miguel Beñarán Ordeñana." http://dbe.rah.es/biografias/134476/jose-miguel-benaran-ordenana.
Regan, Patrick M. *Civil Wars and Foreign Powers: Outside Intervention in Intrastate Conflict.* Ann Arbor: University of Michigan Press, 2002.
Regan, Patrick M., and Daniel Norton. "Greed, Grievance, and Mobilization in Civil Wars." *Journal of Conflict Resolution* 49, no. 3 (2005): 319–336.
Reinares, Fernando. "Who Are the Terrorists? Analyzing Changes in Sociological Profile among Members of ETA." *Studies in Conflict & Terrorism* 27, no. 6 (2004): 465–488.
Reiter, Dan. *How Wars End.* Princeton, NJ: Princeton University Press, 2009.
Rekarte, Iñaki. *Lo difícil es perdonarse a uno mismo: Matar en nombre de ETA y arrepentirse por amor.* Barcelona: Ediciones Península, 2015.
Rekondo, Joxan, and Imanol Lizarralde. "40 años del 'Manifiesto de los 33.'" *Deia*, May 24, 2020. https://www.deia.eus/opinion/2020/05/24/40-anos-manifiesto-33/1040745.html.
Reshi, Manzoor Ahmad. "Kashmir Insurgency: A Review Paper." *World Wide Journal of Multidisciplinary Research and Development* 4, no. 9 (2018): 9–12.
Reuters. "Around the World; Thousands in Basque Area Protest Death of Rebel." *New York Times*, February 16, 1981. https://www.nytimes.com/1981/02/16/world/around-the-world-thousands-in-basque-area-protest-death-of-rebel.html.

Reuters. "Colombian Farc Rebel Unit Rejects Peace Deal, Saying It Will Not Disarm." *The Guardian*, July 7, 2016. https://www.theguardian.com/world/2016/jul/07/colombian-farc-rebel-unit-not-disarm-under-peace-deal.

Ridruejo, Carmelo C. "'Vamos a integrarnos en la vida política para defender lo que pensamos', afirman Joseba Aulestia y Miren Alcorta." *El Pais*, October 4, 1982. https://elpais.com/diario/1982/10/04/espana/402534016_850215.html.

Rivera, Antonio, and Gaizka Fernández Soldevilla. "Frente Nacional Vasco (1933–2019). Pluralismo o Nacionalidad." *Historia Actual Online* 50, no. 3 (2019): 21–34.

Roldán, Javier. "La mano que mató a Berazadi." *El Diario Vasco*, April 8, 2006. https://www.diariovasco.com/pg060408/prensa/noticias/Politica/200604/08/DVA-POL-314.html?ref=https%3A%2F%2F.

Romero, Eduardo Uriarte. "El Proceso de Liquidación de ETA pm." Fundacion Manuel Gimenez Abad, 2010, 1–12.

Rootes, Christopher A. "The Transformation of Environmental Activism: Activists, Organizations and Policy-making." *Innovation: The European Journal of Social Science Research* 12, no. 2 (1999): 155–173.

Ross, Jeffrey Ian, and Ted Robert Gurr. "Why Terrorism Subsides: A Comparative Study of Canada and the United States." *Comparative Politics* 21, no. 4 (1989): 405–426.

RTVE. "Constantino Gómez Barcia." https://www.rtve.es/memoriadevida/detalle.php?id=65.

RTVE. "Eduardo Moreno Bergareche." https://www.rtve.es/memoriadevida/detalle.php?id=59.

Rucht, Dieter, and Jochen Roose. "Neither Decline nor Sclerosis: The Organisational Structure of the German Environmental Movement." Paper prepared for presentation at the ECPR Joint Workshops, Copenhagen, April 14–19, 2000.

Rudloff, Peter, and Michael G. Findley. "The Downstream Effects of Combatant Fragmentation on Civil War Recurrence." *Journal of Peace Research* 53, no. 1 (2016): 19–32.

Rueda, Fernando Martínez. "Religión y Nacionalismo Vasco en el Siglo XX: Aproximación desde el sujeto a una relación compleja." *Hispania Sacra* 69, no. 140 (2017): 721–733.

Rueda, Fernando Martínez. "Telesforo Monzón, el nacionalismo vasco y la Guerra Civil: Historia y Memoria." *Revista Universitaria de Historia Militar* 7, no. 13 (2018): 375–400.

Sageman, Marc. "The Stagnation in Terrorism Research." *Terrorism and Political Violence* 26, no. 4 (2014): 565–580.

Salancik, Gerald R., and Jeffrey Pfeffer. "Who Gets Power and How They Hold onto It: A Strategic-Contingency Model of Power." *Organizational Dynamics* 5, no. 3 (1977): 3–21.

Salehyan, Idean. *Rebels without Borders: Transnational Insurgencies in World Politics.* Ithaca, NY: Cornell University Press, 2011.

Sambanis, Nicholas. "Using Case Studies to Expand Economic Models of Civil War." *Perspectives on Politics* 2, no. 2 (2004): 259–279.

Samuelson, William, and Richard Zeckhauser. "Status Quo Bias in Decision Making." *Journal of Risk and Uncertainty* 1 (1988): 7–59.

Sanchez-Cuenca, Ignacio, and Luis de la Calle. "Domestic Terrorism: The Hidden Side of Political Violence." *Annual Review of Political Science* 12 (2009): 31–49.

Sánchez-Navarro, Angel José, and Michel Vale. "The Political Transition of the Francoist Cortes: Toward the Law for Political Reform (1975–1976)." *International Journal of Political Economy* 20, no. 2 (1990): 8–27.

Sanín, Francisco Gutiérrez. "Criminal Rebels? A Discussion of War and Criminality from the Colombian Experience." Working Paper no. 27, Crisis States Programme Working Papers Series No. 1, 2003, 1–26.

Sarabia, Bernabe. "Violencia adolescente." *Revista Cuenta y Razon de Pensamiento Actual*, no. 106 (1998). http://www.cuentayrazon.org/modules.php?op=modload&name=Publications&file=index&p_op=showcontent&secid=&pnid=1052740202.

Saxton, Gregory, and Michelle Benson. "Means, Motives and Opportunities in Ethno-Nationalist Mobilization." *International Interactions* 34, no. 1 (2008): 53–83.

Schenoni, Luis L., Sean Braniff, and Jorge Battaglino. "Was the Malvinas/Falklands a Diversionary War? A Prospect-Theory Reinterpretation of Argentina's Decline." *Security Studies* 29, no. 1 (2020): 34–63.

Schmidt, Rachel. "Contesting the Fighter Identity: Framing, Desertion, and Gender in Colombia." *International Studies Quarterly* 65, no. 1 (2021): 43–55.

Schulhofer-Wohl, Jonah, and Nicholas Sambanis. *Disarmament, Demobilization, and Reintegration Programs: An Assessment.* Stockholm: Folke Bernadotte Academy, 2010.

Schultz, Richard. "Breaking the Will of the Enemy During the Vietnam War: The Operationalization of the Cost-Benefit Model of Counterinsurgency Warfare." *Journal of Peace Research* 15, no. 2 (1978): 109–129.

Schumacher, Edward. "Domingo Iturbe Abasolo, Exiled Basque Terrorist." *New York Times*, March 3, 1987. https://www.nytimes.com/1987/03/03/obituaries/domingo-iturbe-abasolo-exiled-basque-terrorist.html.

Schuurman, Bart, and Quirine Eijkman. "Moving Terrorism Research Forward: The Crucial Role of Primary Sources." ICCT Background Note June 2013. The Hague: ICCT, 2013. https://www.jstor.org/stable/pdf/resrep17493.pdf?acceptTC=true&coverpage=false&addFooter=false;

Schuurman, Bart. "Conducting Qualitative Research on Terrorism: Finding and Using Primary Sources." *SAGE Research Methods Cases Part 2*, 2019. https://scholarlypublications.universiteitleiden.nl/access/item%3A2975602/view.

Scott, W. Richard. "Unpacking Institutional Arguments." In *The New Institutionalism in Organizational Analysis*, edited by Walter W. Powell and Paul J. DiMaggio, 164–182. Chicago: University of Chicago Press, 1991.

Selznick, Philip. "Foundations of the Theory of Organization." *American Sociological Review* 13, no. 1 (1948): 25–35.

Selznick, Philip. *Leadership in Administration: A Sociological Interpretation.* New Orleans: Quid Pro, LLC, 2011.

Selznick, Philip. *TVA and the Grass Roots: A Study in the Sociology of Formal Organization.* Berkeley: University of California Press, 1953.

Shanahan, Timothy. "The Definition of Terrorism." In *Routledge Handbook of Critical Terrorism Studies*, edited by Richard Jackson, 103–113. London: Routledge, 2016.

Shapiro, Jacob N. "Terrorist Decision-Making: Insights from Economics and Political Science." *Perspectives on Terrorism* 6, no. 4–5 (2012): 5–20.

Shapiro, Jacob N. *The Terrorist's Dilemma: Managing Violent Covert Organizations.* Princeton, NJ: Princeton University Press, 2013.

Shapiro, Jacob N., and David A. Siegel. "Moral Hazard, Discipline, and the Management of Terrorist Organizations." *World Politics* 64, no. 1 (2012): 39–78.

Shils, Edward A., and Morris Janowitz. "Cohesion and Disintegration in the Wehrmacht in World War II." *Public Opinion Quarterly* 12, no. 2 (1948): 280–315.

Shultz, Richard. "Breaking the Will of the Enemy During the Vietnam War: The Operationalization of the Cost-Benefit Model of Counterinsurgency Warfare." *Journal of Peace Research* 15, no. 2 (1978): 109–129.

Shultz, Richard. "Conceptualizing Political Terrorism: A Typology." *Journal of International Affairs*, 32, no. 1 (1978): 7–15.

Silke, Andrew, and Jennifer Schmidt Petersen. "The Golden Age? What the 100 Most Cited Articles in Terrorism Studies Tell Us." *Terrorism and Political Violence* 29, no. 4 (2015): 692–712.

Silke, Andrew. "The Devil You Know: Continuing Problems with Research on Terrorism." *Terrorism and Political Violence* 13, no. 4 (2001): 1–14.

Simon, Herbert A. "Rational Choice and the Structure of the Environment," *Psychological Review* 63, no. 2 (1956): 129–138.

Simon, Herbert A. "Strategy and Organizational Evolution", *Strategic Management Journal* 14 (1993): 131–142.

Simon, Herbert A. *Administrative Behavior: A Study of Decision-Making Processes in Administrative Organizations.* 4th ed. New York: The Free Press, 1997.

Simon, Herbert A. *Models of Bounded Rationality: Empirically Grounded Economic Reason.* Vol. 3. Cambridge, MA: MIT Press, 1997.

Sindre, Gyda M. "From Secessionism to Regionalism: Intra-organizational Change and Ideological Moderation within Armed Secessionist Movements." *Political Geography* 64 (2018): 23–32.

Singh, Jitendra V., and Charles J. Lumsden. "Theory and Research in Organizational Ecology." *Annual Review of Sociology* 16 (1990): 161–195.

Singh, Jitendra V., David J. Tucker, and Robert J. House. "Organizational Legitimacy and the Liability of Newness." *Administrative Science Quarterly* 31, no. 2 (1986): 171–193.

Sinno, Abdulkader H. *Organizations at War in Afghanistan and Beyond.* Ithaca, NY: Cornell University Press, 2010.

Skocpol, Theda. "Review: Wallerstein's World Capitalist System: A Theoretical and Historical Critique." *American Journal of Sociology* 82, no. 5 (1977): 1075–1090.

Snow, David A., E. Burke Rochford, Jr., Steven K. Worden, and Robert D. Benford. "Frame Alignment Processes, Micromobilization, and Movement Participation." *American Sociological Review* 51, no. 4 (1986): 464–481.

Sobek, David, and Caroline L. Payne. "A Tale of Two Types: Rebel Goals and the Onset of Civil Wars." *International Studies Quarterly* 54, no. 1 (2010): 213–240.

Soldevilla, Gaizka Fernández, Miren Barandiaran, and Pau Casanellas. "La documentación de (y sobre) ETA." *Tabula*, no. 14 (2011): 45–57.

Soldevilla, Gaizka Fernández. "'Ya no es todo blanco o negro.' ETA, la izquierda abertzale y el cambio político en España (1974–1977)." *Novísima: II Congreso Internacional de Historia de Nuestro Tiempo* (2010): 411–420.

Soldevilla, Gaizka Fernández. "Agur a las armas. EIA, Euskadiko Ezkerra y la disolución de ETA político-militar (1976–1985)." *Sancho el Sabio* 33 (2010): 55–95.

Soldevilla, Gaizka Fernández. "Aniversario del asesinato de Javier de Ybarra." Blog de Gaizka Fernández Soldevilla, June 21, 2014. https://gaizkafernandez.com/2014/06/21/aniversario-del-asesinato-de-javier-de-ybarra/.

Soldevilla, Gaizka Fernández. "De las armas al parlamento: Los orígenes de Euskadiko Ezkerra (1976–1977)." *Pasado y Memoria* no. 8 (2009): 245–265.

Soldevilla, Gaizka Fernández. "El Compañero Ausente y los Aprendices de Brujo: Orígenes de Herri Batasuna (1974–1980) (1)." *Revista de Estudios Políticos (nueva época)*, no. 148 (2010): 71–103.

Soldevilla, Gaizka Fernández. "Historia de una Heterodoxia Abertzale. ETA político-militar, EIA y Euskadiko Ezkerra (1974–1994)." PhD diss., Universidad de Pais Vasco, 2012.

Soler, Mariano Sánchez. *La Transición Sangrienta: Una historia violenta del proceso democrático en España (1975–1983)*. Barcelona: Ediciones Peninsula, 2010.

Spicer, André, and Steffen Böhm. "Moving Management: Theorizing Struggles against the Hegemony of Management." *Organization Studies* 28, no. 11 (2007): 1667–1698.

Stake, Robert E. *The Art of Case Study Research*. Thousand Oaks, CA: SAGE Publications, 2009.

Staniland, Paul. "Organizing Insurgency: Networks, Resources, and Rebellion in South Asia." *International Security* 37, no. 1 (2012): 142–177.

Staniland, Paul. "Whither ISIS? Insights from Insurgent Responses to Decline." *Washington Quarterly* 40, no. 2 (2017): 29–43.

Staniland, Paul. *Networks of Rebellion: Explaining Insurgent Cohesion and Collapse*. Ithaca, NY: Cornell University Press 2014.

Stanton, Jessica A. "Terrorism in the Context of Civil War." *Journal of Politics* 75, no. 4 (2013): 1009–1022.

START (National Consortium for the Study of Terrorism and Responses to Terrorism). "Data Collection Methodology," 2022. https://www.start.umd.edu/gtd/using-gtd/.

Stedman, Stephen John. "Spoiler Problems in Peace Processes." *International Security* 22, no. 2 (1997): 5–53.

Stevenson, Jonathan. "Northern Ireland: Treating Terrorists as Statesmen." *Foreign Policy*, no. 105 (1996–1997): 125–140.

Stohl, Michael S. "Counterterrorism and Repression." In *The Roots of Terrorism*, edited by Louise Richardson, 57–70. New York: Routledge, 2013.

Stroll, David. *Rigoberta Menchu and the Story of All Poor Guatemalans*. New York: Routledge, 2008.

Sullivan, John L., *ETA and Basque Nationalism: The Fight for Euskadi (1890–1986)*, Abingdon: Routledge, 2015.

Surio, Alberto. "El fantasma de Lemóniz." *El Dario Vasco*, December 4, 2008. https://www.diariovasco.com/20081204/politica/fantasma-lemoniz-20081204.html.

Tajfel, Henri, and John Turner. "'An Integrative Theory of Intergroup Conflict." In *Organizational Identity: A Reader*, edited by Mary Jo Hatch and Majken Schultz, 56–65. Oxford: Oxford University Press, 2004.

Tamm, Henning. "Rebel Leaders, Internal Rivals, and External Resources: How State Sponsors Affect Insurgent Cohesion." *International Studies Quarterly* 60, no. 4 (2016): 599–610.

Tejerina, Benjamin. "Protest Cycle, Political Violence and Social Movements in the Basque Country." *Nations and Nationalism* 7, no. 1 (2001): 39–57.

Tezcür, Güneş Murat. "Prospects for Resolution of the Kurdish Question: A Realist Perspective." *Insight Turkey*, April 1, 2013. https://www.insightturkey.com/articles/prospects-for-resolution-of-the-kurdish-question-a-realist-perspective.

The Guardian. "Comrade Artemio Interview." December 9, 2011. https://www.youtube.com/watch?v=M7hnMy4t3s4.

Thomas, Jakana. "Rewarding Bad Behavior: How Governments Respond to Terrorism in Civil War." *American Journal of Political Science* 58, no. 4 (2014): 804–818.

Toft, Monica Duffy. "Ending Civil Wars: A Case for Rebel Victory?" *International Security* 34, no. 4 (2020): 7–36.

Toft, Monica Duffy. *Securing the Peace*. Princeton, NJ: Princeton University Press, 2009.

Tokdemir, Efe. "Reputation Building as a Strategy for Terror Group Survival." *All Azimuth*, 2021, 1–18.

Tolbert, Pamela S., and Shon R. Hiatt. "On Organizations and Oligarchies: Michels in the Twenty-first Century." Ithaca, NY: Cornell University, ILR School, 2009. http://digitalcommons.ilr.cornell.edu/articles/1011.

Tremblay-Boire, Joannie. "Change Can Be Good: A New Perspective on Mission Drift." University of Pennsylvania Social Impact Working Paper Series, 2013.

Trott, Wendy. "Prospect Theory: Contributions to Understanding Actors, Causes and Consequences of Conflict in Africa." *Stability: International Journal of Security and Development* 2, no. 2 (2013): Art. 43.

Tullock, Gordon. "The Paradox of Revolution." *Public Choice* 11 (1971): 89–99.

uharg, Halvard. "Relative Capability and Rebel Objective in Civil War." *Journal of Peace Research* 43, no. 6 (2006): 691–708.

Unzueta, Patxo. "ETA (p-m) pide el esclarecimiento del caso 'Pertur.'" *El Pais*, August 2, 1978. https://elpais.com/diario/1978/08/02/espana/270856823_850215.html.

Unzueta, Patxo. "ETAm asesinó ayer a José María Ryan, ingeniero de la central nuclear de Lemóniz." *El Pais*, February 7, 1981. https://elpais.com/diario/1981/02/07/espana/350348406_850215.html.

Unzueta, Patxo. "Euskadiko Ezquerra rechaza la acusación de recibir apoyo financiero del Gobierno." *El Pais*, November 15, 1981. https://elpais.com/diario/1981/11/15/espana/374626813_850215.html.

UPI. "Killing of Engineer Sparks Uproar." February 7, 1981. https://www.upi.com/Archives/1981/02/07/Killing-of-engineer-sparks-uproar/8805350370000/.

Urla, Jacqueline. *Reclaiming Basque: Language, Nation, and Cultural Activism*. Reno: University of Nevada Press, 2012.

US Government. *Guide to the Analysis of Insurgency*, 2012. https://www.hsdl.org/?view&did=713599.

Valasik, Matthew, and Matthew Phillips. "Understanding Modern Terror and Insurgency through the Lens of Street Gangs: ISIS as a Case Study." *Journal of Criminological Research, Policy and Practice* 3, no. 3 (2017): 192–207.

Van Den Broek, Hanspeter. "BORROKA—The Legitimation of Street Violence in the Political Discourse of Radical Basque Nationalists." *Terrorism and Political Violence* 16, no. 4 (2004): 714–736.

Varela, Ana Lopez. "El Dramático Secuestro que Mantuvo en Vilo q Julio Iglesias (y a Toda España)." *Vanity Fair*, December 29, 2019. https://www.revistavanityfair.es/sociedad/celebrities/articulos/secuestro-doctor-iglesias-puga-julio-iglesias-eta/23277.

Vinci, Anthony. "Greed-Grievance Reconsidered: The Role of Power and Survival in the Motivation of Armed Groups." *Civil Wars* 8, no. 1 (2006): 25–45.

Vinci, Anthony. *Armed Groups and the Balance of Power: The International Relations of Terrorists, Warlords and Insurgents*. Abingdon: Routledge, 2009.

Vogt, Manuel, Kristian Skrede Gleditsch, and Lars-Erik Cederman. "From Claims to Violence: Signaling, Outbidding, and Escalation in Ethnic Conflict." *Journal of Conflict Resolution* 65, no. 7–8 (2021): 1278–1307.

Voss, Kim, and Rachel Sherman. "Breaking the Iron Law of Oligarchy: Union Revitalization in the American Labor Movement." *American Journal of Sociology* 106, no. 2 (2000): 303–349.

Walter, Barbara F. "Bargaining Failures and Civil War." *Annual Review of Political Science* 12 (2009): 243–261.

Walter, Barbara F. "Designing Transitions from Civil War: Demobilization, Democratization, and Commitments to Peace." *International Security* 24, no. 1 (1999): 127–155.

Walter, Barbara F. "The Critical Barrier to Civil War Settlement." *International Organization* 51, no. 3 (1997): 335–364.

Walter, Barbara F. "The Extremist's Advantage in Civil Wars." *International Security* 42, no. 2 (2017): 7–39.

Walter, Barbara F. *Committing to Peace: The Successful Settlement of Civil Wars*. Princeton, NJ: Princeton University Press, 2002.

Warner, W. Keith, and A. Eugene Havens. "Goal Displacement and the Intangibility of Organizational Goals." *Administrative Science Quarterly* 12, no. 4 (1968): 539–555.

Weber, Max. *Economy and Society*. Edited by Guenther Roth and Claus Wittich. Berkeley: University of California Press, 1978.

Weinstein, Jeremy M. *Inside Rebellion: The Politics of Insurgent Violence*. New York: Cambridge University Press, 2009.

Westendorf, Jasmine-Kim. *Why Peace Processes Fail: Negotiating Insecurity After Civil War*. Boulder, CO: Lynne Rienner Publishers, 2015.

Weyland, Kurt. "Risk Taking in Latin American Economic Restructuring: Lessons from Prospect Theory." *International Studies Quarterly* 40 (1996): 185–208.

White, Barry. "Peace Process: A Question of Definition." In *Protestant Perceptions of the Peace Process in Northern Ireland*, edited by Dominic Murray. Limerick: Centre for Peace and Development Studies, University of Limerick, 2000. https://cain.ulster.ac.uk/events/peace/murray/white.htm#six.

White, Robert W. "From Peaceful Protest to Guerrilla War: Micromobilization of the Provisional Irish Republican Army." *American Journal of Sociology* 94, no. 6 (1989): 1277–1302.

Whitfield, Teresa. "The Basque Conflict and ETA The Difficulties of an Ending." Washington, DC: United States Institute of Peace, 2015. https://www.usip.org/publications/2015/12/basque-conflict-and-eta-difficulties-ending.

Whitfield, Teresa. *Endgame for ETA: Elusive Peace in the Basque Country*. Oxford: Oxford University Press, 2014.

Wilson, James Q. *Political Organizations*. Princeton, NJ: Princeton University Press, 1975.

Wood, B. Dan. "Principals, Bureaucrats, and Responsiveness in Clean Air Enforcements." *American Political Science Review* 82, no. 1 (1988): 213–234.

Wood, Elisabeth Jean. "Civil Wars: What We Don't Know." *Global Governance*. 9, no. 2 (2003): 247–260.

Wood, Elisabeth Jean. "The Emotional Benefits of Insurgency in El Salvador." In *Passionate Politics: Emotions and Social Movements*, edited by Jeff Goodwin and James M. Jasper, 267–281. Chicago: University of Chicago Press, 2001.

Wood, Elisabeth Jean. *Insurgent Collective Action and Civil War in El Salvador*. Cambridge: Cambridge University Press, 2003.

Wood, Reed M. "Opportunities to Kill or Incentives for Restraint? Rebel Capabilities, the Origins of Support, and Civilian Victimization in Civil War." *Conflict Management and Peace Science* 31, no. 5 (2013): 461–480.

Woodworth, Paddy. *Dirty War, Clean Hands: ETA, the GAL and Spanish Democracy*. Cork: Cork University Press, 2001.

Worldometer. Spain Population. https://www.worldometers.info/world-population/spain-population/.

Yin, Robert. *Case Study Research: Design and Methods*. Thousand Oaks, CA: SAGE Publications, 2009.

Yuchtman, Ephraim, and Stanley E. Seashore. "A System Resource Approach to Organizational Effectiveness." *American Sociological Review*, 32, no. 6 (1967): 891–903.

Zabalo, Julen, and Mikel Saratxo. "ETA Ceasefire: Armed Struggle vs. Political Practice in Basque Nationalism." *Ethnicities* 15, no. 3 (2015): 362–384.

Zald, Mayer N., and Michael A. Berger. "Social Movements in Organizations: Coup d'Etat, Insurgency, and Mass Movements." *American Journal of Sociology* 83, no. 4 (1978): 823–861.

Zald, Mayer N., and Michael Lounsbury. "The Wizards of Oz: Towards an Institutional Approach to Elites, Expertise and Command Posts." *Organization Studies* 31, no. 7 (2010): 963–996.

Zald, Mayer N., and Roberta Ash. "Social Movement Organizations: Growth, Decay and Change." *Social Forces* 44, no. 3 (1966): 327–340.

Zartman, I. William. "Ripeness: The Hurting Stalemate and Beyond." In *International Conflict Resolution after the Cold War*, edited by Paul C. Stern and Daniel Druckman, 225–250. Washington, DC: National Academy Presscil, 2000. http://citeseerx.ist.psu.edu/viewdoc/download?doi=10.1.1.460.9657&rep=rep1&type=pdf#page=240.

Zech, Steven T. "Counter-Terrorizing: The Use of Torture in Peru's Counterterrorism Campaign." *Terrorism and Political Violence* 29, no. 2 (2017): 254–276.

Zech, Steven T., and Joshua Eastin. "The Household Economics of Counterinsurgency." *Defence and Peace Economics* 32, no. 2 (2021): 220–239.

Zech, Steven T., and Michael Gabbay. "Social Network Analysis in the Study of Terrorism and Insurgency: From Organization to Politics." *International Studies Review* 18, no. 2 (2016): 214–243.

Zedong, Mao. *On Guerilla Warfare.* Translated by Samuel B. Griffith. Washington, DC: US Marine Corps, 1961.

Zernova, Margarita. "Restorative Justice in the Aftermath of Politically-Motivated Violence: The Basque Experience." *Critical Studies on Terrorism* 12, no. 4 (2019): 649–672.

Zhukov, Yuri M. "Repression Works (Just Not in Moderation)." *Comparative Political Studies* 56, no. 11 (January 2023): 1–32.

Zulaika, Joseba, and William A. Douglass. "On the Interpretation of Terrorist Violence: ETA and the Basque Political Process." *Comparative Studies in Society and History* 32, no. 2 (1990): 238–257.

Zulaika, Joseba. *Basque Violence: Metaphor and Sacrament.* Reno: University of Nevada Press, 1988.

Zuloaga, J. M. "El drama de los atentados sin sentencia: siete muertos y cien heridos en Madrid." *La Razon*, February 2, 2020. https://www.larazon.es/espana/20200202/4qhr4xkejngplopxbsgumh44ei.html.

Index

For the benefit of digital users, indexed terms that span two pages (e.g., 52–53) may, on occasion, appear on only one of those pages.

O

www.ingramcontent.com/pod-product-compliance
Ingram Content Group UK Ltd.
Pitfield, Milton Keynes, MK11 3LW, UK
UKHW041433160926
475595UK00019B/13